CW01455317

THE COUNT OF VIRTUE

Giangaleazzo Visconti
Duke of Milan

E. R. Chamberlin

SAPERE
BOOKS

THE COUNT OF VIRTUE

Published by Sapere Books.

20 Windermere Drive, Leeds, England, LS17 7UZ,

United Kingdom

saperebooks.com

Copyright © The Estate of E. R. Chamberlin, 1965.

First published by Eyre & Spottiswoode, 1965.

The Estate of E. R. Chamberlin has asserted its right to be identified

as the author of this work.

All rights reserved.

No part of this publication may be reproduced, stored in any retrieval

system, or transmitted, in any form, or by any means, electronic,

mechanical, photocopying, recording, or otherwise, without the prior

written permission of the publishers.

ISBN: 978-1-80055-473-3.

TABLE OF CONTENTS

I: THE VISCONTI

OF THE MARVELS OF MILAN

Milan had overshadowed this western corner of Lombardy for a thousand years. In that almost mythical past, when the darkness began to creep across the face of the Roman world, Diocletian had made of it a capital of the west to stay the general ruin and from that recognition of its vitality grew the Milanese consciousness of excellence, of superiority to all other Italians. They developed their own language, a tongue grotesque to southern ears though they themselves maintained that 'it was the easiest of all languages to speak and comprehend'.[1] Their very church became a thing apart, infused with the spirit of their patron saint Ambrose so that it took his name and continued in power and wealth until its archbishops could look down upon the insecure tenure of the bishops of Rome. Under the protection of these Ambrosian priests the people defied the nobles of the plain, created their own laws, learned to call themselves Milanese. Their city, they said, was not only great but unique, for it was the last great city of Italy and the first which the northerners encountered after their passage through the Alps. It was a city curiously regular in both shape and colour, a polygon of rose-red brick, born of the Lombard clay; a city of the plain whence mountains were eternally visible. Eastward ran the endless, fertile plain of Lombardy, a green sea broken by occasional islands of castles and cities. Westward the great plain heaved itself up into the hills of the Maritime Alps and southward the Apennines

---

[1] Bonvesino, cap. III, i.

enclosed Italy proper. Northward rose the Alpine wall, the 'barrier placed by nature itself to keep back the barbaric nations'. The passes of Gotthard and Simplon which pierced that barrier had for centuries echoed to the tramp of armed men but where soldiers could pass so too could merchants with their trains of pack animals. Milan was perfectly situated for the trade of middlemen who bought the wares of western Europe and sent them onwards by the natural highway of the Po to Venice and Genoa and the world beyond. From an early period the merchants of Milan had organized the routes through the Alps, collaborating with local authorities for the policing of routes, the erection of bridges, the establishment of posts high in the mountains where their members could find protection from weather and brigands. While kings and princes grappled and made alliances and betrayed and grappled again the merchants established their own quietly competent international state. These were the men with whom the Visconti first linked their destiny; the solid industrious middle-class who were glad to exchange a chimerical freedom for the protection of a powerful man against the arrogance of the nobles, the tumults of the plebs. Milan's trade was her lifeblood; the woollen industry, the manufacture of the world-famous armour, even her rich agriculture yielded precedence to the humdrum re-distribution of other people's goods.

In the closing years of the thirteenth century a lay brother of the order of the Umiliati took time from his charitable works to prepare a crown for his native city. Bonvesino da Riva's *Of the Marvels of Milan*[2] goes far beyond the stereotyped laude of his day, but Fra Bonvesino was himself an unusual man. A poet of some distinction, a Christian of great compassion, a grammarian of modest fame, the three strands of his nature

---

[2] Ibid.

8

fused to produce an observer in whom sensitivity was strengthened by the scholar's discipline. Milan is for him the first among cities as the rose and lily are the first among flowers, the lion among beasts, the eagle among birds. Rome? Rome is set in a festering marsh whereas Milan is placed in the midst of a sun-drenched plain, its very shape an indication of its excellence for it is 'orbicular in the manner of a circle whose admirable roundness is the sign of its perfection'. He was the first to attempt a scientific calculation of the city's population and economics, appears astounded by what he discovers and expects the reader to be astounded too. 'But though in the proving I shall say things which appear extraordinary, these things are not far from the truth.' He prefaces the figures of which he is uncertain with a prudent 'circa'; he is open about his sources which he obtains from those 'best in the position to know' — tax gatherers at the city gates, butchers, farmers, all those who deal in large quantities of foodstuffs from which some estimate of population can be made. It is as well that he did so, for the most remarkable of his figures concern the population of Milan — 'about 200,000 as I firmly believe' — which makes the city at least twice the size of its major Italian rivals. Villani estimated the population of Florence at some 90,000, while Venice, a hundred years later, returned a figure of 134,600 for the city's first true census. Galvano Fiamma, who stole much of Bonvesino's work to adorn his own, gives no help. Writing in 1340 he employs his predecessor's figure, merely saying 'Such was the state in 1288; it is not for me to say whether it has gained or lost ground in that time.'[3] Bonvesino explains the basis of his calculations, making it quite clear that he has not confused the population of the city with its surrounding district. Milan is divided into 115 parishes each

---

[3] Fiamma, Chronicon extravagans, cap. IX, 2.

of which contains between 500 and 100 families and the daily consumption of grain is 1200 bushels. True, 'there are without doubt cities in Italy which do not eat so much bread as the very dogs of Milan consume', but this figure for the basic food is augmented by the dried chestnut flour which, untaxed, did not appear in the official records. 200,000 is therefore the population of Milan alone; for the state as a whole 'according to my calculations which many assure me to be exact, there are 700,000 mouths of both sexes, including children, living on the surface of the Ambrosian land'. He unwittingly supplies an additional check to his figures with the statement that there are 40,000 men capable of bearing arms in the city and 200,000 in the entire state, proportions not significantly different from Villani's estimate of 25,000 able-bodied men for the Florentine population of 90,000.

Bonvesino's method of proving quality by citing quantity provides a bewildering wealth of statistics. 6000 fountains supply drinking water 'as I have discovered by diligent but not exhaustive search', 150 hotels offer shelter to strangers, 300 public ovens are available for the citizens, private hearths being forbidden for fear of fire. He says little of the industry of the city save to record that 100 armourers are engaged upon the manufacture of the famous armour and 30 bellfounders produce the horsebells peculiar to Milan. The professions are well represented and an indication of the city's wealth is the extraordinary number of religious living at the public expense. There were 10,000 monks of all orders, evident proof of "the natural goodness of the Milanese'. A somewhat better proof of virtue is the existence of 10 hospitals, the largest with 500 beds capable of caring for 1000 patients, together with 28 doctors and 150 surgeons. The city swarmed with notaries — 1,500 of them in addition to the college of jurisconsuls with 120 members. There were 40 copiers of manuscripts, only 8 professors of grammar, but 70 teachers running private schools. So the torrent of figures runs on, confusing in their detail and patchy in their coverage but in their sum giving the impression of increasingly prosperous activity in a city where 'he who would could always find work'.

Two generations later and the picture of a hard-working, thrifty people living well but plainly begins to give place to that of a somewhat softened populace who having tasted luxury begin to expect it as right. Bonvesino could take an innocent pleasure in the fine appearance of his fellow citizens who 'live with decorum but dress with elegance, their women bejewelled as splendid as queens'. By 1340 the trend has gone too far and Fiamma deplores the way in which the new generation is departing from the simple modes of their fathers, aping the foreigner. 'They wear tight clothes in the Spanish manner, ride with enormous spurs like the Tartars. The women curl and frizz their hair, wear clothes of silk and gold, go with their breasts uncovered and endanger their lives with belts of gold fibre as though they were Amazons.' The increasing number of prostitutes makes it economic to levy a tax upon them, the money being used for maintenance of the city walls. So great is their number indeed that, for fear of being confused with virtuous women, they are forbidden to wear their hair in the *coazz*, the Milanese fashion of binding long tresses with ribbon and loading them with precious stone. Lament for the simplicity of times past becomes more general than the boast of time present. 'Then one was rich with little,' Ricobaldo mourns. 'Glory lay in the possession of good arms and horses. They drank little wine; one plate served alike for men and women and the entire family drank from one or at the most two glasses. They had candles of neither wax nor tallow but supped in the light of torches upon green vegetables and little meat.'[4] A bride's dowry then was modest, now it was necessary to prescribe minutely her very trousseau and limit the festivities. Men discarded their sober robes for garments of scarlet silk or of silk contrasted with gold or scarlet wool. Huge pearls covered the clothes of men and women alike. The poorer classes begin to copy the rich in wasteful extravagance and inevitably sumptuary laws make their appearance. They had long been known in Italy but Milan had resisted this artificial attempt to restrict personal expenditure, the merchants having a lively awareness of its potentially disastrous effect on trade. Elsewhere city authorities went to extreme lengths to enforce the laws; Sachetti paints a ludicrous picture of lawmen pursuing women down the streets of Florence in order to examine the stuff of their gowns. It was a symbol both of Milan's increased wealth and subjection to the signore that the first effective sumptuary laws coincided with the establishment of the Visconti. It is a debatable point whether the wealth of the citizens created a softness which made them easy prey for the signore, as the Florentines claimed, or whether the signore, by introducing firm order, paved the way for increased wealth and resultant softness. The result was the same.

THE FAMILY

The great Ghibelline family of the Visconti, two-thirds of whose existence was spent at war with the Papacy, owed its foundation to a Pope. In 1262 Urban IV imposed Ottone Visconti as his own nominee to the archbishopric in an attempt to counterbalance the power of the della Torre, the then dominant family. The attempt was only too successful

---

[4] Verga, cap. III.

from the Papacy's point of view. Sheltered under the wide and legal powers of the archbishop the lay branch of the family rooted itself deep within the state, obtained the Imperial Vicarship of Lombardy from the Emperor, and with his assistance made a final end of their only rivals, the della Torre, whom they had been conjured to destroy. Now rapidly the family outgrew the need for protection and in the ill-defined field of Imperial-papal rights came inevitably into conflict with the Papacy during the Imperial Interregnum. The test of wills came when Matteo Visconti illegally occupied the territory of Angera, and it was probably at this point that some unknown genius of propaganda, in order to substantiate the family's claims over city and state, produced a fable and a banner for them. The Visconti, far from stealing papal property, were but coming into their own, he declared; they were the legitimate descendants of those Counts of Angera who themselves traced descendance from Aeneas. In Milan's great war against Barbarossa the main branch of the family had been eliminated and the survivors were thenceforth known as *vis-conti* instead of *conti*. The fable not only conferred legality upon the usurpation of Angera but, in its explanation of the name of the family, gave it a considerable lift in the world. The Visconti had originally merely held the office of viscount of the empire, but even as the counts had made their own office hereditary so had they, their name and office ultimately fusing. No one troubled to question this novel interpretation of the family's name, but the claim to Angera, with its impudent echo of the Papacy's own forgery of the Decretals, was too much and Matteo, the head of the family, was excommunicated. The fable passed into obscurity but the banner remained.

The viper ensign of the Visconti is peculiarly displeasing, even for this period when heralds were ransacking bestiaries, coupling monster with monster in attempt to keep pace with the demands for arms. Less serpent than dragon, the azure monster coils its body seven times downward to a pointed tail, while in its gaping mouth a red human figure struggles in terror as it is engulfed. A serpent without the human figure had been the ensign of the office of viscount, and in appropriating it the family had also appropriated one of the standards of the free commune. But this new banner, embodying the brazen serpent of Milan's patron saint, was a nobler thing and a more insistent statement of the henceforth identity of interest of city and family than the Visconti's own device, that of a dog chained to a tree. The theft accomplished, justification was needed and justification accordingly appears. The ensign had belonged to a Saracen who had been overcome in the Holy Land by a Visconti and the struggling human is the Saracen himself, placed in the maw of his own serpent for the glory of God and the greater honour of the Visconti. Bonvesino obligingly included the story in his *De Magnalibus* and a generation later Fiamma undertook the actual task of forgery, polishing Bonvesino's account and inserting it into a chronicle of the tenth century. The true origins of the ensign faded from memory, but the Visconti had done themselves a grave injury in appropriating it and the robbed city was ultimately avenged. The image of a snake swallowing a man was a gift for hostile polemics, and even as 'Visconti' became synonymous with Milan so 'Viper' became synonymous with Visconti, the attributes of the snake becoming the attributes of the family, launching it into history with a ready-made label. The Florentines seized upon it, and it was largely due to these attractive and articulate enemies of the Visconti that the appalling reputation of the family arose. Florentine scandals, minted for the temporary purposes of propaganda, passed into permanent currency, for they were the creation of the masters of that dialect which was to dominate the Italian language. From the time that the Visconti appeared as a force upon the Italian scene to their collapse a century later they were in opposition to the Tuscan republic. During that period a succession of gifted writers in Florence laid the foundation of the new culture which blazed into full life during the fifteenth century; the Villanis, Dati, Bruni, Salutati — these writers in recording the history of their city fixed the mould in which the Visconti were to appear to posterity, for during that same period Milan produced no native writers whose bias would have given the necessary corrective. There was no necessary relationship between the presence of the despotic Visconti and the absence of such men. Padua, which was under a despotism as finished as that in Milan, yet produced the vivid chronicles of the Gatari, while republican Siena offered but a few bald compilations; in Lucca, Sercambi's colourful work coincided with the appearance of the despotism of the Guinigi. Chroniclers were at work in most of the cities of the Milanese state, but, with one qualified exception, their work was little more than the compilation of calendars with no attempt at assessment of the ruling family. Pietro Azario, a notary who had served the Visconti in both Tortona and Piacenza as well as Milan, made the attempt in a lively enough narrative, but his account ended in 1364; all other contemporary narratives came from pens bent upon rationalizing Florentine claims to Italian pre-eminence.

With the appearance of the signore in Milan, the constitution of the free city swiftly became an ill-remembered legend. The first bulwark of the Commune to disappear was the executive power of the *podestà*, the one office common to all Italian cities. Established by Barbarossa as sign of his ever-present overlordship, it was the one unqualified good which the Empire contributed to Italy, for the *podestà* stood above all factions, a compromise between the tyranny of the single ruler and the anarchism of the many. The Milanese themselves had tampered with the office again and again, now content with one, now creating two or three, sometimes abandoning it altogether. In this, as with many other of the reforms which strengthened their position, the Visconti merely seized upon and hastened an existing trend. Long before the family obtained absolute power, in fact, the citizens had themselves eroded the authority of the supreme sovereign body, the Grand Council of 1200, transferring its power to the compact and therefore efficient Office of Provisions. The Council was an unwieldy anachronism, but its very size had prevented any one man dominating, whereas the Provisions consisted only of twelve men, vulnerable to pressure. And when determined pressure came, they gave way. On September 20th 1313 the sum of many minor changes produced a complete break with the past when Gianozzo di Salimbene, the last effective *podestà* of Milan, in the name of the people conceded to Matteo Visconti the 'rettore generale' for life. It was a powerful office but it made Matteo no more than the first among equals in the city, and in spite of the absolute power which the Visconti thereafter enjoyed they remained, in theory, elected officials of the city until the establishment of the dukedom. Matteo combined his unique civic power with his existing office of Imperial Vicar of Lombardy and on that twin basis the Visconti despotism was founded. Successive members of the family took care to renew the diploma of vicariate and to obtain the assent of the people, but both became formalities. In the universal breakdown of Imperial authority the diploma became a matter of purchase, while the successive reforms legally instituted by the signore within the city widened the breach between the administration and the executive.

The pattern of the single ruler had long been established in Lombardy. The destruction of Ezzelino Romano in 1259 had been the last unified effort of the free cities against the sweeping tide. The mechanics of tyranny were constant: office, granted by the people and theoretically open to election, was usurped by a family and thereafter remained its hereditary property — Gonzaghi in Mantua, Carrararese in Padua, Este in Ferrara, della Torre and then Visconti in Milan. Machiavelli's theory for the Lombard phenomenon is at once succinct and accurate. 'Cities that are once corrupt and used to the rule of princes can never acquire freedom even though the prince and all his kin be extirpated. One prince is needed to extinguish another and the city has no rest save by the creation of a new lord.'[5] The contribution which the Visconti made to the practice of despotism was their method of transmitting power from one generation to the next. Theoretically, the safeguarding of transmission was impossible, for where power had been obtained by usurpation, rights of primogeniture were meaningless; power came to him who survived and many a would-be despotism came to a bloody end during the struggle for that power. The Visconti solved the problem by an ingenious application of the formula 'divide and rule'. Sometimes as many as three shared the supreme power, but usually the head of the family ruled as signore, supported by his brothers and uncles, each of whom ruled as local lord over some section of the state. Viewed from without, the Milanese State presented the appearance of a monolith, but at close quarters it was seen to be composed of semi-autonomous interlocking segments.

---

[5] Machiavelli, Discorsi, IV.

17

The steady expansion of Visconti power in Lombardy proceeded with an air of inevitability. Milan had lost its freedom but gained an internal stability which, stimulating its commerce, set a powerful example to the city's immediate neighbours. These, no more immune from the Lombard predilection for the single ruler, were yet too close to Milan to set up successful rivals to the Visconti and their absorption into the larger unit was merely a matter of time. Most of them actually requested entry, voluntarily relinquishing sovereignty to share in the greater security of the Milanese State. The citizens of Como spoke for all inarticulate citizens everywhere when, in their petition, they stated that 'because of the frequent murders, rapines and tumults within the city the people are without hope of health save under a lord',[6] a phrase which Machiavelli could have taken as text. The cities retained their established constitutions and enjoyed considerable independence, for the Milanese State more closely resembled a federation than that tyranny beloved of Florentine propagandists. It was a matter of little moment to a citizen of Bergamo or Vercelli or Novara that the titular lord of his city was also the titular lord of Milan. But soon it became a matter of considerable interest to the Visconti's equals and rivals as, the family's hold upon the nucleus of the state established, its ambitions began to move away from the centre. The small buffer states absorbed, then the frontiers of the Milanese State began to touch the frontiers of other, more formidable powers. Here and there the Visconti gained or lost a footing but, accustomed to long term planning, they were content to leave those states which could not be easily engulfed for the attention of future generations. The eastern section of the state was contained by the cities of Padua, Verona, Mantua and

---

[6] Cognasso, SMT V.

18

Ferrara, each under a despot; westward, the frontier was more fluid, for the little lords of Piedmont and Savoy were less able to withstand encroachment, dependent upon a series of complex alliances to retain their independence.

The first real test of the Visconti system of family government came in 1339 when Azzo Visconti died without heirs and five members of the family stood in the line of succession, his uncles Luchino and Giovanni and three young cousins. Luchino was the elder but Giovanni was the archbishop of Milan and a crisis might have faced the city and family had not the Grand Council prudently elected both uncles as joint *signori generali*. Even this would have been but a postponement of the inevitable had it not been for the character of Giovanni. Possessed of immense personal charm, politically able — brutally so if need be — he yet deliberately held himself in the background, occupying himself with those ecclesiastic duties whose complexities were as great as those of the temporal lord of Milan. Luchino pursued the steady policy of expansion of his predecessors until rebellion broke out in Milan itself, the last flicker of the free city. He smashed it with the necessary violence and, though there was no proof that his three young nephews were implicated, he expelled them from the city on the sound enough principle of the herd bull driving off potential challengers. Giovanni said nothing and the nephews — Matteo, Bernabò, and Galeazzo — went into exile. Luchino's anger followed them; he put pressure on the tiny state of Savoy to deny them shelter and even demanded that Avignon should forbid them either marriage, or burial in sacred ground. Irritated by this last touch of personal spite, Bernabò, ever the more impetuous and formidable of the three, began the journey back to Milan intent upon his uncle's assassination. But a woman's hatred travelled ahead of him and it was to Isabella, his own wife, that Luchino succumbed in the January of 1349. It was common knowledge in Milan that she had despatched him to forestall his despatch of her. Luchino seemed to have been altogether blind to the extra-marital activities of his beautiful, restless, and indiscreet wife, and when at last a particularly flagrant example was brought to his attention he fatally delayed action. Under the thin disguise of making pilgrimage to Venice via the Po, Isabella had organized a riverine debauchery of fantastic proportions. En route, the lord of Mantua and the Doge of Venice joined the armada of folly and the number of her lovers and at the journey's end, so rumour said, she was re-united with another lover, her exiled nephew Galeazzo. Long before the gaily bedecked barges had completed the return journey, the voyage's ill fame had spread throughout Lombardy and some of her sister revellers, fearing their own reception, accused her as the instigator to their husbands on return home. They, in their turn hastening to disassociate themselves, informed Luchino who swore that he would 'light a fire that will illumine all Lombardy'. He did not do so. In the last years of his life he was a virtual invalid, tortured by the family complaint of gout, and the lethargy induced probably accounts for his uncharacteristic lack of action. And while he procrastinated Isabella struck.

Archbishop Giovanni succeeded to the supreme power. In most other families Isabella would have met with a prompt end, partisans would have arisen to defend or attack her children and the city would have fallen back into that anarchy which attended the transference of despotic power. But the Visconti had long since learned that family murder as a political tool was a dangerous weapon. Giovanni worked patiently and subtly. His first move was to recall the three exiled nephews. On the face of it the nephews had few expectations, for

Luchino had left four children and the eldest, the six-year-old Luchino Novello, was tacitly recognized as heir. A situation in which three men in their prime played a secondary role to a child was one in which the family tolerance would have been taxed to breaking point. But Giovanni was in firm control and Luchino's heir was accorded all deference until a year after the return of the exiles, when 'on April 28th, Isabella del Fiesco, wife of the late Luchino Visconti, declared by public act that Luchino Novello and Orsina were not the children of Luchino as the people believed but were conceived of Galeazzo, his nephew'.[7] Considering the late Luchino's violent, suspicious nature Galeazzo's achievement of adultery combined with technical incest and lese-majesty over a number of years was remarkable. Archbishop Giovanni had not thought fit to pursue the matter during his brother's lifetime, but his death altered the significance of Isabella's actions. The retention of power within the family, regardless of which member of the family actually exercised it, was Giovanni's sole object in bringing the scandal into the open. Isabella's marital conduct cast a shadow over all her children; the fact that it gave the archbishop an excuse to ensure that power would not fall into the hands of a minor was probably incidental if valuable. In ensuring the disinheritance of Luchino Novello it was also necessary to throw odium upon Galeazzo, and this indictment of one of the three potential heirs gave the strongest possible support to the charge of the child's illegitimacy. It would have been a simple matter to impute his fatherhood to any one of half a dozen distinguished men, but Isabella's assent to her public shaming was probably gained only on condition that the true father be named; that much at least must be allowed in her favour. Even at this stage her skill or beauty or plain luck did

---

[7] Corio, III, IV.

not desert her; she had publicly confessed to the attempted foisting of a bastard into the line of inheritance, but instead of meeting the merited assassin she remained comfortably enough in Milan with her children. The Grand Council of 1200 obediently recognized Galeazzo and his two brothers as the heirs of Giovanni, and the Visconti had yet again safely arranged for the transference of power.

THE FATHER

Five months after Isabella's public announcement Galeazzo married Bianca, the thirteen-year-old sister of Amadeus of Savoy. The marriage was arranged strictly according to the Visconti's tradition of political alliances, but an unusual personal element was the fact that bride and groom were already known to each other. Galeazzo had passed the greater period of his exile at Amadeus' court and Bianca was thus spared the usual ordeal of marrying not only a stranger, but a stranger speaking a foreign tongue. Orphaned at babyhood, she had known no other life than that of Savoy, provincial compared with Milan. Her brother's little capital of Chambéry was unable even to supply the wedding clothes and agents were sent scurrying to Lyons and Châlons to purchase her trousseau, the expenses paid from the two great sacks of gold which Milanese agents deposited in the monastery of Hautcombe. Bianca's purchase price was the first instalment of over three million gold florins which this and the succeeding generation of Visconti expended in dowries for their own daughters and those of coveted houses. It was a token not only of their wealth but of their European ambitions; of the three brothers Matteo was already married to a daughter of the Gonzaghi of Mantua, Bernabò affianced to Regina della Scala of Verona; it was for Galeazzo, the youngest of the three, to

22

forge the first link with France. His marriage in September was overshadowed by that of his brother's which took place on the same day; the Milanese, who ultimately paid for both marriages, were more impressed by the immediate splendour of Verona than by the small and distant state of Savoy, and found themselves more in sympathy with the coarse and vital Bernabò than with the retiring Galeazzo. It was Bernabò who enlivened the festivities with the new sport of jousting which he had discovered on his travels in the north, and after the ceremony it was Bernabò who remained at Giovanni's side at the centre of power while Galeazzo was despatched on an errand of state. It was an important enough task. After years of Giovanni's patient work the vitally strategic city of Bologna had been acquired, the fulfilment of the ambition of two generations of Visconti. Their dominance in Lombardy was essentially a matter of practical politics; the great opportunities lay southward and the acquisition of Bologna was the turning point in their career, for it turned them from a Lombard into an Italian power. The city was the key to the southern route by which invading armies could pass through the Apennines onward into Tuscany and the heart of Italy. Galeazzo went alone to take up his governorship for it was no place to take a young girl. The Papacy who claimed the city was infuriated; the Florentines who were now menaced by it were talking of war and the Bolognese themselves had rung their warbells and flooded into the streets, shouting that they would not be sold like cattle. But sold they were, for Bologna had fallen to those Visconti tactics which preferred bribery to violence and the city was corrupt from within. Nevertheless, it required a firm and skilful hand to steer it through its first few months as a member of the Milanese state and Galeazzo discharged his duty well until a permanent governor was found. Then, in

January 1351, five months after his wedding, he returned to Milan and his young bride. On October 15th 1351 his first legitimate child was born, a boy christened Giovanni Galeazzo which custom shortened to Giangaleazzo. The birth of the future first duke of Milan was an event of little contemporary significance. His father was the youngest of three brothers, all under the absolute control of Archbishop Giovanni; his mother a retiring girl overshadowed by her sisters-in-law. Even his inheritance had been gained by his great-aunt's adultery and not through his father's merit. No special ceremonies marked the child's birth, no ambitious noble craved the honour of 'raising him to the sacred font'. Curiously, Francesco Petrarch, though a close friend of Galeazzo's, stood godfather not to his son but to Bernabò's, earning for that infant an honoured place in Milanese chronology. The unknown person who did a like service for Giangaleazzo was not considered worthy of record and, a generation later, the very year of the birth was unknown although it had by then become a matter of historical importance.

The child was three years old when the great Archbishop, last link with the heroic formative years of the Visconti, died of a trivial operation. Of all the family who achieved the supreme power, Giovanni was the most sane, the most attractive. On shouldering the burden of full power on Luchino's death, he proved himself a statesman of the first rank, possessed of an iron will made stronger by the immense personal charm which could bind the most unwilling to him, even tying the restless Petrarch to one place. Stories of his career made the rounds of Milan, became cherished legends in the chronicles; of how, confronted in the Cathedral of Milan by Papal envoys sent to demand of him whether he were priest or politician, general or archbishop, he raised two emblems, a sword and a cross. 'This is my heritage, the spiritual and the temporal, and with the one I will defend the other.' Or again how, summoned to Avignon to justify himself, he consented to appear — and requested lodgings for 10,000 men. During the five brief years of his rule he had brought Milan up from a Lombard to an Italian power; the state now stretched for the first time in Visconti rule as far south as Bologna, as far west as Genoa. His southward probing had aroused the ever-present fear of Florence; he had been threatened with excommunication; an imperial league had been formed against him. He had not merely survived but at the end of every storm was seen to be a little stronger. Reasonably, he could have hoped for another ten years of life when he submitted to an operation for the removal of a wart, for he was only fifty-nine. His death was particularly unfortunate for Milan. The heirs he left were entirely capable of withstanding the military dangers his ambitions had aroused but they lacked his wide vision, content to fight local wars, unable to see Milan in any other content but that of parochial gain.

The archbishop died on Tuesday October 7th and sovereign power returned to its source, the sovereign people. They lost no time in ridding themselves of the dangerous thing; the Council of 1200 met and delegated one of their number freely to render back their freedom to the dead man's heirs. The ceremony took place on the following Sunday in a public square in the presence of all the people. Their delegate, Boschino Mantegazza, stood holding the three batons of white wood which were the outward sign of power while Francesco Petrarch pronounced the oration. There was a brief and undignified altercation between Petrarch and the astrologer appointed to determine the propitious moment, but at length silence fell and the astrologer 'lifted up his voice and cried "It is now! It is now!"'.[8] Mantegazza handed the batons to the

25

three young men and the transmission of power from one generation to the next of the Visconti was again accomplished. Where before there had been but one lord now there were three, but each was equal, the power remaining undivided. After the ceremony and celebrations each retired to his own castle in the city, the archbishop's palace falling to Matteo as the eldest, Bernabò and Galeazzo entering the castles above the gates of Gio via and Vercellina respectively. From these three massive buildings of reddish brick which rose above the low roofs of Milan each exercised absolute power over the third of the state which fell to him, Bernabò controlling the northern territories, Galeazzo the western and Matteo the turbulent southern. Milan and the recently acquired port of Genoa were held in common and in common too was the overall policy of the state. Nevertheless, equality of authority presupposed equality of ability and the triumvirate suffered a dangerous weakness in the character of Matteo. A satyr, he looked upon the exercise of power merely as a convenient means to satisfy his appetites; his share of the state was allowed to run itself and inevitably the hard-won, vital city of Bologna was lost. He caused his own death. The details of that death were conflicting; some claimed that he died of his own excesses, while the Florentine Villani, ever anxious to pillory the Visconti, reported that Matteo was first poisoned and then suffocated by his brothers. Petrarch, who could have thrown some light upon the first murder of the new regime, diplomatically remained silent, but the brothers' mother cursed them for it upon her death-bed and neither denied it. 'The truth is Matteo died like a dog, without confession, of a violent death perhaps befitting his dissolute life.'[9] Politically his

---

[8] Petrarch.
[9] Villani, M., V, 23.

murder was a wise move for not only did it eliminate a weakness in the state, but it also reduced the likelihood of a clash between the brothers, for he and Bernabò shared too many of the blacker qualities of the Visconti. The state was divided into two, Bernabò taking over the responsibility for the recapture of Bologna.

THE UNCLE

There could be no greater contrast than between these two men who now controlled the largest single political unit in Northern Italy. At thirty-five Bernabò was in the full flush of his violent manhood; a conservative, running his section of the state with the minimum number of officials, attending to everything personally as though it were a private estate. He was educated indeed, 'being learned in the Decretals', but educated according to the older forms, remaining impervious to the new spirit abroad. War was for him no mere instrument of policy as it had been for Giovanni, but the only activity worthy of a man, and to the end of his fife he led his armies personally, the last of the old signori who held with the sword that which the sword had carved. His abiding intellectual passion was the administration of justice, and for all his autocratic temper his judgements were just even if his sentences were macabre. But cancelling his many real virtues was an almost bestial ferocity which, bursting out un-predictably and uncontrollably, placed not only his victims' but his own life in danger. The ferocity, usually accompanied by satyriasis, was a constitutional defect of the Visconti character; allied to it was an equally pathological timidity. The two traits sometimes appeared in the same person; Matteo the Great, having endured the ban of the Church throughout a vigorous life, ended his days in a superstitious fear so great that his sons deposed him as a danger to the house; the late Luchino alternated between bouts of violent activity and extreme lethargy. But normally the defects appeared singly and then were concentrated to an extreme degree. When the paroxysm of rage was upon Bernabò the only person who dare approach, much less attempt to control, the temporary madman was his wife Regina. 'And finally he was dedicated to an astonishing degree to the vice of lust so that his house appeared more to be the seraglio of a sultan than the habitation of a Catholic prince.'[10] His satyriasis, as uncontrollable as his ferocity, peopled Milan with bastards; he himself did not know their total, placing the number at above thirty. All were recognized and, though a demonstration of moral weakness, they were a source of political strength. The illegitimate daughters of the lord of Milan were considered excellent prizes by many a minor princeling or mercenary leader, and with them Bernabò created a net of alliances supplementing the legitimate. Not the least of Regina's tasks was the preserving for her own beloved children the heritage which her husband would have lavished upon natural and legitimate alike.

To this figure from an older cruder past, that of Galeazzo makes an almost theatrical contrast both in character and appearance. 'In Galeazzo II there were almost all the rare gifts of fortune and nature which man could want. Particularly beautiful was he when he followed that fashion of letting his hair, the colour of gold, grow long, sometimes in tresses, sometimes resting on his shoulders in a silken net or garlanded with flowers.'[11] Where Bernabò looked back to the past, modelling himself upon the classic tyrants, Galeazzo with some diffidence reached forward to the dawn light of the

---

[10] Giulini, LXIX, p. 129.
[11] Giovio, p. 91.

Renaissance. He prided himself on his culture; it was he who founded the library which became the glory of the Visconti, and took Petrarch under his protection after the death of Giovanni. And while Bernabò attempted to run the complex affairs of state single-handed, Galeazzo began that delegation of authority which was essential if the State of Milan were ever to become anything more than a transient tyranny. His new methods met with little approval from the more conservative citizens; Pietro Azario spoke for all of them when he claimed that such a delegation created many little tyrants instead of one all-seeing lord. It was Galeazzo's misfortune that Azario, the only contemporary Milanese chronicler, should have been a partisan of Bernabò's, his prejudices becoming the basis of later judgements. Even that clemency which compared so remarkably with Bernabò's brutality arose from nothing but avarice, was the chronicler's opinion. 'To make money he preferred to punish law-breakers with fines rather than with corporal punishment, thereby diminishing his authority and prestige… neither did he keep court in the Visconti manner, rarely if ever entertaining his councillors and officers, and his servants were ill-paid, if at all.'[12] His soldiers, equally badly paid, served him badly and time and again he was obliged to turn to his brother for military aid. Azario judged this an humiliation, but it was a logical consequence of Galeazzo's theory of statesmanship, a theory to which Bernabò must have assented for he never refused aid or made reproach. A more serious consequence for Galeazzo's reputation was that the gossiping writers who could have given the corrective to Azario were little attracted to his court. Bernabò earned and apparently enjoyed the political execration of his enemies, but he also earned a reluctant admiration, coloured by amusement,

---

[12] Azario, XIV, col. 403.

of those who came to know him personally. Contemporaries, if they spoke of Galeazzo at all, did so coldly; the stereotype attacks upon the tyrant were duly made but the embryonic Renaissance prince, overshadowed by his medieval brother, was ignored. Azario was too hostile and the non-Milanese writers too little informed to give the true reason for Galeazzo's apparently lack-lustre character, and if the testimony of the chroniclers alone were to be accepted then he could be dismissed as a mean, retiring man from whose lethargic hands the reins of power were justly taken by his brother. But opposed to the opinions of notaries and merchants was the fact recorded by Francesco Petrarch; Galeazzo was virtually a cripple, grievously afflicted by the family gout and bearing that affliction with a stoic courage which his detractors ignored.

An adequate index to Galeazzo's character was provided by the presence in his court of the most revered poet and scholar then living. Petrarch's decision to reside with a family of such ill fame when he had the choice of almost every princely house in Europe astounded and dismayed his friends. Boccaccio's bitter reproaches summed up the prevailing opinions. 'Rather should I believe that deer should kill tiger and lamb hunt wolf than that Silvano should so act against his own judgement. Oh, Sorrow! where now is his virtue and sanity to become friends with him that should be called Polyphemous or Cyclops... to be subject so to the yoke of the tyrant.' Petrarch himself appears to be hard put to find an answer and, casting round, throws the blame on fate and on the overwhelming charm of that same Polyphemous, Archbishop Giovanni 'who took my hands with great affability and rendered me honour so much greater than my merits, my hopes — and also my desires... Nothing happens according to our plans. I, abhorring the tempest of discord in Parma, had decided to go to live in Mantua, or Padua. Now look at me, resident in Milan! I, that many times had resisted the invitation of the Roman popes, the king of France, the king of Sicily, did not know how to resist this greatest of Italians who prayed me so gently.' Specifically he rejected the accusations of both friends and enemies that he was a courtier of the Visconti brothers. 'I live in their land, not in their house. There come to me from them only the comforts and honours that they are so continually giving me. It is to other men, born for such tasks, that they turn for counsel, for the conduct of public affairs.'[13] In spite of his protestations, Petrarch's position in Milan went rather beyond that of honoured guest. Certainly he had his own establishment in the city and later, tiring of urban life, moved from Milan itself to found an informal academy some three miles away. But his denial that he ever employed his golden tongue in the Visconti cause during his eight years' residence in the State was more emphatic than accurate. On at least one occasion Giovanni obliged him to perform a distasteful duty by sending him to Avignon which he loathed, during winter which he hated. Giovanni's powers of persuasion were admittedly great, but even after his death Petrarch continued to act as unofficial secretary to both brothers in their role of dual lord of Milan and as literary adviser to Galeazzo as a personal friend. The intimacy between the two men grew deeper after the archbishop's death, for although Bernabò was well aware of the propaganda value of Petrarch's presence in Milan the rendering of honour to a clerk, no matter how exalted, was foreign to his nature. As the inevitable rift between the brothers widened so Petrarch identified himself increasingly with Galeazzo's cramped court in the Porta Giovia. Personal

---

[13] Petrarch, Var. 61.

31

relationships counted for much with Petrarch, but even though affection might have blinded him to defects in his friend's character, he was still a better judge than the majority of chroniclers blinded by hatred of all things Milanese.

Galeazzo's court in the eastern sector of Milan was removed from his brother's not only by the physical distance of a few streets but, in its acceptance of a new age, by a whole attitude of mind. The horizon was wider, for visitors from all over Europe came to Petrarch's house — scholars, statesmen, poets, the freemasonry of scholarship transcending political hostilities to include Petrarch's friend and protector. On the other side of Milan the uproarious life of Bernabò's new court at the Porta Romana accurately reflected his own nature. 'Buffoons, pimps and jesters alone form your court,' Matteo da Milano reproached him — after his death. The effect upon the children of both men was profound; Bernabò's sons grew up in the old tradition with its emphasis on physical courage and military skill, indifferent to the new culture which, practised now by the relative few of Petrarch's calibre, within a generation spread through Italy, becoming a potent political weapon as it shed its esotericism. That culture was for Galeazzo's only son a familiar background from his early years. Pedagogy was never Petrarch's strong suit and his influence upon Giangaleazzo's education was indirect, diffused through the general atmosphere of the court. But the impression of his personality upon the child was long lasting. In later life Giangaleazzo treasured above all his heraldic devices — devices which then included the arms of the Empire and of France — the simple ensign of the dove in rays which Petrarch 'with infinite labour' prepared for him as a child. He was nine years old when Petrarch left Milan, old enough to retain a memory of the man who had laid the foundations for that new age on which he himself would build. It was a fitting coincidence that the only personal record of his childhood should link him with the great scholar. As Paolo Giovio told the story the five-year-old child, asked by his father to point out the wisest man in a room full of distinguished people, unhesitatingly crossed the floor and touched Petrarch's robe.[14] It was a slight, if charming, incident but the delighted Galeazzo had it perpetuated in fresco on the wall of his splendid new palace at Pavia.

THE COUNT OF VIRTUE

In the same year that Petrarch left Milan for ever after his eight years' sojourn, Giangaleazzo made his debut on the stage of Italian history with his marriage to Isabella, daughter of the king of France. A.D. 1360 could not have been a more inauspicious year for the Visconti to celebrate a triumph of this rank. In spring there erupted from the north the first wave of mercenaries discharged after the wars in France, at their head the English White Company, the most efficient military machine to strike Italy during that century. They had come at the behest of the marquis of Monferrat, charged to ravage the lands of Galeazzo Visconti, but, once unleashed in Lombardy, no man could claim to control them and they plundered and murdered where they would in concert with their German companions. Even Bernabò with his nascent standing army could not check them; the great cities alone were safe, for so swiftly did the mercenaries move that a man could be snatched from his very hearth and hastened away to ransom before a town or castle garrison could move into action. Hard upon the mercenaries' heels — indeed, brought by them many swore — came the plague. By early summer Milan was abandoned.

---

[14] Giovio, p. 105.

33

Bernabò at first attempted to control the spread of plague within the city with total lack of mercy; not only were the dead with all their possessions burnt but each household struck by the disease was literally sealed within its home and guards placed over the door until all within were dead or recovered. Few enough recovered; Azario calculated the number of dead within the city at 77,000, and though he exaggerated, by late summer they must have equalled the living as all capable of movement escaped the stinking breath of the oven-hot streets. Galeazzo early withdrew with his family, accompanied by Petrarch. Bernabò remained long enough to see the failure of even his draconic measures and then buried himself so deep within the country that by August it was widely accepted that he was dead. The garrison of his castle were ordered to shoot anyone approaching.

The cooler weather of autumn brought an abatement and Milan stirred again into life. The visitation had been more extreme than usual, but plague was one of the conditions of existence, and though there was still high risk of infection a living had to be earned. Only the few had been able to retreat to well-stocked castles and villas; the many had spent the summer wandering like animals in the open country seeking charity where they could. Poorer family groups returned at first to cleanse their homes not only of infected material but also of the corpses of those who had been abandoned in the moment of high peril. The trickle of isolated groups swelled, the merchants returned and finally, in October, the two courts. It speaks much for the resilience of the people that, scarcely two months after the death roll had reached its peak, Milan was preparing for a court ceremony of the first magnitude, a ceremony which would flood the city with guests from a score of other cities and courts.

Giangaleazzo's marriage was a triumph for the entire house of Visconti, for it linked them directly with the most powerful ruling house in Europe. It established a precedent for other alliances beyond the Alps where before they had been, perforce, content with marriages contracted with their Lombard neighbours, lords with as dubious a legality as their own. Petrarch did not return to Milan and the details of the Visconti's greatest matrimonial triumph comes from the pen of a hostile chronicler. Azario noted the event with his customary lack of enthusiasm, preoccupied with the heavy expenses which Galeazzo recouped by increasing taxes. 'To bring her hither endless expenses were made, for he sent captains and nobles without number into France to escort her. And notwithstanding the many deaths from plague then occurring, nor the endless wars that raged within his lands, he was unwilling to be surpassed in magnanimity, royalty and imperial pomp. The prodigality with which the lady was received into his territory hardly bears thinking of.'[15] Giovanni de' Mussi, the chronicler of Piacenza, who usually had a lively interest in Milanese affairs, gave a merely formal account, while the author of the *Annales Mediolanensis*, writing much later, refers the reader to Azario, presumably endorsing his account. In France the garrulous Froissart, inhibited by his dislike of the Visconti from spinning his usual colourful fictions of courtly life, dismissed the affair both coldly and briefly. 'His (Galeazzo's) proposals were listened to because they knew he was rich. He therefore bought the daughter of king John for 600,000 francs.'[16] The Florentine Matteo Villani alone covered the event with the fullness it warranted and Villani's bias is unequivocally demonstrated by his chapter heading — 'How

---

[15] Azario, XIV, col. 404.
[16] Froissart, cap. 75.

the royal house of France allied itself with the Visconti with dishonour to the crown'. Villani's attitude was as much conditioned by his admiration for France as by his thorough dislike of Milan. Elsewhere in his chronicle he could catalogue some of Bernabò's more brutal activities and end the account with a detached 'these cruelties are little worthy of mention (except) as example of the perils that one runs under the yoke of unrestrained tyranny'.[17] But in his chapter on the marriage he abandoned the measured tone of disgust for one of high lamentation. The contract was beyond human misfortune, something to be placed within the category of Act of God, a smaller flood sent to chastise man. 'Considering the grandeur of the crown of France who could imagine that because of the assaults of the king of England — small and poor in comparison — the king of France should be reduced to such straits as virtually to sell his own flesh at auction, an astonishing spectacle in the sight of Christians and most truly an indication of the infelicity of human affairs.'[18] Villani had accurate sources abroad and his reaction probably summed up general European opinion. Formidable though the Visconti appeared to their Italian neighbours, they were parvenus compared with the Valois, their very name an indication of their true status — servants of the Empire whose legal power could be extinguished by a document. But their compact state yielded a crop which sprawling, war-ravaged France lacked; 600,000 pieces of gold, quite literally a king's ransom.

The treaty of Brétigny had placed upon king John the obligation of finding some three million crowns in ransom. In the June of 1360 while John was still enjoying a comfortable captivity in England, Galeazzo made the first overtures.

---

[17] Villani, M., V, 33.
[18] Ibid. IX, 103.

300,000 florins cash down were offered for Isabella and a further 300,000 to be expended in the purchasing of a suitable dowry in France. The offer was not so much accepted as avidly grasped, the marriage being immediately arranged for the following month. But Isabella fell ill of a fever and it was not until the autumn that she began the first stage of her journey to Savoy, where the customary marriage by proxy concluded the financial negotiations. The fief chosen as her dowry was the county of Vertus some eighteen miles from Châlons-sur-Marne and it was from this place that Giangaleazzo took that title of Conte di Virtù by which he was commonly known until his acquisition of the dukedom of Milan. The title, with its ironic double meaning, was to play as great a part in Florentine propaganda as the image of the viper.

The frugal Galeazzo, having parted with a sum larger than the most spendthrift of his ancestors had ever paid out for a dowry, was determined to receive the utmost value for his money. The postponement of the wedding due to Isabella's illness was probably welcome to him for it enabled him to make the most elaborate preparations, even though hampered by his absence from Milan during the plague. In June he wrote personally to Ugolino Gonzaga of Mantua, inviting him to the festivities 'which would be the greatest that Lombardy had ever seen', and throughout the summer ambassadors were sent to all the major Italian powers urging them to send representatives. 'And the lords of Milan commenced to collect jewels, precious stones, silks, gowns, as much as they could find in Italy wherewith to make pompous preparations'.[19] Visconti money had paid indirectly for the trousseau of Bianca of Savoy, but her family had at least purchased the actual materials themselves. The Valois were denied even this face-

---

[19] Ibid.

saving measure; all was provided by the family of the bridegroom. Isabella arrived in Milan on October 8th and Villani sympathetically noted the change which marriage wrought in her status. She entered the Lombard city a princess of France 'regal in habit and bearing, receiving reverences from the lords and their ladies', but marriage submerged her in the family 'and from that point, thrusting into oblivion her royal dignity and nobility of blood, she made reverence to messer Galeazzo and to messer Bernabò and to their ladies'.[20] The festivities given by Galeazzo lasted for three days and more than a thousand guests were entertained in Milan, each with his train of servitors. Bernabò in his turn gave a banquet as lavish as Galeazzo's, united with his brother in proclaiming the apotheosis of the Visconti to all Europe.

Isabella's coming was particularly welcome to the court at Porta Giovia for it conferred much needed prestige upon Galeazzo. Envious of her nephew's brilliant match, Regina della Scala immediately persuaded Bernabò to break the recently arranged marriage between their elder son Marco and a daughter of Padua's ruling house in order to seek a better. The feminine reaction reflected the relationship between the two courts. In the overall affairs of state Bernabò closely associated himself with his brother, but personal relations between them grew more strained within the confines of Milan. As Galeazzo sank into the listlessness of the invalid and the fickleness of the dilettante, so the real burden of power fell upon Bernabò. It suited him well, but Galeazzo's prestige began to suffer. There was no open break between them nor, considering Bernabò's violent nature, any really serious issue, but the hosts of petty vexations created by the division of Milan placed a heavy stress upon the family tolerance. Servants

[20] Ibid.

38

of the one were for ever accusing servants of the other of trespass; once Bernabò himself appeared outside Porta Giovia, armed and on horseback, raging at the insolence of one of his brother's men, demanding that he be yielded up for immediate execution. Galeazzo refused, even though the man was probably at fault, for Bernabò's act in crossing into his sector in that manner was itself technically illegal. The logical solution to the problem was for one of the brothers to withdraw and set up his capital in one of the other cities of the state. It was said indeed that Bianca was ever urging her husband to do so, being convinced that Bernabò meditated poison; but neither could withdraw without placing himself at a disadvantage, either strategically or through loss of prestige. Those cities near enough to maintain the vital daily contact with Milan were too small while those of standing were too distant.

It was this highly dangerous situation which lent an uncharacteristic military ardour to Galeazzo's attempts to recapture Pavia, the city which fifty years before had been part of the Milanese State. The Visconti had never become reconciled to its loss for, twenty-two miles distant from Milan and standing at the junction of Ticino and Po, it was the south-western bastion not only of their State but of Lombardy itself. Galeazzo appreciated that it would provide him with an eminently satisfactory seat, but the Pavese, having tasted independence, had no intention of being engulfed again. Left to themselves, they would perhaps have accepted re-integration after a token resistance had they not fallen under the influence of Jacopo Bussolari, an Augustinian monk who combined the reforming zeal of a Savonarola with the patriotism of a Rienzi. Bussolari cleansed the city of the foul reputation it had gained under its own corrupt leading family, the Beccaria, turning a brothel into a monastery as it was said. The Beccaria sought his life, were defeated and expelled and promptly made common cause with their late enemy, Galeazzo Visconti. Now under mortal danger from without, the Pavese manifested the last revival of republicanism to be seen in Lombardy. Inspired by Bussolari they sacrificed their silks and jewels, not to a fanatic's bonfire but to agents of the distant merchants of Venice, and with the money obtained fought on against the superior forces of Milan. His armies failing, Galeazzo enlisted Petrarch who, in the name of friendship, sullied his own name with unjust and undignified invectives against the monk. At Bernabò's urgent request he even wrote to the Pavese, protesting against the slaughter of dogs within the city, offering to give them shelter with Bernabò's own great packs. The invectives and protests were ignored and the Pavese fought on for three years until at length Galeazzo, again swallowing humiliation, appealed to his brother for military help. Under the undivided weight of Milan the city crumbled. The English mercenaries who had been summoned to aid the city came too late, for while they were still making their way into Italy, an envoy of Galeazzo's was negotiating the terms of surrender with Bussolari. The monk asked for nothing for himself but insisted that the newly established constitution should be honoured. Galeazzo agreed; Bussolari was led in triumph to Milan and from thence to a monastic cell where he spent the rest of his life, and the promises made by Galeazzo were coldly abrogated. It was not for him, Vicar of the Empire, to compromise the rights of the Empire, he declared. Impoverished, starving, without rights save those the new lord wished to concede, the Pavese awaited the conqueror himself. They were more fortunate than they knew, even if they must have been puzzled by the fact that among the swarms of officials who descended upon the city during the first few days were a number of architects. These

40

men, while their legal and military colleagues were engaged in establishing the new regime, began surveying a section of the city. On that site work began on the construction of the Castle of Pavia in March 1360, just four months after the capitulation of the city, testimony to Galeazzo's urgent desire to transform Pavia into his seat. The founding of the castle marked the end of Pavia as an independent city but it also resurrected a glory which had lain dormant for three centuries.

THE COURT OF PAVIA

Four years after the first trenches were dug for the foundations of the castle Francesco Petrarch, comfortably established in one of its rooms, was writing to Giovanni Boccaccio commiserating with his friend on his arduous journey to Avignon, urging him to come to 'this city of Ticinum… now called Pavia which the grammarians tell us means admirable or wonderful. I have now spent three summers here and I do not remember ever to have experienced anywhere else such plentiful showers, such freedom from heat and such refreshing breezes. The city stands in the middle of the Ligurian plain upon a little hill… and enjoys a wide free prospect on every side. By turning one's head ever so little in one direction may be seen the snowy crests of the Alps and in the other the wooded Apennines. The Ticino itself, descending in graceful curves and hastening to join the Po, flows close by the city walls… its two banks joined by as fine a bridge as you would wish to see. It is the clearest of streams and flows very rapidly, although just here it moves more deliberately and has been deprived of its natural purity by the brooks which join it. Lastly in order of time, though not of importance, you would see the huge palace standing on the highest point of the city. I am convinced — unless I am misled by partiality for the founder

— that with your good taste in such matters you would declare this to be the most noble production of modern art.'[21]

Petrarch's blandishment was in vain; not even the opportunity to pass judgement on the most notable palace in Italy could persuade Boccaccio to accept hospitality of the loathed Visconti. But his friend had no such scruples. After his departure from Milan, Petrarch had taken up residence in Padua, but each summer he joined Galeazzo at Pavia, watching the enormous building arising from the chaos around it. The coterie Petrarch had built up in Milan had left with him, so that for Galeazzo the great city was nothing more than an administrative centre, governed from the comfortless castle at Porta Giovia in unpleasant proximity to his brother. His family remained in Milan but he himself spent all available time in Pavia, his presence urging the workmen on to a speed the more remarkable considering his parsimony. Speaking of his architectural activities elsewhere, Azario remarked that 'he wished to have masters, workers and carvers for very little or nothing, from every part and in every trade. In the cold of winter or the heat of summer, in rain, in all conditions, work went forward. But what was worse so soon as one wall was built it was pulled down and another erected nearby and because these walls were made in a hurry, with poor materials, cracks appeared and soon they fell.'[22] Azario either knew little of architecture or Galeazzo had learnt his lesson, for there could have been nothing gimcrack in the construction of a building which has survived 600 years with only minor alterations. The workmen must have been treated in a manner just short of slavery, for by the autumn of 1365 the castle was

---

[21] Petrarch, Sen. V, ep. 1.
[22] Azario, XIV.

considered fit for habitation; in October Galeazzo with his family left Milan for ever.

The city which he and his son were to make a kind of Versailles had once overshadowed Milan itself, for it had been the ancient capital of the Lombard kings and its capture by Charlemagne signalled the end of their dominance in Italy. Approached by the great road from Milan it presented a gloomy, formidable face, created by the centuries of warfare its strategic value had caused. Dominating were the towers, 150 and more of them, most of them already in their fourth century, soaring pinnacles of brick which rendered dark the already narrow streets. They had been architects of chaos, for each had housed its egoistic fragment of society, providing a secure base from whence rivals and the desperate government itself could be defied. But with the coming of the Visconti and the smashing of faction they had lost their primary function and were in decay. On that same northern slope of the city was a castle as bleak as the towers, that erected as instrument of suppression by Matteo the Great during the Visconti dominance fifty years before, more recently used by Galeazzo during his prolonged visits while his own more elegant home was in construction. From the south the city appeared more open, almost gay, for here the waters of the Ticino lapped the walls and the forests were cleared for husbandry. Pavia was virtually an island in the plain. The Ticino swept round it before running on to join the great river route of the Po five miles away; northward lay the Carona which Galeazzo diverted to form the moat for his new castle, and the Naviglio Grande, the newly built canal which connected the city with Milan. Two days' journey from the sea though it was, Pavia was a port of some distinction, developing an impressive war fleet during endless conflicts with its riverine neighbours, expanding a merchant fleet which, bringing goods from Milan via the canal, could transport them onwards to the Adriatic. But in spite of its strategic and economic importance, Petrarch's description of it as a city for pleasure was essentially correct. It was an oasis in the heat of the Lombard summer, its *contado* astonishingly fruitful even for Lombardy. Galeazzo carved out a great estate as a fitting park for his castle, but so richly did game swarm in the whole area that the rigorous game laws of the Milanese *contado* were not necessary, indications of a condition which approached the idyllic. Bernabò's laws were based on the uncontradicted assumption that the life of a peasant was something less valuable than the life of a boar.

Galeazzo gave every indication of happily resigning from that tense and violent life which characterized Milan. His letters to the neighbouring lord of Mantua showed a relaxed, and indeed a happy, man for whom the problem of transporting a pair of black swans from Mantua ousted the problems of holding his own with his brother. The swans have died for the weather was too hot; would Gonzaga be good enough to send another pair by boat. If they be covered with straw and the straw kept wet they should arrive in good condition. Gonzaga is requested to lend carvers and painters for the embellishment of the castle and his advice sought from the experience he had gained during the construction of his own great palace. A pair of rascally Venetian weavers escape with a quantity of gold thread and a great deal of effort is expended in bringing them to book. He informs Gonzaga of how his health improves daily for regularly he rides along the cool banks of the Ticino, breathing the scented air of the woods which press close. There needed only one thing more to fill his domestic cup and in March 1366, five months after taking up residence in Pavia, it was granted to him with the birth of his first grandchild.

Giangaleazzo was nine years old at the time of his marriage in 1360 and his wife Isabella perhaps three years older. Child marriages were common enough, the bride, especially, frequently taking first communion just before the marriage ceremony, and custom ensured that a political necessity did not result in a moral outrage. The legal age of puberty was twelve and until he reached that age Giangaleazzo and Isabella were treated as the children they were, their marriage unconsummated. In his thirteenth year they began cohabitation, but thence departed from custom for they remained under the parental roof. The close bond which knit Galeazzo's family together was so strong that not until his father's death did Giangaleazzo have his own household. It was a voluntary submission and it had a profound effect upon his character, for throughout his formative years he remained under the direct influence of his mother, Bianca. It was fortunate for Isabella that influence was benign. The household which the adolescent princess entered was presided over by a woman of rare gentleness, ten years older than herself, speaking the same language and, with her husband, setting an example of domestic felicity rare in princely houses. Azario thought it worth while to remark that Galeazzo remained faithful throughout his life, not even possessing the customary mistress, and so attached to his wife as to allow her to persuade him in political matters. Isabella, bought to further Visconti ambition, found a security in Pavia which had been utterly lacking in her father's chaotic court. Three months after her arrival in Milan, Petrarch had gone to Paris on Galeazzo's behalf to congratulate the king on his recent release and to bring him news of his daughter. She had charged him to say that she could not be treated with greater kindness nor be in a place which she could love more, he assured her father. According to Petrarch's own account, John seemed to be more interested in hearing him discourse on scholarly matters than to learn of his daughter's fate. Villani's jibe of 'flesh auction' was better aimed at John the Good of France than at Galeazzo, tyrant of Milan.

Isabella's infant was christened with his father's name in May and Galeazzo took the opportunity both to display his new castle to public admiration for the first time and to blazon his augmented dynastic status. Apart from Giangaleazzo, he had only a daughter, Violante, and in a society much of whose strength was founded upon the marriage potential of children he was at a disadvantage. Compared with his brother, who saw each year an increase in his family whether legitimate or illegitimate, Galeazzo had only the most limited opportunities; nevertheless, for both his children he contracted marriage alliances more brilliant than had ever been known among the Visconti. His ability first to marry his son into the French monarchy and then his daughter into the English was largely a matter of finance; Bernabò, freer with his money, preferred to spend it on soldiers and fortresses, assuming that those who wished to marry into the Visconti would be willing to pay for the privilege.

The negotiations for the marriage of Violante to Lionel, duke of Clarence, had taken nearly two years; Humphrey de Bohun came to Pavia in 1366 to discuss the possibilities, but it was not until April 1368 that the treaty was signed in Windsor. In return for Violante's solid dowry of 200,000 florins and certain Piedmontese cities, Lionel was bringing the glamour of his father's name, some shadowy rights in Ireland which he had spent ten years vainly trying to acquire, and very little else. In

England it was taken for granted that one day he might be king of all Italy, English imagination expanding the few Piedmontese burghs into half Galeazzo's territory and assigning the lord of Milan an importance in Italian affairs which he would have been surprised to be thought to have possessed. Lionel arrived in Lombardy in May 1368 with a train of some 2000, but the preparations made for his welcome outshone even the ostentation of the English. A marriage of such importance could take place only in the capital of the Milanese state and Galeazzo's family moved into Milan for the occasion. Again it was a Visconti triumph and again Bernabò identified himself with his brother, even though he was in the midst of a war which threatened to topple the entire Visconti structure. Lionel was met at the Porta Ticinese by Galeazzo and his wife, accompanied by their son and daughter-in-law. Giangaleazzo led a group of thirty knights, all vividly dressed as for a joust; it was the nearest the seventeen-year-old youth had yet come to military experience, while his cousins had already been blooded in their father's interminable wars.

The wedding took place on the 15th of June outside the shabby cathedral for there was no room within for the great press of people. And afterwards there followed that banquet the tale of whose almost Oriental extravagance spread throughout Europe. It would have turned a harder head than Lionel's, this introduction to the Italy which gave him the kiss of death three months later; even the Milanese, accustomed to the political extravagance of their rulers, deemed it a kind of natural wonder, Corio and the Milanese Annalist cataloguing the interminable courses and gifts as though they had been poured on to the city by a deity. The citizens themselves were probably hungry enough, for there had been rain that year from February through to May and crops were poor, but they were not quite desperate and no unseemly disturbance marred the splendour. The Visconti guards were competent and there was hope of charity, 'For such was the sumptuousness of the banquet that the meats that were brought from the table would sufficiently have fed 10,000 men'. The banquet was held in the open courtyard of a palace, probably that of Porta Giovia, and though the men present must have run into the hundreds, only fifty women were present. Bianca should have presided at their table, for it was her daughter's wedding, but it was the imperious Regina who did those honours, dominating her sister-in-law even as her husband dominated his brother. Petrarch was present at the high table, come, with a stoic courage, to honour his friend; on that same day his beloved grandson had died in Milan. It is probable that Geoffrey Chaucer was also at that table with Lionel and the Visconti brothers, having come to Italy with Lionel and now making his first contact with the Visconti and the profligate generosity of a despot. There were eighteen courses to the meal but each was double, one of fish and one of meat, the woods and streams and pastures of western Lombardy scoured to provide the choicest meat: veal, trout, quail, partridge, duck, heron, chicken, rabbit, eels, sturgeon, Corio's list was an inventory of the fauna of Lombardy. But the meal itself provided only a framework for a demonstration, vulgar but overwhelming, of the wealth of the Visconti, acting almost as a kind of trade fair for the products of Milan. The marshalling and distributing of the fantastic variety of gifts fell to Giangaleazzo, for he was acting as steward at his sister's wedding banquet, for once in a position of authority over his four cousins. 'Chief of the choice youth' Stowe referred to him, a remark which no Milanese chronicler would have dreamed of using, for the sons of Bernabò were already public figures while few Milanese would have even recognized the son of Galeazzo. Accompanying the first course — itself bizarre enough for it consisted of sucking pigs spouting fire — came couple after couple of the famous greyhounds and bloodhounds of Milan, each with a collar and leash of velvet and silver. Admired and then conducted off by servants of the recipients, they were followed by suits of the beautiful Milanese armour, all bearing the crest of Visconti and Clarence; great rolls of silk and brocade from the looms of Milan were brought in, ceremonially offered to Lionel, and despatched to join the rest; goshawks and sparrowhawks filling the air with the tinkling of their silver bells, garments liberally covered with pearls and trimmed with ermine, jewels, clasps, girdles, a dozen fat oxen, war horses bearing lances, shields and helmets, tourney mounts gaily caparisoned — the incongruous spate of gifts could have left little time or space for the enjoyment of the meal.

Lionel departed to his new estates in Piedmont after the festivities, apparently intending to take up the life of an Italian nobleman. In October he and Violante went on a short visit to her family in Pavia; he never left the city. His death was due entirely to his own intemperance, for he had made no concession to the new circumstances in which he found himself, but conducted himself throughout the Lombard summer as though he were at home in England. The ubiquitous and undefined 'fever' of Italy took him off, but inevitably there was a cry of poison even though his death was manifestly a catastrophe to Galeazzo, who thus saw the edifice raised at enormous expense shattered at his feet. The English knights still being entertained in his territories, led by Edward le Despenser, swore revenge and called upon all English mercenaries in Italy to join them. The mercenaries prudently ignored the call, but 2000 incensed and veteran soldiers, activated as much by thought of loot as desire for revenge, presented Galeazzo with a grave problem. He drove them out at length and they united with his enemy, the marquis of Monferrat, leaving him to ponder the value of alliances founded solely on money. But the ingratitude of the English and the destruction of his political hopes swiftly dwindled to nothing in comparison with the storm which, gathering for over a decade, threatened to sweep him, his brother, and the Milanese state from the face of Italy.

II: THE GEOGRAPHICAL EXPRESSION

THE FOUR POWERS

The land was in the final throes of the anarchy which had seized it a millennium before. A century hence, and those convulsions could be seen as heralds of new life as well as of death, the agony of half a hundred minor cities the prerequisite for the Renaissance glory of half a dozen. But for the nameless mass of people it seemed that, in this fourteenth century, every horror which God had devised for the trying of man and man for the torment of his neighbour was poured upon the peninsula. 'O happy posterity, who will not experience such abysmal woe and will look upon our testimony as a fable.' Petrarch's cry was wrung from him by the horrors of the plague, but the plague was only one of the three traditional scourges which, singly and in combination, swept the land unchecked. The sword was never sheathed and as delicately balanced economic forces were destroyed in fratricidal warfare, so famine followed. Plague, sword, and famine; these were the sole constants in a disintegrating society. Central authority was dead, the envious cities leaguing only to tear down any of their number which seemed about to dominate. The Communes, the last attempt of free men to build free societies, had long since decayed although the forms continued. The coming great autocracies were still in process of establishing themselves, their legal power still vested in the people so that when tyrants fell the ancient constitutions were swiftly and easily re-established. But the tyrants always returned. In the free cities governments and constitutions changed with bewildering speed, and with each change exiles by the thousand were thrust out to wander and plot the downfall of their city with its external enemies. In the chaos the mercenaries rose, a new phenomenon among ancient hatreds, exerting unpredictable stresses on the tottering society. The twin supra-national authorities of Papacy and Empire which should, in theory, have placed a curb upon the fratricidal tendencies were themselves engaged in combating their charges and each other. Here and there some few figures stood out momentarily above the general ruck: Rienzi the Tribune of Rome, fired by the ideal of resurrecting the City, momentarily dragging his fellow citizens up with him, becoming himself corrupt and ending his career butchered in a gutter; Catherine of Siena, balancing her life between heaven and earth, plunging into the drab and dubious world of papal politics and, perhaps greatest miracle of all, emerging unsullied if unsuccessful; Dante following a splendid, sterile dream of Empire, living long enough to see the hollowness of both Empire and Emperor; Petrarch, succeeding Dante in the hopeless task of recalling the Emperor to Rome, later aiding Catherine in the thankless one of calling the Pope, becoming embittered in both causes as Dante had done; these were among the handful of people whose thin voices proclaimed a goal above immediate self-preservation, an ideal a little higher than the enslavement of a city by its neighbour. But the four mutually exclusive forces of cities, mercenaries, Papacy, and Empire, in rending each other tore down the fragile structures raised by reasonable minds. Those minds were centuries too late or centuries too early; the Empire Dante sought to reinstate was a sonorous ghost; the federation Rienzi sought to establish needed six centuries more of bitter experience. The cities, blindly following their instincts of survival and growth, more truly diagnosed the Italian need;

that coalescence had to precede federation, the hundreds becoming dozens before they could again become one.

The Cities

Throughout the peninsula, confusion is the only characteristic which appears at first sight. But even in this welter where evanescent powers arise with all-embracing claims only to disappear like mists, where every path seems to peter out or become lost in a tangle of motives and ambitions, two forms appear to give scale and orientation. Milan and Florence were at once the symbols and results of the diverging path of their time. The Lombard despotism and the Tuscan republic had both known the earlier ideals of the Commune; both cities had sporadically suffered the tyrant and had thrown him out; each had known the clangour of partisan struggles within its walls. Each had followed a different path in its attempt to find relief from anarchy although a century later the paths met again and became one. Milan sought peace by creating the despot or, more accurately, by allowing him to create himself. Florence cut down her dominant figures when they became too strong, distributing power as far as humanly possible among all citizens. The elaborate and sometimes fantastic methods adopted to ensure that all Florentines should enjoy the exercise of power occasioned endless turmoil in the city. 'Numquam in eodem statu permanserunt', Marco Foscari observed with some scorn, for to the Venetian, accustomed to an established constitution, the upheavals in Florence seemed to be based upon a fundamental frivolity. But a Florentine could reasonably retort that the vaunted political stability of Venice was based on the absolute rule of a minority, a situation differing little from open tyranny to the unprejudiced eye. Both these cities lay claim to the title of 'Republic', but so did every other city not under the rule of an hereditary monarch. Corio could refer to the Visconti Milan of his grandfather as 'Republic' or 'Commune' quite simply and without irony. Outside the open despotisms the concept of individual freedom was narrow enough; in Florence perhaps 5000 out of a population of some 100,000 enjoyed full rights; in Siena citizenship was strictly hereditary or conferred as reward for individual merit. Florentine theory, however, still favoured democracy even though her practice was usually at variance. Her great and growing commercial wealth, though it brought her into conflict with her immediate neighbours, naturally constituted her as leader of those cities which, though discordant about means, still agreed as to the main goal — a society whose leaders were elected by at least some of the people. Florentine leadership was ultimately gained by default of others. Venice remained aloof from the troubles of the peninsula, interfering only when her own land communications were threatened. The cities of the Lombard plain, first occupied in swallowing each other, were themselves swallowed by their great neighbour. The Papal States, which might have formed an influential bloc, was the territory of the most finished autocrat of them all. The power of the Tuscan cities shrank as that of Florence increased. Rome was a city in a nightmare, its desolation broken only by ferocious local brawls. It carried still the magic of its ancient name, so that on those rare occasions when it lifted its head from the mire Italians looked towards it with quickening interest. But the city could neither lead nor follow any national movement, and after the tragedy of Rienzi it was dismissed from the calculations of most. Naples, trapped in its complex web of hereditary hatreds, was incapable of exerting that influence which the antiquity of its monarchy gave her and was, for most Italians, but a discordant sound upon the southern horizon. At those rare periods, therefore, when the independent cities ceased their internecine warfare and grouped for a common cause, it was Florence who led them. Florentine reasons for the city's God-given role were plausible. 'The liberty of this city appears to be all the more secure the broader the belt of free peoples surrounding it. Therefore, everyone ought to be readily convinced that the Florentine people are the defenders of liberty of all people, since in defending them, they also make the defence of their own freedom less difficult.'[23] So the Florentine Chancellor, Coluccio Salutati, wrote to the Lucchese, seeking to allay their apprehensions and, incidentally, draw them into the Florentine strategy. Florence was ever fortunate in having golden-tongued apologists for her politics.

The Mercenaries

The condition of virtually permanent warfare throughout the land destroyed the last true guarantee of the free cities, the armed citizen-soldier. It became impossible for a man to follow his own trade and yet render adequate service to his own state as it expanded its frontiers or was obliged to protect them from the expansion of others. And with the total breakdown of centralized authority coinciding with the need for ever more soldiers, the armed companies of mercenaries arose. The *Compagnie di Ventura* were brigands, but they were successful brigands who had learned to render themselves indispensable. Their employers gained nothing more than the maintenance of a ruinous *status quo*: those who did not employ them fell from the ranks of first-class powers. The role of the citizen-soldier was now not even secondary for his presence on the battlefield told not of his own courage but of his city's

---

[23] Valeri.

poverty; yet his disappearance heralded the end of the Communes.

In 1176 the citizen-soldiers of the Lombard League led by Milan met, held, and smashed the professional army of Frederick Barbarossa; in 1289 the last battle between citizen-soldiers was fought at Campaldino when Florence finally crushed Arezzo. Legnano gave the young Communes confidence in their ability to defend their identities; Campaldino set a seal on the fear that soon there would be no citizens left to inherit, the slaughter of citizen by citizen was so great. The progress of emancipating him from military service was approved by tyranny and republic alike, the former because it was easier to keep an unarmed population in check, the latter because the dislocation of trade had an appalling effect upon the economy. The obligation to serve had included all males between the ages of fifteen and seventy and the all-embracing age group ensured the suspension of all normal life when war broke out. In each city the wealthier citizens, who normally furnished the vital cavalry, compounded for a cash settlement and turned their defence over to professionals who were discharged after each war. The system worked well enough until 1342 when Werner of Urslingen, a German mercenary recently discharged from the service of Pisa, persuaded his fellows to remain together as a company instead of dispersing as hitherto. Thus simply the Great Company, the first of the *Compagnie di Ventura*, came into existence and inaugurated a new political pattern in Italy. The companies approached the status of nomad States with an internal order that many a small faction-torn city might have envied. Discipline, though strict, could be enforced, for each man knew that nowhere else could he find such a combination of profit and security. They were, again, far truer democracies than the so-called republics. A company might come into existence only through the personality of its commander, but his decisions off the battlefield were subject to the approval of the constables and marshals in council, and these in their turn were elected by the soldiery. No longer now could a city treat with half a dozen small groups, playing one against the other, but was obliged to enter into formal contract with a company numbering possibly 10,000 men. The contract signed, the Companions became legal soldiers; but their methods of life remained unchanged, for their sole object was the extortion of blackmail whether it were labelled pay or plunder. Lucius Landau, *condottiere* of the Great Company, spoke for all mercenaries when replying to the Papal envoys who had requested him, as a good Christian, to spare Papal territories. 'My Lords, our manner of life in Italy is well known — it is to rob, plunder and murder those who resist. Our revenues depend on ransoms levied in those provinces which we invade. Those who value their lives can buy peace and quiet by heavy tribute. Therefore, if the Lord Legate wishes to dwell at unity with us then let him do like the rest of the world — that is to say Pay! Pay!'[24]

The companies which dominated Italy during the middle years of the century were entirely foreign. 'In truth, their military success was more owing to the cowardice of our men than to their valour and military virtue,'[25] was Villani's judgement, but in this he erred. The foreign mercenary had no stake in the land, fought for neither life nor honour but for pay, and a state could therefore employ him without fearing his political ambition. In order to ensure this most states inserted a clause in the contract stipulating that no citizen — and

---

[24] Gregorovius, VI, 2.
[25] Villani, F., XI, 81.

57

particularly no exiled citizen — should be a member of the contracting company. Until 1360 the companies were for the most part composed of Germans and Hungarians, but in that year, as a result of the treaty of Brétigny, English companies began to make the passage of the Alps. Among them was the White Company, commanded by the East Anglian John Hawkwood who was to become the greatest foreign *condottiere* in Italy. He had fought at Crécy and Poitiers and taken their lesson to heart, but it was not only his military skill which brought him to the height of his profession; a rarity among mercenaries, he could not be bribed. The companies he led took part in the usual blackmailing operations during the brief periods of peace, but when once he had signed a contract he fought with a devotion usually found only in militia. He married a daughter of Bernabò Visconti's and though he did not scruple to attack his father-in-law during the course of business, for twenty years maintained a curiously warm relationship with him. Bernabò trusted him as he trusted no other of his generals or even his sons. A dour, hard, but just man, Sachetti's anecdote of him summed up not only the man himself but the philosophy of all his colleagues. Saluted by a pair of wandering friars with the customary 'God give you peace', Hawkwood snarled back 'God take away your alms!' Astounded, the friars protested that they but wished him well. 'How so,' replied Acuto (Hawkwood). 'Is not begging your profession and is not war mine? If you wish me peace how shall I live? So I say — God take away your alms!'[26]

Before the coming of the English, the heavily armoured man on horseback dominated the battlefield. Cavalry was compact, mobile and expensive and was therefore the weapon of the professional, widening the gap between him and the citizen-

---

[26] Sachetti, *Novelle*.

soldier who possessed only his own two legs. Native and foreign horsemen were, with one exception, alike encased in metal from head to toe — helmet, body-armour, shield, gauntlets, greaves, together with lance and sword making a ponderous weight which, though irresistible in a grand charge, hampered mobility and totally incapacitated the wearer if he were unhorsed. The exception was the Hungarians whose arms and tactics had changed little over 1000 years; they were virtually mounted archers, relying for protection upon their incredible agility, their armour being simple jerkin and helmet of leather. Foot archers and crossbowmen were in the minority until Hawkwood revolutionized their role, bringing their numbers up to approximately half the total strength of a company. His bowmen continued to be armed in the English manner, their sole weapon, apart from the great longbow of yew, being a knife. The longbow swiftly demonstrated its superiority over the crossbow but it nevertheless remained an exclusively English weapon, and when the English themselves disappeared from Italy, the longbow went with them. Throughout the century it had no real rival as a missile propellant, even though artillery had established itself by the 1350s. The German companies sometimes dragged bombards around with them and possessed what appear to be grenades and crude handguns, but the cumbersome nature of these uncertain new weapons made them little in favour with a soldiery whose chief value lay in their mobility. There were no prolonged sieges of cities in Italy to favour the development of monster guns, although a few appeared in Lombardy where the terrain was more suitable for their use. The Lord of Verona employed three gigantic ribaulds or multiple bombards against Hawkwood at the battle of Castagnaro in 1387. Drawn by four horses and standing more than twenty feet high, each of the monstrous weapons possessed 144 tubes arranged in three storeys and could fire twelve salvos of twelve balls in succession. Theoretically a deadly enemy against a massed enemy, they were in fact useless, being first stranded by the swift movement of the armies and when at last brought into action were captured before the tedious business of loading was completed.

Hawkwood continued the English practice of dismounting his cavalry in battle, organizing his forces on the basic unit of the 'lance', a method which became adopted throughout Italy. The lance consisted of three men, cavalier, squire and page, the two former being the fighting component who, dismounted in battle, would together wield the great lance in the manner which Villani vividly described. Villani came to know the English well — too well for his liking. 'These English were all lusty young men, most of them born and brought up in the long wars between France and England; warm, eager and practised in rapine and slaughter… with very little care for their personal safety but in matters of discipline very obedient to their commanders.' Their ability to fight in the close season of winter amazed him. It was a thing unusual even among the Romans, he declared, and could find no one but Hannibal with whom to compare them. Significantly, he remarked upon their fighting formation. 'Their manner of fighting in the field was almost always on foot, their horses being given in charge of their pages. The body they formed was very compact and almost round, each lance was held in the same manner as the spear is held in hunting wild boar. And thus close embodied, with their lances pointed low and with slow steps, they marched up to the enemy with terrible outcry and very difficult it was to disunite them.'[27] This compact body bristling with

---

[27] Villani, F., XI, 81.

lances discharged the mercenaries' two main needs — the profitable prolonging of a campaign with the least danger to themselves. The formation might lack the glamour and swift advantage of the conventional cavalry charge, but the company was admirably placed to take up the defensive should it fail to triumph by sheer weight. Obligations were discharged by bringing the enemy to even a temporary halt, and the time consumed in the subsequent regroupings earned yet more pay. Local battles might be frequently bloody, but grand strategy was almost impossible to plan with such untrustworthy material. And in between wars they reverted to banditry. Again and again leagues were proposed and even formed against them, but on each occasion some city, grasping at the opportunity to establish a brief ascendancy, would break the agreement and hire a company and the league would collapse in the resultant scramble for soldiers.

The Papacy

There were not lacking Italians who understood that the absence of a central authority was the ultimate cause of the social chaos. The century was five years old when the Papacy removed itself to Avignon, thereby exacerbating that problem of its temporal power which had forced it to enter the arena on the same terms and with the same objects as the meanest of cities, depriving it of its possible role of arbitrator. The temporary absence became protracted into the 'Babylonian captivity' which did not end until the return of Gregory XI in 1377, and that return merely precipitated the worse evil of the Schism. Avignon could with some justice claim that it offered the Papacy a security quite lacking in the gloomy violence of Rome, but inevitably the Curia degenerated into a pensioner of the French throne. Yet still it claimed those revenues and privileges which it had enjoyed as an Italian institution and to enforce those claims appointed legates who could not have been better chosen to enrage Italians. 'Demoni incarnati,' St Catherine called them roundly, 'evil pastors and rectors who poison and putrefy this garden.'[28] Bitter though it was to witness the Pope as a French captive, infinitely more bitter was it for Italians to submit to the demands of foreign legates and watch the wealth from Italy pass into the hands of foreigners. One by one the cities broke away from their allegiance. The brief national unity formed in the 1370s under pressure of foreign arrogance was subject to too many internal stresses to survive. Nevertheless, a war led by Guelphic Florence allied with Ghibelline Milan against the Papacy ensured the effective end of the two great factions which had divided Italy. In a little over a generation the ancient definitions of 'Guelph' and 'Ghibelline' were modified until they became no more than rallying cries. In the middle of the century Villani could identify the Guelphs as 'those that follow Holy Church in the affairs of the world', while the Ghibellines were 'those that follow the Empire whether it be on the side of true believers or no'. In 1420 Leonardo Bruni, in redefining the statutes of the Florentine *Parte Guelfa*, stated: 'If one considers the community of the Guelphs from the religious point of view it will be found to be connected with the Roman Church; if, however, from the human view, then with Liberty'.[29] Such a definition would have been meaningless to Villani and to the thousands who had lived and died in the name of Guelph before the war with the Papacy. But to an Italian who had seen the dying unshriven, the new-born unbaptized, his goods sequestered in the name of that Papacy, 'Guelph' as a concept of liberty must

---

[28] Harleian MS. 3480; 185 (1).
[29] Baron, p. 15.

be for ever divorced from the source of its being.

The Empire

And as the Papacy embroiled itself deeper in temporal struggles, so Italians looked beyond the northern mountains to Caesar's heir, the half-mythical memory of the *pax romana* so briefly revived by Charlemagne and Leo III returning to haunt them. There was, for them, no break between the uncouth Germans with their high titles and the Emperors of the ancient city. Annalists had but one sequence for all the Emperors from Augustus to the reigning Charles IV; during their coronation in Rome Emperor and Empress were still lodged in chambers called Livia and Augustus; their processions were still adorned with the wolf, eagle, and dragon standards.[30] But even this awesome lineage was raised to greater heights by the Christian infusion which saw in Emperor and Pope not the conflicting authorities they became, but a duality appointed by God, the one to rule over the souls of all men, the other over their bodies. Rarely was this harmony attained. Papal power increased at the expense of its ordained protector until that day of jubilee in 1300 when Boniface VIII could disclose himself to the pilgrims, throned and crowned, shouting 'Ego, ego sum imperator'.[31] Yet as the actual power of the Emperor waned,

---

[30] Bryce, pp. 249, 258, 260. The colder modern view is summed up by Emerton (Humanism and Tyrant, p. 8): 'What was called the Empire was really a national kingdom, the kingdom of the Germans... accepting a foreign culture and an alien religion, imposing itself on less forceful peoples to the north and south and then decorating itself with the borrowed symbols of a sham imperialism.' It is unlikely, to say the least, that Italian merchants would assent to the disbursing of several millions of gold for the purchase of rights from a Germanic sham.

[31] Bryce, p. 109.

the ideal of the universal monarch increased so that the Imperial nadir coincided with the appearance of its most able apologia, the *De Monarchia* of Dante. Henry VII came in answer to Dante's summons. Hailed as saviour by Guelph and Ghibelline alike, his progress was at first all triumph, but inevitably he became trapped in the complexities of Italian politics, drawn into narrow struggles for ignoble aims, was bewildered alike by the violence and the disillusion which met him, and in the end died shamefully. *De Monarchia*, intended to be the trumpet call for the risen majesty of empire, became its requiem. Nevertheless, in 1354, a German king was summoned again into Italy to take the crown and bring peace to a tortured land, but where Henry had come in majesty, the progress of his son Charles IV 'was more as a merchant going to mass than an emperor going to his throne', the merchant Villani observed sardonically.[32] Charles's journey through Italy was undertaken simply to obtain the crown and, through it, peddle his vicariates and exemptions for solid golden florins. At Rome itself he was allowed to stay only the few hours necessary to receive his consecration and from there he was hurried out to return north 'with the crown which he had obtained without a sword thrust, with a full purse which he had taken empty to Italy, with little glory for manly deeds and with great disgrace for the humiliated majesty of the Empire'.[33] Petrarch, who had implored him as passionately as Dante had implored his grandfather, joined Villani in condemning him. 'If thy father and grandfather were to meet thee in the passes of the Alps what thinkest thou they would say? Emperor of the Romans but in name, thou art in truth no more than the king of Bohemia.'[34] But Petrarch was looking back to a dead Golden

---

[32] Villani, M., V, 54.
[33] Ibid.

Age while Charles accepted the current age of iron. Lord of the world in theory, the emperor had nothing with which to support that title than the resources of his own nation, so that every descent into Italy was accompanied by a wrangle over money. In order to obtain the reluctant financial aid from his own country, he was forced to make far-reaching domestic concessions. In Italy, the Italians who summoned the Emperor of the Romans to settle their disputes voted money to the German king with the deepest reluctance as though the mere incantation of his sonorous powers sufficed. Yet side by side with their contempt for his physical powers was the unquenchable belief in his office as the source of all legality, the ultimate lord of Italy.

CRUSADE AGAINST MILAN

Five days after Violante was married to Lionel, in distant Siena Donato di Neri recorded with sober thankfulness: 'The Emperor has left the cathedral of Prague helm on head and sword in hand, come to acquire the places of the Church — and the places of the Empire.'[35] The Emperor was the theoretic head of an anti-Visconti league which stretched halfway across Europe from Avignon to Naples, from Siena to Hungary, a league which included Guelphs and Ghibellines, ancient monarchies and new republics sworn to uproot and destroy the Viper's nest in Lombardy. In his continuous probing southward Bernabò had at last touched off a virtual national alliance. He could not have avoided it had he wished, for the struggle to regain Bologna had fallen to him as dominant partner and lord of eastern Milan. The loss of Bologna in 1354 had again penned the Visconti within

---

[34] Petrarch, Fam. XIX, ep. 12.

[35] *Cronaca Senese.*

Lombardy; their attempts to regain it would form the pattern of Italian politics for the next half-century, for the fate of the city affected almost every power in Italy. The construction of the League had taken years, for though all hated and feared the growing power of Milan, mutual hatreds and suspicions were almost as great and Bernabò had for long been able to play one against the other. But the great Papal Legate, Egidio Albornoz, noble priest, consummate soldier, and wily politician, had skilfully exploited the common factor in all the Italian states, the fear that one of their number might become pre-eminent, and as the fruit of his legation presented Urban V with a workable military league. Once more the theory of Empire was brought out to seduce Italians; Christ's secular vicar, the Emperor, was come in support of the spiritual. Urban, it seemed, had forgotten or preferred not to remember the Imperial shame of a decade before when this same Charles IV, *imperator terrenus*, had played the part of merchant.

The Visconti policy of divided rule had long enabled Galeazzo to pursue his preferences independent of his brother. The two sections of the State ruled from Pavia and Milan were separate states for practical purposes, each lord free to pursue the path he best saw fit. And the path which Galeazzo preferred emphatically did not lead to that turmoil in which Bernabò rejoiced. Nevertheless, enemies of the Visconti did not trouble to distinguish between the brothers and against his will Galeazzo found himself drawn in. Bernabò beat off the first attack with accomplished ease, the Emperor proved as venial as ever, Urban died and the League collapsed. But Milan had now become the target for a Holy War; Gregory XI excommunicated Bernabò, 'that son of Belial', and European forces were again set in motion against the Lombard city. From the south the armies of the Tuscan allies began to march, while from the north-west a Papal army prepared to move down through the Piedmont hills. The defence of the western territories fell to Galeazzo, its focal point the city of Asti which for years he had been sieging in vain. His attempt to reduce the city in the summer of 1372 was no more successful for Asti now was strongly defended by the Count of Savoy, charged personally by the Pope, and at length Galeazzo was forced to appeal to his brother. Hard pressed though he was in the south, Bernabò detached 400 lances and hurried them to the west under the command of the English *condottiere*, John Hawkwood.

It was at this critical point of Milanese fortune that Galeazzo determined that his son should at last win his spurs. At twenty-two years of age it was Giangaleazzo's first appearance upon a battlefield and his tardy attempt to prove himself ended in humiliation for himself and near disaster for Milanese arms. The young Count was already a knight, having been dubbed when only two years old by the complaisant Charles IV. But that honour was common — too common for many. 'How art thou sunken, unhappy dignity,' Sachetti wrote, protesting at the universal degradation of a once noble order. 'A few years ago everybody saw how even the workpeople down to the bakers, how all the wool carders, usurers, money-changers and blackguards of every description became knights. Of all the long list of knightly duties, what single one do these knights of ours discharge?'[36] Certainly Giangaleazzo had done little to warrant that honour, avoiding even the endless tourneys which provided most Italian knights with their main purpose. The too-loving, feminine atmosphere of Pavia which wrapped him round during his childhood and early manhood encouraged in him traits which would have been derided in a more robust

---

[36] Sachetti, nov. 153.

court. The son of a great house would have expected to have been blooded on the field of battle by the time he was sixteen, captain of his own company by his twenties. Giangaleazzo remained safely in the great castle of Pavia; as he later demonstrated, he did not waste his time there, but an adolescence spent in study was poor preparation for the harsh military life deemed to be an inescapable factor in the making of a signore. Even his father's wise policy of centralization of government worked against him; his cousins had long since been appointed to cities of their own, lords in their own right and, though under the iron dominance of their father, had gained the habit of command. Presumably the Count of Virtue was inducted into the problems of government at his father's councils, but from all indications he was merely a mild and studious young man with neither political nor military experience nor even the shadow of power.

The disaster at Asti was not altogether Giangaleazzo's fault. He was placed in command of his father's army, working in conjunction with Hawkwood's brigade, and had it been left at that there could have been little doubt of the outcome. The combined force, under Hawkwood's experienced generalship, was quite strong enough to overwhelm the city. But accompanying Giangaleazzo were two of his father's councillors 'on mandate from the lord Galeazzo and his wife Bianca who did not wish to see the lord Count of Virtue placed in danger, to be killed or captured as are the frequent events in war'.[37] Their mandate was far-reaching, reducing the Count of Virtue to a mere figurehead so that he remained a passive spectator during the inevitable and bitter arguments which arose from the division of the force. Bianca had an additional reason to fear the results of the siege of Asti, for its

_____

[37] de' Mussi, col. 514.

defender was her brother and, though such situations were common enough in the network of family alliances which held Italy together, the affection she inspired in both husband and brother rendered the situation unusually delicate. The councillors discharged their duty only too well. Hawkwood decided that a heavy frontal assault upon Asti would be successful, his military commanders agreed but Giangaleazzo's guardians demurred. The *condottiere* scornfully replied that 'he did not choose to regulate the conduct of military affairs according to the council of scriveners'[38] and when the scriveners refused to allow the Count's contingent to be used in the attack, he raised camp and marched off. Galeazzo complained to his brother who promptly halved Hawkwood's pay and as promptly Hawkwood deserted the Visconti and went over to their enemies. Bianca's solicitude tarnished her son's reputation, lost the Visconti their most able general and placed Pavia itself in imminent danger. Giangaleazzo retreated to Pavia with the remnants of the besieging army before the triumphant onslaught of the Savoyards. The lateness of the campaigning season alone saved the city and after ravaging the very gardens of the castle the enemy withdrew. But their withdrawal was only a preliminary to a grand multi-national onslaught upon the Visconti which should send them tumbling. The Emperor, in a sudden burst of enthusiasm, withdrew the Vicariate of Lombardy from the brothers; legally they became usurpers and outlaws, deprived of all rights over their cities. Some of the smaller states under Galeazzo's control took the opportunity to rebel and Galeazzo was forced into active warfare again to reduce them. But meanwhile the strategic assault for which the Savoyards had been withdrawn was set in motion. Hawkwood, at the head of an army which

---

[38] Ibid.

included a French detachment, repelled an attack upon Bologna and began to march across Lombardy with the intention of meeting the Savoyards in the heart of the Milanese state. Such a union would have been disastrous and Bernabò, reversing the usual roles, sent out a call for help to Galeazzo who promptly responded. A relieving force was raised and the command given to Giangaleazzo.

Galeazzo's anxiety for his son to retrieve prestige after the humiliation of Asti was laudable, but family affection outpaced common sense. So at least Bernabò thought, for on hearing of the identity of the commander he immediately despatched one of his natural sons, Ambrogio, to ensure that the relieving force arrived intact. Ambrogio was in his own right a soldier of distinction, having led his own mercenary company, and Giangaleazzo accepted the escort of his experienced cousin without demur. Together the two hastened westward across the plain, but en route came news that Bergamo was on the brink of rebellion, and after a hasty consultation, Ambrogio took 300 lances and hurried northward to suppress it. Giangaleazzo continued on in sole command; there was little danger for his force was twice the size of the nearest enemy unit, a brigade under the command of Hawkwood. So confident was the young Count in his ability that he actually sought out the formidable Englishman, offered battle and, after a short, sharp struggle of little more than an hour, was totally successful. The enemy force broke up and Hawkwood himself retired to the top of a small hill with his bodyguard; the victory was complete and Giangaleazzo could at last claim to have entered manhood. But when he had decided to continue the march without Ambrogio he had overlooked the fact that the bulk of his army was composed of German mercenaries. Ambrogio would have known instinctively that mercenaries were as vulnerable at the moment of victory as at the moment of defeat. The loot which formed the largest part of their pay was to be gathered and it required a skilled commander to force them to keep good guard whilst the plunder was harvested. Giangaleazzo did not have that skill, his mercenaries fell to their usual habits and Hawkwood, with his ability to make swift assessment followed by sudden action, reorganized the few who remained with him and swept down upon the loot-gorged men. The Germans fled and Hawkwood's cavalry crashed into the Count's bodyguard. Giangaleazzo was hurled to the ground, helmet and lance lost, and he would infallibly have fallen prisoner if the Milanese contingent had not fought with extreme gallantry, protecting him while a fresh horse was found. Many nobles fell prisoner but he was able to retreat from the field, while Hawkwood, prudently allowing for the return of the Germans, marched off after a signal and unexpected victory. The actions with and against Hawkwood were the total of Giangaleazzo's military experience; he never again took the field. The cause of both humiliations lay as much in his upbringing as in his character. The defeat at Asti stemmed directly from his mother's oversolicitude, while that of Montechiaro was caused by simple inexperience. He had shown valour enough in deliberately seeking out and giving battle to the toughest veteran in Italy, and a defeat at the hands of Hawkwood was something of which a twenty-two-year-old youth did not need to be ashamed. Yet both defeats confirmed him in inclinations which he later erected into political principles; war was best left to the professionals and foreign mercenaries were to be distrusted. It proved a valuable lesson.

The war in which Montechiaro was but a minor skirmish was drawing to its end and with it was ending a chapter in Italian history. For over thirty years the Visconti had acted as a catalyst in Italy, for fear of them had fused the disparate forces of the peninsula into near-national alliances again and again. The Papacy had used that fear to hem in the family which ceaselessly disputed its secular authority. But now while Gregory in Avignon planned the destruction of the Visconti with his Tuscan allies, his legates in Italy, with a blind treachery, attempted to profit from the war weakness of the cities and so drag them back under direct Papal control. The dormant suspicions of Avignon flared into open hatred. Florence, hitherto the staunchest supporter of the Papacy, proclaimed a war of liberation and even held out her hand to her most determined enemy. Bernabò took that hand; neither partner had illusions about the other, but Lombard and Tuscan for once had a common enemy. Galeazzo refused to follow his brother; utterly fatigued, an old man in his late forties, in the January of 1375 he passed over much of his powers to his son, reserving to himself the ultimate authority but in effect leaving the running of the state to Giangaleazzo, leaving him free above all to make peace with the ever-pressing enemy in the west and so draw back from the storm about to burst over Italy. Gregory, observing from distant Avignon the ruin of Papal hopes in Italy, resolved to come in person and despatched Robert, cardinal of Geneva to prepare his coming. He could have chosen no worse tool than this lame and squinting man whose appetite for blood was unappeasable. Robert left France at the head of a company of those Breton mercenaries whom even the English and German veterans in Italy loathed and feared. The terror of their coming paralysed Florence, made even Hawkwood uncertain of the wisdom of continuing in office as the Florentine captain-general. The Breton's route lay across the territory of Pavia and in return for peace Giangaleazzo came to an arrangement with them. The cardinal ceded to him those territories which the Papacy had captured and in return forced him to sign a league against every other power save only Bernabò and the Emperor. Galeazzo ratified the agreement and the Bretons went down into Tuscany and the Marches to massacre and to plunder and to raise in Italian breasts such an ecstasy of hatred against the Papacy that even the pleadings of St Catherine could not assuage. The ailing lord of Pavia and his retiring son were alike ignored in the general storm, but under its cover in March 1378 the Count of Virtue prepared and executed his debut into Italian politics.

Secondotto, marquis of Monferrat, was the present lord of that city of Asti which had been for so long an irritant in the Visconti flank. In an attempt to resolve the problem Giangaleazzo's sister Violante, widowed after only three months' marriage, was given in marriage to the fifteen-year-old marquis in 1377. It was therefore natural that, when Secondotto needed assistance to throw out a German adventurer who had succeeded in occupying the city, he should turn to his new relatives. Giangaleazzo not only provided a company of lances but, signal mark of esteem, led them himself in company with Secondotto. The warlike preparations doubtless impressed Secondotto but, as Giangaleazzo well knew, they were unnecessary for the citadel of Asti remained in loyal hands and on approach of an apparently determined force the usurper fled. In sincere gratitude Secondotto allowed his brother-in-law to make certain alterations in the military and civil governments which put the effective control of the city in his hands, 'pretending to do so in the name of his relative, and thus the most prudent Count, with love and without the slightest danger, obtained the dominion of that city of Asti which his father… in spite of uncountable expense had never been able to obtain'.[39] Secondotto 'recognizing his error' hastened back to Pavia to complain but, receiving the answer he might have expected from Galeazzo, departed in high rage to seek a champion. His quest ended with sordid tragedy, for he was stabbed to death in a stable by a servant whom his bestial rages had infuriated. In Asti Giangaleazzo put into movement the administration which a century of Visconti experience had perfected and returned to Pavia, taking with him his sister widowed for the second time. He had reason to be satisfied with himself, for the whole operation had been conducted with a smoothness which belied his youth and apparent inexperience. On his own chosen field he had proved himself a master.

On August 4th 1378, six months after his son had gained his political spurs, Galeazzo died. A man more unfortunate in his time than evil in his nature, he would have been happy to play the part of dilettante, but was instead dragged at the heels of his furibund brother. He died as he had lived, overshadowed by Bernabò, ignored, his death passing unnoticed outside the state. But even as his lethargy had permitted Giangaleazzo to gain priceless experience in statesmanship, so his lacklustre character stood his successor in good stead. The Count of Virtue had no towering figure to be measured against and could establish the state in the manner he thought best.

LORD OF PAVIA

The new lord of Pavia was twenty-seven years of age; two military humiliations and a piece of political trickery were his sole claim to notice. His succession to an important state passed as unnoticed as his father's death, for he shared with Galeazzo some quirk of character, a coldness or an

---

[39] Corio, III, 6.

indifference which gave no material to the most inventive of chroniclers. And yet behind the apparently insignificant front there must have been already some indication of the later grandeur, some magnetism which drew to him men capable of making valid judgements of character, for later they proved themselves capable of moulding Italy. Within two years of his succession the names of the men who were to accompany him throughout his career were already appearing on his documents, their faces familiar at the court. Some came from outside the state, from Verona, Lucca, Crete, men already famous in their own world but prepared to identify their career with the unknown young lord of Pavia. His father's own councillors and generals, assessing his qualities from a lifetime's knowledge and balancing them against the qualities of the lord of Milan, decided to continue in his service.

The only existing contemporary portraits of Giangaleazzo are the single sketch by Pisanello, a half-destroyed wooden panel by an unknown hand in which the young Count of Virtue is shown with Petrarch, and the formal miniature by Imbonate in the Missal of Sant'Ambrogio. But in the Certosa of Pavia, Cristoforo Romano's brilliant sculptures for Giangaleazzo's tomb and the great painting by Bergognone both preserve a vanished source of illustration. Both artists were working at least a century after their subject's death, but they had as model the still vivid murals of the Castle of Pavia which were executed during his life.[40] The most characteristic

---

[40] In 1583 the Consiglio Generale of Pavia, at the request of Aldus Manutius, sent to him a drawing of 'messer Francesco Petrarcha with the colours according to the picture that was in the castle', evidence that some of the murals were intact at that date. An additional, anatomical, vindication of Bergognone's accuracy was provided when Giangaleazzo's tomb was opened in 1889; the unusually large skull

feature in all the portraits, a feature appearing even in Imbonate's stiff work, is the expression of melancholy, of withdrawal, which sits upon the heavy, fleshy face. The florid good looks of the father are missing and neither is there any indication of the gloomy strength of the uncle. Physically, the Count of Virtue shared the bulky stature and fresh colouring of the Visconti; in his portraits the hair of reddish-gold is cut short and sensibly, the beard pointed and straggling in mandarin fashion. Sober in dress, frugal in habits, studious by inclination, there was little to attract contemporaries of the young Count, while the portrait of the Duke he was to become, though limned in vigorously, was too heavily coloured by the hatred of political enemies. The most valuable assessment of his character by a contemporary comes from the pen of the 'Minerbetti' chronicler, a Florentine. 'Minerbetti'[41] is a temperate and attractive writer, preserving a sardonic reserve for miracles and heroes, capable of objective and even sympathetic judgement of enemies — save one. He bore for the Count of Virtue a bitter and unrelenting hatred which could only have sprung from a personal source. Throughout the chronicle his reasonable air so charms that when he comes to his peroration on 'the most great evils and treacheries and deceits made many times by Giangaleazzo, late Count of Virtue and now styled duke of Milan', the reader is already disposed to accept his version. His analysis of Giangaleazzo is able enough, but it is followed by a tirade so bitter and personal, with crime piled upon fantastic crime without regard to

was in an excellent state of preservation with even a few reddish-gold hairs upon it.

[41] The chronicler is anonymous; the work was first credited to a transcriber and later to a Piero Minerbetti in the possession of whose family it long remained.

evidence, motive or inherent probability, that the temptation is to dismiss the assessment along with the accusations. It would be unfortunate, for 'Minerbetti' was an excellent judge of character and his portrayal of Giangaleazzo includes most of the elements which appear in other sources — the physical timidity, the intelligence, the suppleness of morals. 'This was a man very grand of person and subtle of intellect, learned in grammar and wise in the ways of the world. Very affable and blandishing in words but that which he promised he had little intention of performing. He was not robust in person but weak and timorous and always lived with fear... rarely leaving his castle at Pavia save at night.'[42] In all this 'Minerbetti' is on uncontroversial ground. All Italy was to bear witness, as Secondotto of Monferrat already could, to the affable man who promised smoothly but did not perform. But 'Minerbetti', losing control of his pen, rushes on to paint a scarcely human portrait. 'He was the most criminal man in the world and worked the most vicious malices and crimes than any other man of his time. Proud, avaricious, luxurious, adulterous.' The chronicler was preoccupied to the point of morbidity with poison and therefore the Count emerges as the arch-poisoner of all time and the catalogue of deaths which follow is little short of ludicrous. In the hurly-burly of the wars which Giangaleazzo precipitated, hard words in plenty were thrown about, but 'Minerbetti' alone pursues the same theme through both peace and war and the Count's later reputation can probably be attributed to this single source, the distorted truth embellished further, mushrooming to proportions which even 'Minerbetti' would not have recognized.

The first Milanese historian, Bernadino Corio, substantially endorsed the Florentine a century later but toned down the

---

[42] 'Minerbetti', XIV, A. 1402.

more extreme details. 'This most excellent prince was a very prudent and astute man but of solitary life… timid in adverse fortune, most audacious in prosperity. And he deceived many… In his needs he promised much but maintained little. Ambitious to spread his name throughout Italy, more than any other Italian prince he was most fortunate in his enterprises.'[43] Solitary, timid, unscrupulous, ambitious, so the main elements of Giangaleazzo's character begin to appear, but it was another thirty years after Corio before the first attempt was made to solve the paradox of how such a man came to dominate all northern Italy. The biography written by Paolo Giovio is little more than an essay of perhaps 3000 words, but within its compass he attempted to examine Giangaleazzo's actions in terms of his personality instead of by the traditional retailing of anecdotes. By the time he came to write his *Life* all human links with Giangaleazzo had long since descended to the grave and the Visconti State itself had passed into history. But sufficient of its institutions remained from which Giovio could draw conclusions as to its effective founder. The political immorality was a matter of common knowledge; Giovio was more concerned with the intellectual capabilities of his subject. 'He was not distracted from business by the pleasures of hunting or hawking, nor by gaming nor by the delights of women, but exercised his body temperately to conserve health and refreshed his soul with discussions with wise men and with frequent reading… He was accustomed to give himself up to meditation during solitary walks, to hold discussion with those most experienced in every branch of affairs, to quote instances from annals of the past.' Giovio emphasized his love of careful order, his ability to plan with minute detail while yet keeping the grand pattern in view. 'He used to say that in the

---

[43] Corio, IV, 1.

management of the things of the world both domestic and abroad there was nothing better than order.'[44] The picture which begins to emerge is that of a studious introspective, a man preferring his own company yet sociable when politics demanded, physically timid yet capable of decision.

Giangaleazzo inherited that constitutional timidity which was a recurring factor in the Visconti character. Denied thereby the customary means of action while yet possessed of immense capabilities, he turned inward, exploiting to the full the rare academic resources available at Pavia. Friends and enemies alike remarked upon his deeply studious nature. He was a mature man when he succeeded his father and all his actions indicate that during the years of his minority he had closely examined the mechanics of power and had waited only the opportunity to put them into practice. His control of the state was firm from the moment he took over. His action in immediately reducing his personal allowance by some 500 florins per month was doubtless a calculated attempt to win favour during the first few weeks, but thereafter his reforms, particularly those touching taxation, were based less on politics than economics. The resultant reductions in taxation earned him a valuable measure of support. In the vexed matter of ecclesiastic rights he made it very clear that he would brook no interference within his state, threatening with death whosoever should recognize any bishop not nominated by himself. Such an act was not the courting of disaster it might once have been, for in the very year in which he succeeded the Papacy was rent by the Schism and from the beginning he turned the fact to his advantage. Officially he proclaimed that either Pope could be recognized within the state, privately he refused to commit himself to the support or the enmity of either. He retained his

---

[44] Giovio, pp. 106, 107.

neutrality to the end; while all Christendom was passionately engaged, coldly he employed the religious disaster as a political weapon.

The small court of Pavia over which he now ruled differed little from the old. His mother remained its mistress, for Isabella of France had died at the age of twenty-four in giving birth to her fourth child. The 'fever' which had delayed her marriage was evidence of an already delicate constitution further weakened by a series of pregnancies. The chronicler of Piacenza who had ignored the death of the late lord of Pavia, found room for an epitaph for the young Countess of Virtue which went considerably beyond the usual formal statement of grief. Her illustrous antecedents roll off his pen with sonority, but nevertheless he sounded a note of genuine loss. 'Her death occasioned both the lord Galeazzo and the lord Count Virtue and all their subjects great sorrow at the loss of so noble a lady, good and wise, humble, pious and virtuous, fruitful of children and especially such noble children. We shall not see her like again in this world.'[45] Isabella left no inheritance except the beauty of her daughter Valentina and, perhaps, the melancholy of her husband. The extraordinary affection in which Giangaleazzo held his only daughter hints that his marriage, like his father's, was unusually happy. This, a few books to be added to the growing library, and four children were Isabella's legacy. But the children also inherited her frail health; the little boy who had caused her death himself died seven months afterwards, her firstborn died four years later at the age of ten, and the surviving boy, Azzone, was continually ailing. To the personal grief which must have assailed the Count was added the political problem; a daughter and one sickly son to be set

---

[45] de' Mussi, col. 512.

against the fourteen legitimate children and uncounted bastards of his uncle Bernabò.

Since the departure of Galeazzo had left him all-powerful in Milan, Bernabò's character had steadily deteriorated, his rages becoming ever more common, his violent arrogance increasing. 'Don't you know, fool, that I am Pope and Emperor and Lord in all my lands and that neither the Emperor nor even God himself can, on these my territories, do that which I do not wish to be done,'[46] he stormed at the archbishop of Milan who had dared to voice a complaint. The year after Giangaleazzo's accession to Pavia, Bernabò divided his territories amongst his sons, following the Visconti policy of divided rule which, in his case, was to prove fatal. Marco, as eldest, had half of Milan, Lodovico was installed as lord of Lodi and Cremona, Carlo as lord of Crema, and the baby Mastino ruled Brescia under his mother's regency. Such a division of the state was a necessity considering Bernabò's personal method of government, but though in theory his sons could now sign themselves as lords, in practice they were merely his lieutenants and he made explicit orders that his edicts overruled theirs. Nevertheless, Marco's installation as lord of half of Milan was the first clear indication of the precarious position in which Giangaleazzo was placed. Half of Milan belonged to him as his father's successor and he still retained a garrison in the castle of Porta Giovia. Marco's authority was presumably limited to Bernabò's half of the city, but the line of demarcation made concrete the political dichotomy. One of Giangaleazzo's first acts had been to obtain a renewal of his father's Imperial vicariate which had automatically lapsed on the death of the Emperor Charles IV in November 1378. Charles's son and successor Wenceslaus

---

[46] Romussi, V2, p. 347.

made no difficulties in confirming the Count's possession of the western cities of the Milanese state while taking care to recognize Bernabò's rights over the rest. Bernabò himself did not trouble to go through the formalities of obtaining a renewal of his own vicariate; for all its high legality the diploma tended to go to him best able to hold it. For twenty-three years Bernabò had been the dominant lord in Lombardy; he had shared the rule honestly enough with his brother, but there was little guarantee that he would continue to respect the claims of the new lord of Pavia. A ridiculously trivial incident early brought the fact home to Giangaleazzo. The *podestà* of Monza had captured an errant hawk which Bernabò claimed as his own and, refusing to give it up, Bernabò promptly prepared to march in and arrest him. Monza was under Giangaleazzo's jurisdiction and he protested, receiving in answer an insulting letter. The Count replied, mildly but with courage. 'We have before given you our opinion that the hawk did not bear your sign and that it was given to our captain of Monza by one of your own subjects in the presence of Rodolpho. But whether the hawk be yours or not, the territory of Monza is ours and we pray you refrain from sending such letters,' Bernabò's reply is almost incoherent with rage. 'If it does not please you I shall send you no more letters, neither white nor black, nor send ambassadors... But it would be as well to remind you that at the time of Luchino, when I was but a boy, I killed a man with my bare hands for insulting our house. I am not disposed to suffer injury without avenging it. You say that you do not wish me to interfere with your affairs. By Holy Mary! there is not one person to you so dear that I will not punish if he offends me.'[47] The letter's implications were clear; Bernabò was willing to allow the situation to remain only so long as the Court of

[47] Novati, in ASL 33, 1906.

Pavia conducted itself as the subordinate it was. Its ultimate absorption into Milan must have seemed inevitable to him and to further that aim he imposed upon his nephew a series of marriages with his own children. The matrimonial alliances envisaged a degree of consanguinity remarkable even for the Visconti. The Count and his son Azzone were to marry Bernabò's daughters Caterina and Elisabetta respectively; Valentina was to be given to Bernabò's third son Carlo, while Violante, the unfortunate twice-widowed sister of the Count, was apportioned to Lodovico. A sheaf of dispensations was needed and duly obtained from Urban, glad of the chance to bind the turbulent family to his cause. Corio states that for the Count's own marriage both Clement in Avignon and Urban in Rome were approached for the necessary licences, Giangaleazzo insisting on preserving his neutrality in the Schism. Not all the projected marriages came to fruition; Azzone died before he could become his own father's brother-in-law and Bernabò later found a better match for Carlo. But the Count and his sister were duly included in Bernabò's family group.

Giangaleazzo had been a widower for eight years. Shortly after his accession to power he had made a bold attempt to marry the orphaned Maria, heir to the throne of Sicily, a marriage which would have made him king in the south and lord in the north. But the very size of the ambition brought about its downfall, for it infringed the interests of too many powerful parties, not least those of his uncle. Bernabò as a Visconti was deeply impressed, but Bernabò as senior partner in the Milanese state demanded wide concessions in the event of the marriage taking place. The preliminary negotiations were successfully concluded, the bride married by proxy and a fleet sent to escort her back to Italy. The fleet went no further than

Pisa, for while all Italy had been debating the matter, Peter of Aragon quietly assembled his own fleet, destroyed the Visconti's and abducted Maria. The Count had insufficient resources to permit the luxury of revenge and he resigned himself to the loss of the Sicilian crown. A few months afterwards he accepted Caterina, the chronicler of Piacenza assuming that he did so to placate Bernabò. Certainly there was little enough to gain and much to lose. The 100,000 florins he received as Caterina's dowry was a paper transaction for it was returned soon after as the dowry of Violante, and it needed little insight to perceive that Caterina, duly schooled, was to be a spy in Pavia. Nevertheless, in his dependent position, an outright refusal was impossible and on November 15th 1380 the marriage was celebrated in Bernabò's favourite church of San Giovanni in Conca in Milan. It did not in fact extend Bernabò's covert control over Pavia, for Caterina was too glad to escape the atmosphere of her father's court to prejudice her position with her husband, but neither did it bring the Count his much-needed heir. Eighteen months afterwards his position was indeed worsened with the death of his sole surviving son Azzone. Of all the children of Isabella which provided him with a direct link with the French crown Valentina alone was left and she, only twelve years old, was already in pawn to Bernabò. Without heirs, with little military or financial resources, the Count of Virtue found himself playing by necessity that role which his father had played from choice — chorus to Bernabò.

In the last years of his life the old lord of Milan was blossoming forth as a statesmen, leaving behind the rough-and-tumble warrior-tyrant whose horizon lay no further than the frontiers of his own state. In 1382 the affairs of distant Naples took a new turn which involved all Italy. Charles of

Durazzo was come from Hungary to avenge the death of his kinsman, the late husband of Giovanna, queen of Naples, reputed by some to be whore and murderess, defended by others as the most unfortunate woman alive. Urban espoused Charles, creating him king of Naples while Giovanna yet lived, and she in desperation stretched out her hand to France, adopting Louis of Anjou as her heir in return for his immediate protection. The state of Milan suddenly threatened to become the route of march of two armies no more mutually hostile than they were hostile to Italy itself. Bernabò proposed a national league. 'I and the Count of Virtue will between us put up 2000 lances while you will contribute 1000', he wrote to Florence in the November. '3000 lances well armed and well paid will be sufficient to rid Italy of the barbarian. We are ready with all our hearts to unite with you and with the others for the salvation and defence of all Italians. If you — Florentines, Pisans, Sienese, Perugians and all the cities of Tuscany and the Marches — will contribute to the expense we will assume the burden of defending Italy from the union of barbarians that wish to disturb the peace.'[48] He had excellent personal reasons for such a union, but the grand strategy outlined did for once display an ideal loftier than the usual parochialism. It came to nothing as all free leagues of Italians came to nothing. Florence and a few other cities sent ambassadors to Milan, but the discussions dragged on until the incentive of danger had passed and Bernabò's own interests demanded alliance with the barbarians beyond the Alps. Louis of Anjou descended into Italy, infeudated in his turn with Naples by Clement of Avignon, the contending holders of the Papal tiara fighting out their differences over the prostrate body of the city. In Anjou's coffers was the stolen wealth of his dead brother Charles V of

---

[48] ASL 38 (2), 1911.

France, but he needed yet more money, and as so many others before him had done he turned to the deeper coffers of Milan, offering his son Louis in marriage to Bernabò's daughter Lucia in exchange for money and troops. The opportunity of making Lucia heiress to the Neapolitan throne was not to be missed and Bernabò accepted, immediately putting down 40,000 florins on account. Now hopes in Milan ran high; this marriage apparently secured, there was much talk of another between that of the little Elisabetta, released by the death of her cousin Azzone, and the brother of the king of France. It remained talk, heady presage of future greatness, but meanwhile Bernabò forged yet another link with France at the expense of Giangaleazzo. The betrothal between Valentina and Carlo was broken and Carlo affianced and rapidly wed to Beatrice d'Armagnac. In August the Angevin army arrived in Lombardy, encamping near Pavia. Thither went Bernabò with all his court to pay respects to the French duke who might one day make his daughter queen of Naples; thither too went the Count of Virtue, taking with him Valentina, who could hope for no such glory as Lucia's but in whose veins coursed the same Valois blood as ran through the veins of Anjou. The courtesies exchanged, the ponderous army moved slowly across the Milanese state, feted as it went, then turned southward to Naples and death — death, not from wounds but from those southern diseases which had melted even greater armies than this. Anjou died, but his claim on Naples was transmitted to his son and Lucia was thus brought even closer to the throne.

It is presumably at about this time that Giangaleazzo began to realize that the division in the state of Milan could be removed only by force. Bernabò himself seemed content to allow matters to drift, for he was an old man, no longer eager for war and in particular a civil war. The Count might appear to be a timid young man, but he had managed to bind to himself some of the foremost professional soldiers of the day; a civil war placed heavy stresses upon loyalties and there were few important Milanese who had not experienced violence at Bernabò's hands. But though he might be disposed to let the situation remain there was no certainty that his sons would follow the same policy after his death. Corio makes the specific charge that, encouraged by their mother, they were actively plotting against their cousin. Regina 'was by nature impious, proud and audacious, insatiable after riches and in a manner that her children and especially Marco conspired against Giangaleazzo her nephew for cupidity of his dominions, which was the principal cause of the ruin of Bernabò and of his sons as we shall show'.[49] Each of the sons was aware that he could look forward to only one-fifth of his father's share while his cousin held one-half of the entire state. From a very early period Giangaleazzo must have realized that the problem was merely postponed, but as yet there had been no challenge grave enough to warrant an attempted *coup d'état*. Now the Angevin alliance brought that challenge, a potential menace to be weighed against the potential failure of an attack upon Bernabò.

The actual details of the coup which Giangaleazzo planned were simple enough, requiring only as guarantee the absolute loyalty of a handful of men. But a vital prerequisite of the plot was that Bernabò should have no suspicions, not merely of the Count's intentions, but of his ability to form such intentions. There was the additional need to persuade the interested Italian powers to remain neutral when the time came. Bernabò helped him in this latter; unable to resist the temptation of meddling

---

[49] Corio, III, 6.

in Tuscany he earned the cordial resentment of the Florentines. They even turned to Giangaleazzo for help, and though he carefully made no move which might arouse Bernabò's anger or suspicions 'he showed great friendship for those with whom messer Bernabò was on hostile terms — and especially for the Florentines'.[50] Nevertheless the enemies of Bernabò did not automatically become his friends. Suspicion and dislike of the Visconti were far too deeply engrained in most Italian minds for him to be able to count upon any assistance in a family quarrel. Italians as a whole would regard themselves the winner whichever Visconti succeeded in eliminating the other. In the last resort he had only one weapon, surprise; to forge it he adopted a show of timidity which, though rooted in his nature, in its consistency was the result of a conscious application. 'He pretended to become Catholic and religious and made a show of despising the things of the world and gave himself over to contemplations, devotions and abstinences, abandoning all delightful things and beautiful raiments and began to dress himself in clothes of grey, thus hiding his treacherous intent behind the visage of a lamb the better to deceive those who trusted him and especially his uncle.'[51] The exaggerated pietism whereby priests surrounded his every waking hour, the exaggerated timidity whereby armed men surrounded him whenever he went out of the castle, would have been ludicrous in any other person but a Visconti. But Bernabò had seen the defect of timidity in other members of his own generation and its appearance now in the Count merely confirmed him in his decision to allow that branch of the house to mewl itself into extinction. He did not lack warnings; apart from what his own common sense should have told him he received detailed

[50] Morelli, p. 492.
[51] Gatari (A. 1385), p. 232.

information that the Count was collecting troops even though not at war. 'Let him throw his money away; it shall avail him nothing',[52] was his sole response. Thirty years of absolute power had blinded him, and in that same year of 1384 he lost the only counsellor whose advice he ever noticed and whose bitter jealousy of Giangaleazzo might have persuaded him to anticipate the Count's move. Regina della Scala died on the 18th June, taking to the tomb her ambitions for her sons, her pride, her steadfast support of her husband. She was fortunate in the time of her death for she left her husband almost on the crest of fortune. Louis d'Anjou died in September and Bernabò immediately wrote to the duchess of Anjou, offering condolences and help to Louis' heir. The duchess thanked him, her son sent a ring to Lucia to whom he was already married by proxy, and in January 1385a Valois family council in Paris discussed the possibilities of a new Neapolitan expedition. On February 28th the king authorized the new attempt; in April the duchess conferred with Clement and it was decided to send ambassadors to collect Lucia and consummate the marriage. The cup was now raised to Bernabò's lips and there seemed nothing that could prevent him drinking.

'News of the great feasts and high revelries' came to Giangaleazzo in his retirement at Pavia. The challenge was now explicitly framed; he was either to allow Bernabò to unite himself with France or to stake his own life on a single act. 'The friends of the Count said to each other with downcast eyes "Now what will he do with the men all here assembled. Oh! God guard the Count in these days."' He is warned not to go near Milan; his mother seeks him out and adds her graver warning, 'Bernabò is making fresh alliances with France. If he becomes related he will seize upon your sovereignty.'[53] In

---

[52] Giulini, Lib. 72.

those last taut weeks Bernabò threw aside all pretences of respecting his nephew's independence. In February he married his infant son Mastino to a daughter of the della Scala of Verona, and without reference to Giangaleazzo made over certain territories in the Veronese which the Count held as mediator. There arrived the inescapable point when Giangaleazzo, the hater of violence and of hazard, was forced to hazard his life on an act of violence.

---

[53] Medin, ASL, XVIII.

III: THE LORD OF MILAN

COUP D'ÉTAT

On the evening of Friday May 5th 1385 Giangaleazzo left Pavia with an unusually large bodyguard, ostensibly on pilgrimage to Varese. His route ran past Milan and he had expressed a desire to pay his respects to his uncle, a desire which Bernabò agreed to satisfy. Friday night was spent at Binasco, roughly ten miles from both Milan and Pavia, and on the Saturday morning the Count, with a few chosen companions, rode on to Milan where Bernabò was awaiting him outside the city gate. By early afternoon the lord of Milan was a prisoner and the entire state was in his nephew's hands.

Such were the bare facts of the story which almost every chronicler in Italy recorded. During the actual moment of encounter only a few people were immediately involved, but not all the survivors were the Count's well-briefed men. A courtier of Bernabò's, Medisina da Desio, escaped to Padua and it is probably from this first-hand source that Galeazzo Gatari, the chronicler of Padua, wrote his detailed account of an event which all deemed incredible. 'Truly, it was an act of God and not of man,'[54] de' Mussi recorded in Piacenza, a judgement later endorsed by Corio. 'This thing, I think, in those days was marvellous and unheard of because he whom almost all the universe held in fear and honour was by a timid youth made prisoner, and in defence of such a high lord not one friend raised himself and in a lightning flash he was tumbled from the summit of power.'[55] In Lucca Sercambi

---

[54] de' Mussi, col. 544.
[55] Corio, III, 7.

seized on the event to deliver one of his moral apostrophes;[56] in England Chaucer heard of it and shook his head over the fall of such a man, this 'grete Barnabo Viscounte, god of delyt and scourge of Lumbardie'.[57] Morelli in Florence uneasily pondered the effect upon his city[58]; Froissart recorded it as a case of dog eating dog.[59] The versions of the affair are many, but actual contradictions rare, and it is possible to pinpoint the exact moment when a great state came into being. All the vital details were recorded — save one; the reason for Bernabò's astonishing stupidity. Lombardy had become accustomed to the fact that the Count travelled abroad only with a large bodyguard, but the escort he took with him on that Friday evening numbered no less than 1200 men. Dati says that over their arms and armour they wore pilgrims' robes, carried olive branches and sang hymns;[60] they possibly did, but it is still remarkable that the suspicious Bernabò — who habitually created a zone around his every residence within which trespassing meant death — should have been tricked by so simple a ruse. It can only be assumed that the Count's pose had so utterly deceived Bernabò that the request for a meeting outside the city walls seemed fully in keeping with a poltroon's fear of violence. However the request was phrased, sometime during the Saturday morning Bernabò rode out of the city, accompanied by his two sons Rodolfo and Lodovico, through the *pusterla* Sant'Ambrogio. Again, the choice of the Sant'Ambrogio must have been Giangaleazzo's. The natural meeting place would have been at the Porta Ticinese where the

[56] Sercambi, CCXCVII, p. 240.

[57] Chaucer, 'The Monk's Tale'.

[58] Morelli, p. 292.

[59] Froissart, Chap. CLVIII.

[60] Dati, p. 18.

road from Pavia ended, but a meeting there would have taken place under the eyes of the large permanent garrison whereas Sant'Ambrogio was merely a secondary gate with only the actual guards on duty. And finally, as though doing all in his power to help his enemy, Bernabò sent his sons ahead, accompanied by Medisina da Desio, to meet the Count en route. The 'Lament for Bernabò' then pictures the old man awaiting his nephew 'under an arbour near to the city gate' with a yearning of a father waiting a dearly loved son

> 'Dov'e il mio figlio, dov'e lo mio Conte
> Dov'e la luce ardente dei Vesconte?'[61]

Some few miles away the blazing light of the Visconti was putting into motion the last act of seven years' planning. The twenty-two-mile journey from Pavia to Milan could have been comfortably accomplished in a morning, but the overnight halt at Binasco had been planned in order to leave the majority of the escort behind — far enough to be discreetly out of sight, near enough to be at swift call. Accompanied by three of his generals, Jacopo dal Verme, Gugliemo Bevilacqua, and Antonio Porro, and a detachment of troops, Giangaleazzo greeted his cousins affably 'and took their hands with a false smile'. Unobtrusively, his escort gathered round them, pressing them in towards the centre. Neither of the brothers suspected anything, presumably accepting their position in the centre of the escort as an honour naturally due. But Medisina's suspicions were aroused particularly when dal Verme and Porro, having conferred with the Count, quietly slipped away to return a little later. He hurried back to Bernabò. 'My lord, I do not wish to go contrary to you but I think you should not

---

[61] Medin, ASL XVIII.

go to meet your nephew, for it appears to me that he does not come to do you honour but to make battle, so many armed men does he bring.' But Bernabò merely laughed. 'You have little sense — I tell you I know my nephew,' and mounting his mule rode off to meet the company.[62] The two groups met and mingled, the Count took his uncle's hands in a gesture of greeting and called out an order in German. There seems to have been a momentary misunderstanding for one of the German mercenaries put hand to sword with the obvious intention of striking Bernabò when a voice, unidentified but probably Giangaleazzo's, called out 'Do not strike him'. The German dropped back and dal Verme grasped Bernabò's baton of office, saying 'You are a prisoner'. 'Have you the audacity—' Bernabò began, but dal Verme cut him short with a laconic 'It is my lord's command.'[63] Bevilacqua then rode into Bernabò, cut his sword belt and left him helpless. Throughout, the old man seems to have been paralysed by astonishment and when he did find coherent voice it was to make an almost ludicrous plea. 'Son, why do you do this? I have no other good but yours; all that I have is yours. Do not betray your own blood.' His enemy's reply was brief, prepared with an eye to future apologetics. 'It is necessary for you to be a prisoner for you have many times tried to kill me.'[64] No further time was wasted; Bernabò with his sons were hurried round the circuit of the walls to the gate of Giangaleazzo's own castle of Porta Giovia and secured there while the vital operation of 'riding the streets' was accomplished. The lances brought up from Binasco entered Milan through Giovia and galloped through the narrow streets of the city before barricades could be

---

[62] Gatari, p. 233.
[63] Annales Mediolanenses CXLVII.
[64] Morelli.

erected, seizing the strongpoints. The Milanese rose, not to avenge their fallen lord but to acclaim the new one. 'Long live the Count of Virtue' was the cry, with the significant addition 'Down with the taxes'. The humdrum hope of tax reduction went far to smooth the changeover, the Count's clement policy in Pavia bearing fruit in Milan. By Sunday morning the city was quiet in his hands. Bernabò's own castle of Porta Romana was seized with its enormous treasure early in the operation, but the mob was allowed to work off its excitement with the sacking of his palace and a burning of the tax books.

Simultaneous with the reduction of the city was the rounding up of Bernabò's many sons. Most were soldiers and, although they had no political rights whatsoever, with the companies they commanded they could have presented a formidable threat to the new lord. Yet by the 10th of May all the more important had been picked up. Two legitimate sons remained at large, the twenty-four-year-old Carlo and the five-year-old Mastino. Two of Carlo's children were in Milan and were taken into custody, but Carlo himself was in his own city of Crema twenty-five miles away. The news of Bernabò's downfall reached him only a few hours afterwards, for on that same Saturday he wrote to his brother-in-law John Hawkwood, the Florentine captain-general. The letter[65] was brief and written in obvious haste, for after giving Hawkwood the incredible news that the despised Count of Virtue had captured Bernabò, Carlo went on to claim that the fortress of Porta Romana 'is held in my name'. Carlo was either misinformed or, more likely, was attempting to put the best face on a hopeless matter, for his object in writing to Hawkwood was to get immediate aid. If family ties were not enough then, he hinted, money might be forthcoming. Hawkwood did nothing, for there was nothing he

---

[65] Temple-Leader, Doc. LIII, p. 349.

could do. Florence was extremely unlikely to give him permission to meddle in Milanese affairs; even had he received permission he would then have had to induce his troops to fight, without pay, for the unpopular sons of a universally hated man. Carlo's tenure of Crema was brief. Giangaleazzo's generals made a rapid tour of the state and in most cases the very rumour of their coming was sufficient for the cities to open their gates and freely accept the new lord. Crema was no exception and Carlo fled scant hours before dal Verme entered. From Crema he went to Parma 'where timidly he remained in the castle, but knowing the citizens to be not too much for him he rode to Reggio, from thence to Mantua and finally to Germany to his own relative the duke of Bavaria, where he remained until he had spent all his money'.[66] The Count was glad enough to see him go, acceding to the request of Gonzaga of Mantua that a safe-conduct should be supplied him. By May 22nd almost all the cities had been swept into the net; Lodi, Bergamo, Soncini, Crema, Parma, Reggio, so the tale went, until at length only Mastino's city of Brescia held out. Medisina da Desio had brought the child there out of immediate danger and for three months held out against the Count's troops. Antonio della Scala offered help but, isolated in a state which had gone over totally to the usurper, Medisina's loyalty had little more effect than a delaying action and in August a truce was arranged. Mastino was taken to Venice and later a pension was accepted from the Count in lieu of the child's rights.

The most vital of Giangaleazzo's immediate tasks proved the easiest, the formal recognition by the Grand Council of Milan coming as a corollary to the fact of possession. But it was also necessary to obtain the approval of the neighbouring states and

---

[66] Corio, III, 7.

on the Monday his chancellor, Pasquino Capelli, drew up a hasty justification for the *coup d'état*. Dated from Milan on the 8th May, the letter was not intended to be a formal accusation of Bernabò — that would come later — but an *aide-memoire* to Visconti ambassadors in interested cities. It rehearsed the injuries which the Count had suffered at the hands of his uncle and gave a drastically edited account of the events of the Saturday morning. The Count and his escort were peacefully riding past Milan, Pasquino wrote, when Bernabò and his sons fell upon them and in sheer self-defence they were obliged to overcome the attackers.[67] It was the first of many distortions which Giangaleazzo was obliged to give to an essentially illegal act, but Italian reaction ranged from the non-committal to the favourable. Lucca, Pisa and Savoy sent token forces at his request and Venice sent a congratulatory embassy. But not all his skill was able to win the whole-hearted favours of Florence. The mob rejoiced, for Bernabò had been a symbol of all they feared and hated, 'but certain wise men said "we rejoice at our own misfortune for that which was ruled by two men is now ruled by one and both are our enemies"'.[68] Nevertheless on 13th May the Signoria decided that their reply should be '*onestà*', a protean adjective which their Chancellor correctly interpreted as 'prudent', and on the following day he sent his reply, congratulating Capelli on his lord's escape and uttering the usual pious hopes for future peace.

Three weeks after the *coup*, with Milan firmly under control and the neighbouring states indifferent or friendly, Giangaleazzo deemed it safe to move his prisoners from Milan. Lodovico and Rodolfo were taken to Lodi and Bernabò to his own country castle of Tresi, accompanied by Donnina Porro,

[67] ASL 33, 1906.
[68] Morelli, p. 292.

the favourite mistress whom he had recently married. The 'Lament' says that it was at her own request that Donnina joined him, and certainly the license which Giangaleazzo allowed Bernabò's officials and illegitimate children argues that she could have remained free had she wished. But in any event her vigil did not last long, for by December Bernabò was dead, received back into the Church of which all his life he had been a deadly enemy, 'with tears and great devotion receiving the divine Sacraments, continually asking pardon of God for his past sins, beating his breast saying "Cor meum contritum et humiliatum Deus meus non despices"'.[69] His body was brought back to Milan and buried with all the honours of a lord of Milan — all save one; there was no baton of office in the dead right hand, Bernabò's death raised the inevitable rumours of poison. Gatari claimed that the Count attempted no less than three times to despatch his prisoner, an accusation capped by 'Minerbetti' with his statement that Giangaleazzo not only poisoned Bernabò but later murdered his swarming progeny in one grand holocaust. Dati quotes the Count himself as saying that the Blessed Virgin Mary, in a dream, had ordered the despatch of the tyrant; Corio transmitted the accusations with the additional information that the poison had been administered in a dish of beans. Thereafter, the rumours were repeated as fact. News of Bernabò's death was doubtless welcome enough to the Count, but it was little more than a tying up of loose ends. At seventy-six the old man was a spent force; senility and complacency had thrown him into his enemy's hands. His sons — dull, lumpish men who fell as easily or docilely accepted pensions — were nonentities without him, incapable of creating serious opposition. None of the many charges of poison laid against Giangaleazzo was

---

[69] Corio, III, 7.

capable of sustained proof and this least of all. Wanton cruelty was not his nature and to risk, unnecessarily, an accusation of murder at the very time when his notaries were drawing up a legal indictment of Bernabò would have been folly. But though he could repel any such charge the later accusations of usurpation came nearer home. As the memory of Bernabò's crimes dimmed, as Giangaleazzo himself grew to be the greatest threat ever produced by the Visconti, so the dead lord of Milan became something of a martyr, his overthrow a means of attack upon his successor. Both Sercambi and Chaucer independently remarked upon that aspect which shocked many. 'You knew well that messer Bernabò was your uncle, your father-in-law; your children were his nephews, his were your cousins. Certainly the act was cruel.'[70] So Sercambi apostrophized him, while Chaucer addressed Bernabò, sympathizing that

> 'Thy brother sone, that was thy double allye
> For he thy nevew was, and sone-in-law
> Within his prisoun made thee to dye.'[71]

Giangaleazzo could have justifiably claimed that such a close relationship was forced upon him, but the illegality of the act remained. It presented Giovio with his greatest difficulty when he came to write Giangaleazzo's biography; he excused it by arguing that the destruction of a tyrant was permissible and that Bernabò's policy of fragmenting the state between his sons made his removal politically beneficial to the Milanese. Nevertheless, he concludes, it was from this act that Giangaleazzo's later bad reputation grew. Yet Giangaleazzo

---

[70] Sercambi, CCXCVII, p. 240.
[71] Chaucer, 'The Monk's Tale'.

had an apologia made for him by no less a person than the humanist Chancellor of Florence, Coluccio Salutati. Eight months after he had transmitted the Signoria's reply in his official capacity, Salutati wrote personally to his friend Andreolo Arese, a member of the Count's chancery. Salutati's letter was a considered defence of Giangaleazzo which arose from his scholarly preoccupations, quite distinct from any attitude he might have to adopt as a servant of the Guelph Republic. His thesis was similar to Giovio's; Bernabò was a tyrant and therefore it was not only a right but a duty to depose him. Giangaleazzo, the only Lombard lord who had the courage to do so, acted virtuously; he should not be accused of injustice for does not Seneca say that it is licensed to bind tyrants with iron. 'Now Italy can rejoice and the lords of Este, Verona and Padua be tranquil. Now Liguria and Emilia, Genoa, Bologna and Florence can enjoy peace. Now can Venice breathe. No other action was more salutary than this done by Giangaleazzo whom his uncle had derided as an inexperienced boy until the time had come for his well-merited punishment.'[72]

The Count of Virtue would have done well to have left his defence in the dignified hands of the Florentine but, driven by the ever-returning Visconti need to demonstrate legality of succession, he ordered the Chancery officials to prepare a justification fuller than the hasty letter of May 8th. An army of clerks was set to work examining the criminal records, recording gossip, preparing what was intended to be the final indictment of Bernabò. Pride of place was given to a verbatim reproduction of the diploma of vicariate granted by Wenceslaus to Giangaleazzo in 1380. Even though Bernabò had not troubled to obtain a similar diploma his rights were

---

[72] Salutati, Ep. V.

recognized and a recitation of Giangaleazzo's own claims was therefore totally irrelevant. Nevertheless those claims were ritually paraded. Bernabò's personal cruelties followed at full length — the hangings, the impalements, the quarterings, thefts, rapes; someone with an astute ear to public feeling developed that aspect of Bernabò's interest which particularly offended Italians — the vast pack of hunting dogs which were quartered on the citizens who guaranteed the animals' condition with their lives. Then came the 'causes and reasons' which impelled the Count to act against his uncle. Item: Bernabò attempted to murder both the Count and his mother. Item: when Galeazzo was sick and rumoured dying Bernabò attempted to seize the castle of Porta Giovia. Item: he or his wife Regina made certain spells so that Caterina, wife of the Count, was unable to conceive. Item: he introduced a woman into the Count's household to spy upon him. Item: he treated the Count with contumely as though he were a mere boy. Item: even though of senile estate he held many women in concubinage, eighteen of whom were simultaneously pregnant.[73] So the lengthy list went on, but though the Chancery clerks were hardworking, the Chancery propagandists were as yet unskilled and the total effect of the indictment with its unselective mixture of the trivial and the damning was somewhat ludicrous. Yet not even Bernabò's many dispossessed heirs denied the graver charges and the *Processus* served its immediate purpose of establishing a gloss of legality.

THE RECONSTRUCTION OF THE STATE
Giangaleazzo remained in Milan only long enough to secure physical possession before returning to his preferred home in Pavia. Immediately ahead of him lay an enormous task. The

---

[73] Annales Mediolanenses CXLVII, cols. 788-800.

State had doubled in size as a result of his coup; for the first time since 1339 a single lord again ruled it and the old, casual method of government, already creaking, would have broken down under the new strains to which he intended to subject it. The speed with which he introduced a series of drastic reforms argues that they had been planned to the last detail long before he made the final move against Bernabò. A few days after the Grand Council formally recognized him as lord of Milan he ordered a complete revision of the statutes; eleven years were to pass before the work was completed, for the commission was laying the foundations of a law code which thereafter endured for centuries. Certain vital changes in the constitution had to wait until the new statutes were ratified, but in the interim a mass of administrative detail could be cleared. Two primary and frequently conflicting considerations were in Giangaleazzo's mind: the desire to create a truly homogeneous state and the need to recognize the identities of the communes composing it. One of his first acts as lord of Milan was to circulate the cities of the state requesting the governors to furnish names of potential officials. Merit alone was to be the test; the first list from Reggio was rejected as being composed 'ex affectione'. The stipulation that no candidate would be able to hold office in a city where he had near relatives was aimed at the elimination of corruption, but its secondary effect helped towards uniformity, for it weakened local patriotism; an able man, denied office in his native city, would move to another. In his need for competent administrators Giangaleazzo chose men not only from all levels of Milanese society but also citizens of foreign and frequently hostile cities, some of whom were exiled, some seeking fortune, all attracted to one of the few courts where the sole test was efficiency regardless of party or class. 'He used to say that there seemed to him to be no more worthwhile activity than that which acquired singular men',[74] Giovio said of him years later; but Giovanni Conversino, the Count's contemporary, while praising him for his generosity towards learning 'which surpassed all others', emphasized, 'I do not say for poets and scholars, whom he most rarely appointed, but doctors and jurisconsuls.'[75] Giangaleazzo's need for lawyers came second only to his need for soldiers, for he was attempting to make a single working unit out of dozens of once independent states, each with its ancient and complex constitution. There was a limit to the numbers of officials with the necessary legal training whom he could hope to recruit from outside the State, and he therefore gave every encouragement to the University which was already in being in Pavia. There had been a law school in Pavia since the eleventh century, but it had become moribund by the time that his father conquered the city. The despot achieved what the republic was unable to do. Determined to re-establish the glory of Pavia, Galeazzo sent out an edict in 1361 ordering all students within his state to attend at Pavia, 'and if they shall frequent other universities they shall immediately be sent for and, by compulsive means, constrained to come to Pavia'.[76] The Commune protested that it could not afford the luxury of subsidizing a university, but Galeazzo ignored the protests though he alleviated the burden slightly by making over certain taxes to the Commune for the upkeep of the University. His firmness ultimately paid dividends and when Giangaleazzo took over the institution there were some thirty professors, each receiving a stipend of up to 400 florins a year. There was an arts faculty and later a college of theology under the direct

---

[74] Giovio, p. 106.

[75] Baron, p. 491.

[76] Corio, III, 5.

control of the Holy See, but canon and civil law were the prime objects of study. Professors of the University formed part of the Count's privy council and vice versa, establishing a process of cross-fertilization so that students had first-hand knowledge of the problems of government and the Count was able to have advice of the foremost legal minds of his day. His own mind was bent towards the study of law, his State needed bureaucrats and it was therefore natural that law should be erected above all studies in the University. It was natural but unfortunate, for at about the same time there began to move through Italy the first current of that change which has since been given the name of humanism. The Visconti who had sheltered Petrarch allowed their enemies to gather in the great humanist's disciples, ensuring that their histories would be written with an anti-Visconti bias. Giangaleazzo later became aware of the lack of humanist scholars and made an attempt to correct it, but the University had by then become confirmed in its legal path.

The Count created two recognizably distinct administrative bodies within the state as opposed to the haphazard group of relatives and favourites which had hitherto advised the signore. His privy council, composed of trusted soldiers, politicians, and financiers, had direct access to him, while a general council, distinct from the communal offices, saw to the day-to-day running of the State. At the head of the Privy Council was the aging Pasquino Capelli, once chancellor to the Count's father and now probably the most influential man in the state next to his master. Capelli habitually signed himself as chancellor to the Count, but the term was still indistinct, his real power not clearly delineated, so that when a rival later arose he found himself fatally vulnerable. But now it was to Capelli that ambassadors presented themselves and from whom chancellors of other states would seek favours. A man of high scholastic ability, discreet to the point of colourlessness, his importance grew as the scope of the Chancery widened. A century later Giovio gave a first-hand account of the extraordinary care with which Giangaleazzo kept records of his manifold activities. 'I myself have seen in the armoury of his archives marvellous books in sheepskin which contained year by year the names of captains, *condottieri* and old soldiers and the pay of each. There were also registered copies of every letter which he despatched to various powers and received in return.'[77]

Azario had complained that delegation of authority led to the creation of many little tyrants. It was a just complaint, the obvious weakness of any growing bureaucracy. The Count attempted to correct it by developing the venerable communal process of the *sindacato*, the examination of each official's accounts at the end of his term of office. None were exempt; even the *podestà* was obliged to render his accounts and be prepared to answer the complaints of dissatisfied citizens. An extension of the principle enabled the central government to keep an observer in every commune noting local expenditures, present at the debates of the city councils, unobtrusively establishing the principle that, though identities of the individual communes were recognized, the state was superior to all. Early in his reign the Count laid down the basic conditions of citizenship which applied to all the cities of the state; the conditions were by no means onerous — five years' continuous residence and the possession of not less than 500 florins' worth of fixed goods — but some of the communes objected. The poaching of tax-payers from neighbouring cities was a recognized means of increasing revenue throughout

[77] Giovio, p. 107.

Italy, but as the Milanese state grew, such poaching merely resulted in an imbalance; when Brescia requested permission to citizenize certain rural localities it received a firm refusal. But many of Giangaleazzo's sensible attempts at reform met deep-rooted traditions whose eradication would have created a serious weakness within the state. The species of *Quo Warranto* which he instituted theoretically solved the ever-pressing problem of tax exemptions. After the inquisition the Treasury announced that henceforth only concessions granted *de jure* would be recognized, but in practice the *ex gratia* concessions continued and flourished, for tax exemptions as means of political reward were as vital as those for the encouragement of trade. An example of the problem which faced Giangaleazzo was the exemptions granted to the Visconti family itself. Even the Treasury did not know the total number, although an indication is given by Corio's list of those who attended the duke's funeral in 1402. At least thirty-seven branches of the Visconti existed in the state, some powerful and wealthy, others possessing little more than their great name. Motivated by pride or poverty, some allowed friends to share their exemption by fictitious contracts or by the painting of the Viper ensign on goods and houses. Total abolition of the right would have been damaging to prestige; all that could be done was to correct too obvious abuses as they came to official notice.

The administrative reforms in the state, though necessary, were largely the rationalization of existing methods; it was in his creation of a standing army that Giangaleazzo, most unwarlike of the Visconti, departed from precedent. He began by clearing the ground of the last remnants of feudal power. Tax collectors had complained that the rural barons were presenting themselves not with respectable groups of servants but with long trains of armed men, arrogant and dangerous. Henceforth the barons were forbidden to have more than four men in such companies under threat of heavy fine, and in the same edict of April 1386 was promulgated an absolute prohibition of arms throughout the state. A milder prohibition of the previous November had been ignored and the ban was extended to all persons within the state. Even foreigners were ordered to deposit their personal arms on entering a city. It was a reasonable measure within the cities where the soldiers of the garrisons or officers of the Commune were present to maintain order, but in the country districts it occasioned real hardship. The Count was petitioned by agricultural workers who pointed out the peculiar danger of their position and requested permission to carry arms. The answer was an unqualified refusal; their own tools were defensive arms enough. The disarming of the citizenry was the logical conclusion of that process which had begun with the abolition of the free militia in favour of mercenary companies. Arms now were carried only for the purpose of private brawls and private armies; both were repugnant to the lord, for the one disturbed the peace of the state and the other threatened his dominance.

The heyday of the foreign mercenaries was past; in all Italy only the Florentine Captain-General, John Hawkwood, served as a reminder of the humiliating days when the totality of Italian military power had been in the hands of English or German mercenaries. In 1379 the entirely Italian company of St George, in defending the Roman Pope at San Marino, had smashed the company of the Bretons and introduced a new type of *condottiere*. He was always an Italian, frequently a minor lordling whose companies were composed of loyal retainers instead of the chance-gathered companies of foreigners. The new men were the military superior of their predecessors, but their employment created a new danger to their masters. The foreign mercenary had fought for cash; the Italian mercenary was tied to his *condottiere* by feudal loyalties and the *condottiere* was himself frequently motivated by political ambitions. It required considerable skill to exploit his capabilities while avoiding the danger of introducing a rival into the state. The Count continued to make contracts with separate companies in the usual fashion, but instead of discharging them between wars he retained many on an unofficial basis. The device enabled him to keep a large force at readiness and to exert continual pressure upon his opponents during peace. Others had exploited the marauding tendencies of discharged mercenaries in order to harass unfriendly cities, but it was Giangaleazzo's control through his generals which turned sporadic spite into a considered weapon of policy. In his creation of a general staff the Count's isolation stood him in good stead. He had no equal within the state, neither son nor brother nor uncle to turn to for support, but in compensation there was no one within the state who could demand high position as of right. His brother despots were supported by close relatives who, even if loyal, were not necessarily militarily efficient; in the free republics generals chosen for their military skill were hampered by consultations with politicians jealously guarding their rights. Giangaleazzo was free from both limitations. His general staff was composed of men with dual responsibilities — political generals or military politicians — who could make decisions on the spot from their knowledge of the overall position. It was a dangerous precedent and under his weaker successors it proved fatal, the State itself falling prey to the professional soldier Sforza. But from the days of Pavia through to the peak of his success the Count received unswerving loyalty from his generals. Loyalty was perhaps natural from such Milanese citizens as dal Verme or Porro for whom service to the Visconti was a family tradition, but the foreigners who came to fight under the banner of the Viper identified themselves as closely with Giangaleazzo's interests. Some were his social equals or superiors: Paolo Savelli, Roman aristocrat and finished soldier, came from a family beside which the Visconti were vulgarians; Gugliemo Bevilacqua had served the Scaglieri in Verona in the highest offices until exiled by Verona's ferocious young lord. Others were rough professionals who had fought their way to the top like Ottobuon Terzo or, like Niccolo Diversi, were solid citizens who had turned to arms as a means of advancement. Carlo Zeno had been a Venetian admiral; Giovanni Ubaldini was a noble from the Tuscan hills. The diversity of their origins was of incalculable value to Giangaleazzo, for he was able to receive first-hand information, evaluated by trained minds, of the resources of potentially hostile powers. The pay they received was handsome, but they could have received as much from any other wealthy state with the possibility of political power thrown in. In his ability to bind such men to his cause Giangaleazzo gave ample indication of his ability to bind all Italy to Milan.

BETROTHAL OF VALENTINA

The Count's major reforms were introduced during the brief breathing space between the *coup d'état* of May 1385 and the opening of his first war in 1387. Thereafter, the accelerating pace of events forced him to postpone plans for a truly unified state and to modify or even abandon reforms already commenced. Time was his primary enemy; time — and the network of family alliances which Bernabò had created. Two months after the fall of Bernabò, his fifteen-year-old granddaughter, Isabella of Bavaria, became queen of France on her marriage to Charles VI and the Milanese family feud became an element of French politics. It was fear of an alliance between Bernabò and the Valois which had forced Giangaleazzo into action to prevent the marriage between Lucia Visconti and the duke of Anjou. The limited objective, with its incalculable results, was totally successful. Bernabò as head of a great state willing to contribute to French interests was one thing; Bernabò as a helpless prisoner was another, and the Angevins hurriedly disentangled themselves from the now embarrassing proposals, even considering an alliance with Bernabò's usurper. The proposal to marry Valentina to the duke of Anjou came to nothing, but it was a significant indication of Giangaleazzo's sudden elevation to a European reputation. Six months before he had been obliged to accept Bernabò's younger son for that same daughter and then stomach the insult when a better match was found elsewhere. Now he could negotiate a marriage at the highest levels, and after the failure of the Angevin proposal began negotiations for the marriage of Valentina to the Emperor's half-brother. It was at best a second choice and, though the negotiations went smoothly, Giangaleazzo kept in constant view the possibility of a French alliance. Some believed that his attitude towards France was deeply coloured by the fact that he was a Savoyard on his mother's side and his daughter was herself half French. Certainly there might have been a sentimental predisposition, but it was stiffened by the sudden threat of Bernabò's granddaughter becoming queen of France. With Carlo Visconti able to claim aid from the powerful Armagnacs and the duke of Bavaria now linked to the throne itself, it was imperative that some counterbalance be constructed in France. The ideal counterbalance would have been a marriage to the king's brother, Louis of Touraine, but Louis was himself about to marry the daughter of the king of Hungary and was even styled, somewhat prematurely, 'king of Hungary'. Louis left France in September 1385 for his wedding, but his bride was abducted before the ceremony and, accepting the situation with ungallant equanimity, he returned home. Giangaleazzo immediately commenced discreet enquiries in Paris and as a result French ambassadors came to Milan in May 1386 to discuss a possible marriage between Valentina and Louis. The discussion was successful but the price was high — too high for most Milanese. Valentina's dowry was to consist of half a million of gold together with the city of Asti and other Piedmont territories, but even this was hot all. She was the Count's only child and therefore a clause was inserted in the contract stipulating that, should the Count die without male issue, the State of Milan would pass to his daughter — or to her descendants. 'Thus the crime of May 1385 swiftly showed its tragic consequences. In order to resist his persecuted cousins and their German protectors, Giangaleazzo was obliged to bind himself in an irreparable manner to the French monarchy, abandoning... a precious territory and ensuring the passage of the State to the sons of Valentina who would be French princes.'[78]

To those who signed the contract the clause was probably nothing more than the satisfying of a legal necessity by the covering of all contingencies, no matter how remote. There could have seemed no real possibility that this mortgage would ever be foreclosed, for the Count and his second wife were young and healthy. Caterina in fact later presented her husband with two male heirs who ultimately succeeded him, but they in

---

[78] Cognasso, SMT, V, p. 577.

their turn died without heirs and the State automatically fell to Valentina's descendants. No one in France troubled to enforce the claim and for a century and more the contract gathered dust; yet it remained valid and the claim ultimately presented by Louis XII of France was paid for in Milanese blood. Superficially the marriage was a resounding triumph, for not only had Giangaleazzo at last allied himself directly with the first throne in Europe, but by ceding his Piedmontese territories to his son-in-law he ensured that the vulnerable western approaches to the state were in powerful and friendly hands. But even this proved a hollow triumph in his own lifetime and Valentina's legacy earned him the condemnation of generations of Milanese. 'Truly with sinister augury and singular damage to Italy and to France was this arrangement made because in order to have this legacy was born a long and terrible war of which even now we cannot see the end', Giovio wrote in the fifteenth century.[79] Three hundred years later Giulini remarked that 'the wars which Lombardy suffered because of her (Valentina) has made her name odious among us'.[80] The proposals were unpopular even at the time they were made. Corio supposed the reason to be that the Milanese were far more in favour of an alliance with the splendour of the Empire than with the ambiguous French, but de' Mussi in Piacenza gives an earthier and more probable explanation.[81] High politics meant nothing to the average citizen, but increased taxes did, and the enormous dowry of 450,000 florins meant a burden to every city. Piacenza alone was ordered to find 20,000 florins.

---

[79] Giovio, p. 109.
[80] Giulini, Lib. LXXIV, p. 500.
[81] de' Mussi, col. 548.

Valentina was married by proxy in January 1387 and from then on was styled duchess of Touraine, but over two years passed before she finally left Pavia, a delay almost entirely due to the difficulty of collecting the money for her dowry. The state could have paid even this enormous sum with comparative ease, for the total annual revenue was some 1,200,000 florins, but scarcely a fortnight after his daughter's wedding Giangaleazzo commenced the first of his major operations, the war against della Scala of Verona, and the greater part of the dowry money was used for military purposes. No one was better aware than he of the uncertainty of a marriage until its consummation. Valentina might be styled 'duchess of Touraine' even as her cousin Lucia could once have styled herself 'duchess of Anjou'. But Lucia was still an unmarried girl and the same thing could happen to Valentina should another, more advantageous, marriage present itself for Louis. Yet Giangaleazzo had little choice; to have delayed the marriage would have been to lose Louis altogether, and though the Veronese war was not of such pressing moment, circumstances forced him into the business of robbing Peter to pay Paul. In September 1387 collection for the dowry began, the smallest hamlet contributing its share. Government officials made a forced contribution of two months' salary and even the customary tax exemption on wine for the court was waived. The need to raise money conflicted with the need to retain that reputation for clemency which had helped him to secure power. A year after the collection was begun Reggio had still not paid its share and the Count wrote a remarkably temperate letter urging the city to do so. 'I should like to concede you further time but it is not possible for time is creeping up upon us. We have taxed you only 2000 florins, a sum much under that which you should be taxed, taking the entire sum into account without which the consummation of so important a marriage cannot take place.'[82] The request is followed by a warning; the money shall not be collected unjustly but from each according to his ability to pay. But though Valentina remained in her father's care her bridegroom's agents hastened to secure what could be secured. Bertrand Guasco, governor of that County of Virtue which never saw its Count, was nominated as Valentina's procurator for the complex work of examining the financial structure of Asti and arranging for its passing over to the French. Matters there went smoothly enough, but not all the Piedmontese cities of the dowry were minded to become French citizens at the stroke of a pen. Giangaleazzo personally ordered the rebels to recognize the duke of Touraine, but he was ignored and the French had their first taste of attempting to control turbulent north Italians. The Count could not be blamed for the aggressiveness of his late subjects, but later a more embarrassing matter was disclosed. Asti's revenue was found to be considerably below that guaranteed and he was asked to make up the deficit. He refused and the long wrangle dragged on while Valentina waited. But while she waited the war with Verona grew wider, the prize greater, so that her father was forced to dip deeper into the money collected for her dowry.

---

[82] ASL XXIX, 1, 1902.

IV: LORD OF LOMBARDY

THE DESTRUCTION OF DELLA SCALA

On news of Valentina's proxy marriage, Fillipo Corsini, Florentine ambassador to Paris, urgently warned his fellow citizens of its possible consequences. 'The lord of Milan has 2000 lances permanently under arms; he has the keys of the Empire; if we give him time to breathe and to ally himself with the French we are lost.'[83] The perspicuous warning went unheeded, for the Count of Virtue was still an unknown quantity to his contemporaries. In Italian eyes the overthrow of Bernabò, though dramatic enough, was merely a family quarrel; even that action, it could be argued, had been forced upon the Count through sheer self-preservation. On his previous record it could be hoped that the threat from Milan was at least suspended as the State entered upon a period of consolidation after two generations of violent expansion. Blessed with the wisdom of hindsight, later Florentine writers were to claim that their government was from the first aware of the boundless ambitions of the Count of Virtue, that they knew from the beginning that his goal was an Italian crown and the destruction of republicanism in Italy. In truth, no man knew the workings of the mind of the thirty-five-year-old man who now paused in brief survey of the field before him. It is possible that the appearance of the *coup d'état* was also its reality; that having disposed of the personal danger which Bernabò represented Giangaleazzo might indeed have been content to pursue the domestic path of ordering the State of

---

[83] Cognasso, SMT, V.

Milan into a pattern pleasing to his logical mind. His plans and motives can only be conjectured, their outlines traced through the archives of interested cities, their details filled in only from the gossip of courtiers and chroniclers, for his own archives, housed though they were in three different cities, were all destroyed after his death. He had no confidant to betray his secrets, yet all were laid bare in those same archives which so impressed Paolo Giovio. 'Whosoever should wish to write a just history could desire no more of abundance or authenticity because from these books one may easily discover the reasons of the wars, the councils and the successes of the enterprises.'[84] Giovio's intention was merely to produce a series of elegant essays upon Milan's great family and it was no part of his task to record the Count's voluminous personal archives in Pavia; it was nevertheless unfortunate that he did not attempt even a selection, for he was the last scholar to view them before they were carried away by the French and ultimately destroyed as valueless paper. The state archives housed in the Castle of Milan were destroyed in the rebellion which established the Ambrosian Republic in 1447; the few archives preserved in Vertus in France were destroyed when the duke of Buckingham sacked the city. It was a peculiar irony that the one aspect of his administration in which Giangaleazzo probably took personal pleasure, and which could have provided a rebuttal of hostile propaganda, should have perished in its entirety.

That side of Giangaleazzo's character which delighted in solitude and study might have disinclined him to engage in the ruthless Italian struggle, yet in the existing conditions the power which sought merely to preserve the *status quo* inevitably fell victim to dynamic neighbours. He himself had proved that

---

[84] Giovio, p. 107.

personally with the destruction of Bernabò, and the peninsula was littered with the corpses of once free communities which had failed to see that expansion was an ineluctable factor of independence. The years of study spent in the obscurity of Pavia had made him familiar with the techniques of power, techniques which the precision of his mind and the strength of his will could turn into formidable weapons, given the backing of a great state. He now had that backing, for Milan, its territory, its subject cities, its great wealth, were all at his sole command. And even while he was assessing the resources at his disposal a situation arose in eastern Lombardy which invited him to the greatest Visconti enterprise, the eastward expansion of the State, which no Visconti could have ignored.

Franceso Carrara, lord of Padua, had extended his own frontiers at the expense of Venice. The Venetian Serenissima, usually indifferent to the affairs of the peninsula, were presented with a brutal challenge, for Carrara's act threatened to cut the Republic totally from the mainland. Too weak to interfere directly, for they were suffering still from a disastrous maritime defeat, reluctant to abandon their almost traditional neutrality, the Serenissima found a catspaw in Antonio della Scala, lord of Verona. The Scaligieri were now drawing to the end of their days, a living example of the rise and degeneration of the tyrant. The family had begun to climb under Can Grande, host to Dante and great general. His nephew Mastino had surpassed even him, dreaming of founding an Italian kingdom, but with his death collapse of the family started. His two younger sons slew the elder; of these two one murdered the other and died leaving only two bastards. Again the bloody tragedy was repeated when Antonio murdered his brother in 1381 and reigned alone. Bernabò Visconti attacked him, claiming Verona through his wife Regina, granddaughter of

Mastino. Antonio held his own and with the disappearance of the formidable Bernabò felt himself secure. So contemptuous was he of the new lord of Milan that he was unwise enough to help Bernabò's son at the siege of Brescia and turned his attention elsewhere — to Padua whose lord had been the most outspoken in condemning his past actions. The Serenissima subsidized him and Padua and Verona clashed in Spring 1386. Into this tangle of personal hatreds and political ambitions, a tangle where a false step would bring down the weight of Venice, the Count of Virtue stepped.

The only writer who covered the entire Paduan tragedy from the Count's first delicate moves to the end two years later was the Paduan chronicler Galeazzo Gatari. The title of his work amply indicates his bias, for it is the 'Chronicles of the House of Carrara'[85] not of the city of Padua; the people indeed are mentioned directly only once, for all his details are subordinated to one aim — the glorification of the Carrarese. Gatari's use of direct speech and provision of minute information sometimes seems suspiciously glib, but certainly none could have been closer than he to the centre of events. In 1378 he was Carrara's treasurer; as one of the Anziani of the Duomo quarter he received Carrara's renunciation of office in 1388 and was one of the ambassadors of the people who

---

[85] Galeazzo Gatari discontinued his chronicle in 1389, but his son Bartolomeo brought it up to 1405, the year which saw the total destruction of the house of Carrara. A second son, Andrea, heavily edited their work in an attempt to create historical perspective. Writing nearly fifty years afterwards, he was aware of the value of details to which they were indifferent and though he excised much of what they wrote, he added more from other sources. The 1915 edition of the Chronicles has restored all his cuts with the valuable addition of his redaction.

waited upon Giangaleazzo with the articles of surrender. The Chronicles, for all their obvious prejudices and romantic defects, provide rare first-hand accounts of Giangaleazzo; it is as though Gatari trained a powerful spotlight upon his beloved House and when members of that House moved, the spotlight followed, shining briefly upon those with whom they came in contact. Gatari's fitful illuminations of the Count of Virtue show more detail than the entire Milanese chroniclers put together.

Gatari was convinced that, from the first, Giangaleazzo was playing Verona and Padua against each other, ready to support either as advantage dictated. In June 1386 della Scala was heavily defeated at Brentelles by the Paduan army under the great Tuscan general Giovanni Ubaldini. Immediately after the battle Giangaleazzo sent Gugliemo Bevilacqua to Padua congratulating and offering help, 'but craftily and fraudulently he sent to Verona and thus the Count of Virtue played with two mantles'.[86] The defeat at Brentelles had done nothing to diminish della Scala's arrogance. Again Venetian envoys came to Verona bringing gold; Carrara pleaded with him, pointing out that the defeat of either of them could please only their common enemy Venice, but della Scala ignored him and with Venetian aid pressed the Paduan armies hard all through the winter of 1386-7. Ubaldini went personally to Tuscany to gain the assistance of John Hawkwood, and with the almost legendary general in command near-defeat was turned into crushing victory at Castagnaro in March 1387. Antonio della Scala was deeply disheartened; he had thrown almost his entire resources into the battle and, left to himself, would probably have heeded Carrara's renewed requests for peace. But Venice

---

[86] Gatari, p. 255.

came forward yet again with encouragement and money and he again prepared for war.

Giangaleazzo had as yet declared for neither party and della Scala in his weakened condition deemed it wise to sound his hitherto despised neighbour. Stefano di Picardi was sent hastening to Pavia bearing a rich gift, instructed to voice a suspicion. The Count accepted the one and dispelled the other. It was impossible for him to treat with Padua, for did he not look upon della Scala as a son? But Picardi had barely quitted Pavia with the dubious comfort that the Count regarded his master as a near relative when Giangaleazzo sent for the Paduan ambassador at his court, Giacomo Turchetto. He told Turchetto of Picardi's mission and added that the Venetians had also attempted to draw him into a league against Carrara. Up to now he had managed to avoid making a decision, but soon his hand would be forced. Turchetto thanked him most gratefully and asked him to delay his decision while he conferred with his master. The Count agreed. But Turchetto was no fool; he wrote to his master giving him the gist of the conversation but warned him to have a care in whom he confided, for the Count was well informed of both Paduan and Veronese affairs — and was a friend of neither state. Nevertheless Carrara had little choice; behind the puerile spite of della Scala was the deep hatred of the Serenissima who would know no rest until the House of Carrara was totally eliminated. Veronese troops massed for the third time; Hawkwood had returned to Tuscany and in desperation Carrara sent to Pavia. Giangaleazzo made a great show of being obliged to consult his council, but at length agreed to the proposals for a league and for the divisions of the spoils. He, through his wife Caterina, daughter of Regina della Scala, was to have Verona while Carrara took Vicenza. He had one additional request however; he would like Carrara's generals Ugolotto Biancardo and Giovanni Ubaldini to be seconded to him. Carrara agreed. The Count's policy of engaging skilled men was well known, but the secondment of Biancardo and Ubaldini had a secondary effect which Carrara overlooked in the joy of completing the league; their withdrawal left him without a single professional general of any standing.

The months of careful work was at an end. All della Scala's potential allies had been bought or frightened off; Venice still was imponderable, but the Serenissima never threw good money after bad, and having estimated della Scala's chance of success under the new alliances, coldly left him to his fate. On April 17th 1387 the Count sent his formal Defiance to Antonio della Scala. It was a florid letter, skilfully expanding a modicum of fact into a mass of accusations, della Scala is reproached with giving aid to the besieged city of Brescia, his treacherous action is compared with Giangaleazzo's own altruism when he did all in his power to save Verona when Bernabò was attacking it. His activities then, in fact, had been limited to holding certain territories as arbitrator. Nevertheless 'with what sweat, what vigilances, what fatigue, what solicitude we did all in our power to raise the near defeated city of Verona… and all this you have forgotten. We would have done great things for you for the love we bear you. But now listen to how you have responded to the many benefits made you.' della Scala received the dukes of Bavaria when they came 'with ponderous armies' to avenge Bernabò; he conspired with Carlo Visconti; and finally 'to augment your faults you rendered vain the negotiations for marriage between us and the princes of Germany'.[87] Open war was therefore to exist between them from April 23rd.

---

[87] Corio, III, 7, p. 331.

Antonio della Scala was a depraved man, cordially hated by his subjects and equals, yet there was a certain pathos in the picture of him, the last of a great race, desperately striving to extricate himself from a situation in which his own arrogance and stupidity had placed him. When he had commenced his adventure a year before his sole object had been the destruction of Carrara in the east; his reaction to the unlooked-for danger in the west was utter surprise. He called his councillors together on receipt of the letter and they confirmed what he already knew; there was no conceivable means of defending himself from both Milan and Padua. His only means was to plead, and plead he did, grovelingly. He denied everything; everything was the result of enemy gossip. It was true that he had brought his army on to the Brescian *contado*, but that was in response to the movements of mercenaries and the Count benefited from his action as much as he did. He admits his non-existent debt to Giangaleazzo for the latter's attempt to bring about peace between himself and Bernabò. But as to the accusation that the dukes of Bavaria and Carlo Visconti were on his territory, the truth is that these people had urgently asked him to let them through in order to complete their secret designs for an attack upon the lord of Padua. 'And these are the frauds, these the deceits that our dearest father has received from the hands of his son.'[88]

The letter was totally ignored, but Giangaleazzo thought it worth while to make a gesture to Italian opinion by giving the Florentines a brief account of the matter. The Signoria contented themselves with the cautious reply that they were sure that he would not unleash a war for frivolous reasons, but prayed him to remember the advice of Cicero and not make a war greater than that necessary to elude the snares of the

[88] Ibid., p. 334.

122

enemy.[89] The Count had little need of such advice; war was for him the unavoidable end of politics, not its beginning, and long before his armies marched the true work had been done in council chambers and private rooms where the skilful manipulation of ambitious men could take the place of the blind hazards of violence which he loathed. Immediately after the declaration of war he issued a proclamation to the Veronese people saying that he had come to relieve them of an intolerable tyranny, an appeal which had no immediate effect but was remembered by some of the Veronese at a crucial moment later. Certain highly secret instructions were also issued to Guglielmo Bevilacqua, the exiled Veronese, and to Giovanni Ubaldini. Then he waited while Francesco Novello, son of Padua's lord, earned new glory for the Carrarese, conducting himself like a new Hector on the battlefields of Lombardy. When at length the retiring lord of Milan moved, his armies struck like a knife, cutting off Verona to north and west, leaving the heroic Francesco to strike his useless postures in the south, della Scala appealed to the Emperor, offering him both Verona and Vicenza. Wenceslaus accepted and his envoys came to Pavia, demanding peace and informing the Count that della Scala was willing to cede to him the territories already occupied by the Milanese. Giangaleazzo 'gave them fine words' but immediately summoned Giacomo Turchetto, telling him to write to his master, urging him not to make peace for in a very short time Verona would be in their power. At the same time he wrote to Bevilacqua ordering him to complete the matter in hand before a peace treaty could rob him of the greatest prize. Turchetto again warned Carrara that the Count was probably contemplating some act of duplicity, but Carrara was now in

---

[89] Ibid., p. 340.

too deeply to draw back and obediently he rejected the Veronese proposals in his turn.

Turchetto was not the only puzzled man in Pavia, for Giangaleazzo's own advisers were urging him to accept della Scala's offer. But where they were obliged to base their judgement on guesswork, Giangaleazzo's action was based on solid knowledge of what was actually happening in Verona. Bevilacqua was in contact with some of his fellow citizens who, for a consideration, were prepared to introduce him into the city with a small band of soldiers. Behind all the political and military preparations Giangaleazzo was making use of the most ancient and certain of political tools, an injured man's desire for revenge. It argued much cold courage on the part of Bevilacqua, for he came of a well-known family in Verona, and had any citizen recognized him and reported the fact to della Scala, swift death would have been the end. But during the night of October 17th he and his companions remained safely in the gate-house of San Massimo while half a mile away Ubaldini launched an attack upon Santa Lucia. At dawn Bevilacqua's small party ensured the entry of the main army. Even at this eleventh hour della Scala believed that his personal popularity could yet bring victory, and with the few loyal soldiers remaining he mounted and coursed the city crying 'Viva la Scala'. There was not the slightest response from the citizens and the wretched man retired to his castle and sent for Bevilacqua. Only the Count knew the full details of what passed between them, but on the following night della Scala, recognizing reality, fled to Venice. 'And in such a manner with great ignominy ended and fell from apogee the great house and family of Scala that had maintained themselves with consummate pomp for eighty years.'[90] It was now the turn of Carrara.

FALL OF PADUA

Four days after the fall of Verona Francesco Carrara sent his natural son, the Conte da Carrara, to take over Vicenza as had been agreed in the pact. En route, the young Conte met a soldier who gave him the remarkable news that Ugolotto Biancardo, Visconti's general, was already established in the city. Uncertain whether or not Biancardo's presence was part of the campaign or had a more sinister meaning, the Conte sent the soldier on to Padua, asking for instructions — and incidentally losing valuable time. His father ordered him to do the obvious thing — go on to Vicenza and ask Biancardo what he was doing there. Biancardo's reply was simple; he w s holding the city for his master until its future was decided by its own citizens. This account of Gatari's[91] implied that Giangaleazzo was engaged in double-dealing, but, probably from a desire to show his beloved Carrarese in a favourable light, Gatari suppressed a vital piece of evidence which Corio later supplied.[92] The Vicentinese loathed the house of Carrara; indeed, they had not only requested Giangaleazzo to take over the city but had sworn that, if he did not, they would rather deliver it to flames than return to the rule of Padua. The Conte reported to his father and he was ordered to return. The next round lay in the council chambers of Padua, Pavia — and Venice.

Giangaleazzo's first reply to Carrara's reproaches was a simple lie; he had neither troops nor officials in Vicenza. Carrara had barely received this reply when firm news came that Milanese officials had been appointed to the city.

---

[90] Ibid., p. 341.

[91] Gatari, p. 303.

[92] Corio, III, 7, p. 342.

Giacomo Turchetto was sent hastening to Pavia, was received courteously and treated to a remarkable explanation. 'Certainly your lord has reason to complain... but it is not my will that these officials have been appointed. They are there on behalf of Madonna la Contesa', his wife; he could do nothing as both Caterina and his councillors were opposed to him. Turchetto was asked to write to Padua, explaining, but the Paduan replied that he had no intention of writing any such thing for he would not be believed. 'I myself that have heard you do not believe it.' The Count himself must write. Giangaleazzo merely replied 'I will not write and as for yourself do so or not as you please.'[93] Turchetto gave way, informing his master that Bevilacqua was on his way to Padua with more promises, and telling him in addition that Venetian ambassadors had arrived in Pavia — for what purpose he did not know.

The purpose was soon very clear. The Serenissima had never looked upon della Scala as other than a means of attack upon Padua, della Scala had fallen and their cold logic dictated an alliance with his conqueror — still against Padua. Now what had been a local quarrel suddenly seemed to be growing and the non-Lombard states took alarm. Florentine suspicions were based as much on their traditional anti-Milanese attitude as on real fears, but their ambassadors sent to Pavia in October 1387 reported a disquieting incident. Finding that they had arrived too late to make peace between Visconti and della Scala they offered their congratulations. The Count accepted, remarking that the fall 'of that unwary lord' had been unfortunate considering his magnificent forbears. He followed up the smooth hypocrisy with an oblique threat, saying that many unemployed mercenaries were again at large. 'He then brought Ubaldini into the presences of the ambassadors and demanded

[93] Gatari, p. 307 (Andrea's redaction).

many things of the Florentines if they did not wish to be overrun and sacked.'[94] It was a disquieting change of front from the mild and studious late lord of Pavia. The Florentine Signoria responded by destroying the castles of the Ubaldini family in the Apennines and made vigorous attempts during the early spring of 1388 to bring about peace between Venice and Padua. Venice had no desire for peace, intending at last to eliminate the danger on her frontier, but neither had the Serenissima any intention of assisting the Count save as a by-product. On March 31st they disburdened themselves of a sibylline utterance. 'The Senate is treating with the Bolognese and Florentines but what shall be the result is uncertain. Meanwhile the orators of the Count promise great advantages to the Republic but lack full powers to conclude. The Senate desires that these powers should be sent — then we shall see.'[95] Stripped of its subtleties the statement was plain enough — state your offer. The Count did so; he would contribute 1500 horse and 1000 foot, bearing the brunt of the actual fighting, while the Republic would contribute 100,000 ducats for the first year; Padua would fall to the Count and Treviso to Venice. The Florentines abandoned the conferences while continuing to make unofficial efforts. Their eyes were opening to the real dangers. 'Every day we are meditating on the perils that we see,' Salutati wrote. 'Fear increases and it is not possible for us to be tranquil seeing how imminent is this terrible war… which brings with it many other perils.'[96]

The Florentines were not to know that Giangaleazzo was running because he could not walk. The coinciding of two advantageous projects had committed him simultaneously to

---

[94] 'Minerbetti', XXXIV, A. 1387.

[95] ASNXXVI, 1921.

[96] Cognasso, SMT V, p. 539.

the financing of the Veronese war and the collection of Valentina's dowry, della Scala destroyed and Valentina still unwed, he would have preferred to bide his time, but Venice now was eager for the final attack upon Padua. Such an opportunity might never occur again and therefore, in May, he assented to the publication of a league between himself and Venice with the nominal addition of Ferrara, Mantua and Udine. Again the brunt of the fighting was borne by Milanese forces, the Venetians deploying their mercenaries along their own frontier. Carrara was outmatched and knew it; in the east his most deadly enemy had actually placed troops in the field, while in the west was the young man whose political cynicism and ability only he, della Scala and the dead Bernabò really knew; between them Padua lay like a nut for the cracking. But the true reason for the extraordinarily rapid collapse of Padua is dismissed by Galeazzo Gatari in a single paragraph. 'The citizens waited with joy for what would happen, for they wished to be under the domination of the Count of Virtue, who falsely had a good and perfect fame. And for another reason; for more than twelve years messer Francesco had been at war and the citizens were exhausted in body and money and they all wished to change lords in order to be at peace.'[97] In the crisis Carrara threw himself upon the mercies of his councillors. 'There is no one to turn to. The Emperor is bound to the wishes of our enemy. The king of Hungary (God rest him) is no more; the duke of Austria will not move without a great deal of money — and I have no money, for the expenses of the war with della Scala were great. Neither Florence nor Bologna wishes to become involved and in any case the marquis of Ferrara, ally of Visconti, has closed all the passes into Tuscany. Therefore for God's sake counsel me in what

---

[97] Gatari, p. 310.

manner our State may be saved and our person not fall into peril.'[98] The counsel he received was anything but disinterested, for those councillors not in the pay of Milan or Venice had long since become disenchanted with the Carraresi. He was advised to sell Padua to Visconti and go to Treviso. His son Francesco Novello protested, citing with an unhappy choice of historic parallel the fortitude of Priam after Hector's death. The old man withdrew from the chamber and the weary discussion went on; a suggestion of assassination was made which Novello rejected indignantly, but a compromise was reached. Francesco il Vecchio would abdicate and Novello would assume the state, the argument being that neither Giangaleazzo nor the Venetians hated him as they hated his father. Three of the councillors then went in search of il Vecchio and disclosed the plan to him, 'to which the lord made no reply but stood as though mute, all the time holding his sceptre in his hand and biting at it as though in anger'.[99] But at length he said that night was the mother of thought and that he would give a reply in the morning. He remained in his state of acute indecision for some days, first accepting the proposal, then toying with the idea of sending yet another embassy to Visconti. At length the threat of open revolt by the citizens forced him into action; he would resign the power to his son and go to Treviso. On Monday June 29th the speech of renunciation was made to the assembled citizens, who received it in total silence. 'Minerbetti' adds that he offered the sceptre but, no one accepting it, he placed it upon the table and left Padua for ever, still in silence. But even if the change of government would have made the slightest difference it came too late; on the following morning Milanese heralds brought

[98] Ibid., p. 312.
[99] Ibid., p. 314.

their master's formal declaration of war. Novello immediately wrote to Pavia, pointing out that he was now lord of Padua and that the accusations in the declaration could not possibly be intended for him. But Giangaleazzo merely remarked 'Sons of cats are fond of mice' and continued his preparations.

Francesco il Vecchio had brought his troubles upon his own head, but he was a wily politician, experienced after a decade of running battle with Venice. Gatari's portrait of his son is that of a romantic, a brave, generous man of high ideals. Though coloured by affection it was accurate enough, for through all the tragic years that lay ahead, no person could accuse Francesco Novello of lacking either moral or physical courage. It was left to the sardonic 'Minerbetti' to give the corrective to Gatari's eulogy. Novello was 'a valorous soldier — but a fool, with little sense'.[100] Prepared to fight the war single-handed, he was yet totally unaware that the majority of his generals and courtiers were but awaiting the chance to go over to the successful Milanese. Summer that year was cold beyond living memory; food grew scarce, and while his enemies were able to draw supplies from abroad, the Paduan state knew famine. Novello had only his own courage and limited military ability to oppose the combined attack of the foremost generals of Italy gathered under the banner of the Viper. By November dal Verme had smashed through into the Paduan heartland; again the citizens trembled on the edge of revolt, again a Carrara called a council and received pessimistic answers. 'There is no money.' 'You cannot hold the people by force.' A messenger was sent to dal Verme to treat of possible peace. The Milanese replied that his commission was to see that not a house was left standing in Padua. Nevertheless 'tell your lord to go with his children to my lord, *messer lo Conte di Virtù*, and with them

---

[100] 'Minerbetti', VIII, A. 1388.

throw himself into his arms and ask for nothing but of his good grace'.[101] Novello received the news uncertainly; throughout he had been convinced that a man-to-man talk with the Count would resolve all difficulties, but such a measure at this stage might be construed as weakness. Again the people decided their lord's course of action, this time with no mere 'general murmurings' in the outlying territories but with a fierce riot in Padua itself. Novello accepted dal Verme's suggestion in principle; he insisted that he was not capitulating but was merely making an armistice while affairs of state were discussed at the highest level, dal Verme agreed; he agreed to a meticulous contract in which the Milanese would 'temporarily' take possession of Padua to keep order during the lord's absence; he promised faithfully to return the city to that lord should the talks fail. It is an indication both of his naivete and nobility that Francesco Novello believed that the contract would be honoured, that he would be free to return to his city after having been in Visconti's power. Il Vecchio, hearing the news, was beside himself with rage, declaring that Novello was no son of his but a bastard; but il Vecchio knew rather more of politics than of honour, a characteristic he shared with the Count of Virtue who, so soon as the 'temporary' garrison was installed in Padua, ordered three days of rejoicing throughout his state. Novello made the dangerous journey to Milan to find himself coldly received and informed that the Count had retired to Abbiategrasso because of the plague. From then on he knew the bitterness of suing from weakness, Giangaleazzo deliberately avoiding him while the Paduan tragedy drew to its close. Francesco il Vecchio was taken into custody, 'the whole time cursing and blaspheming his son', and Treviso handed over to Venice according to the treaty. There were rumours

---

[101] Gatari, p. 331.

131

that Giangaleazzo contemplated keeping the city for himself, but such an act would have been a stupid courting of disaster at the end of two expensive wars. Indeed, on November 27th the Milanese general in Treviso passed on a letter to the Doge of Venice from his master in which the Count explicitly ordered the cession of all claimed territories to Venice. 'It is our intention that in this affair and in all others at all times we shall so comport ourselves that the signoria of Venice shall be content with our vicinity and friendship.'[102] Both the Count and the Serenissima were well aware of the necessity for the most scrupulous conduct. Two great Lombard states which had acted as insulators had ceased to exist so abruptly that there had been no time for adjustment; Milanese and Venetian frontiers now touched.

Meanwhile in Padua a brief but astonishing resurrection took place. No living citizen had ever taken part in a communal election, yet without difficulty the old forms of government were revived, the people again exercising absolute sovereignty. Nevertheless the first act of the new government was to draw up a treaty of submission to Giangaleazzo and elect ambassadors to take it. Galeazzo Gatari was one of their number, all dressed magnificently at the Commune's expense to convey thanks to the Count 'who has brought us from slavery to liberty, from darkness to light, leading us from death to life'. The thirty-eight chapters of the instrument were crammed with an envenomed indictment of the Carrarese and their servants. The Count was asked to ban and exile them in perpetuity, to pity the wretched citizens afflicted by years of ceaseless war, and to take under his benevolent protection the state of Padua while recognizing the rights of the citizens.[103]

---

[102] Pastorelli, p. 184, n. 24.
[103] Gatari, p. 349.

On the way to Milan the *ambassade* passed the cavalcade of Francesco il Vecchio. The old man desired to speak with them but, in embarrassment, they refused and continued on to Abbiategrasso where the Count was still in residence. Their leader had a long and private consultation with him and then the Count came to them in person 'embracing each one with great love and one by one demanding his name'. He accepted their charge and in reply to a question relative to the Venetian triumph said, 'If God permits, it shall not be long before these two states — that is to say Padua and Venice — shall stand equal. Neither then will be able to taunt the other.'[104] Returning to Milan the embassy met Novello still waiting for the Count 'to see if it was possible to make an accord', and again in embarrassment they were forced to reject a request for an interview.

For two months Novello waited in vain for the long promised conference with the Count before his eyes were opened to reality. His assent to the transference of Padua was a mere formality which the Count certainly desired, but not with any great urgency. Giangaleazzo allowed a few tempting rumours to leak from Pavia; he was contemplating giving Lodi to Novello, or if not Lodi then Crema or possibly some other honourable appointment. His policy of waiting at length paid dividends, for in January 1389 Novello formally ceded the city and state of Padua without further qualifications. In obedience to his promises to the Paduan envoys, the Count distributed some minor posts among the citizens who had helped him, but the city was far too important a bulwark to allow of any real independence. Spinetta Malaspina took up residence as governor and Bertoletto Visconti as *podestà* and gradually the upper levels of the Paduan administration were flooded with

---

104 Gatari, p. 358.

Milanese officials. Novello had one last demonstration to make of his undoubted courage and utter lack of discretion. His plot to assassinate the Count was carefully planned — save that one of his many confidants kept Giangaleazzo minutely informed. Gatari says that the Count made little of the plot and certainly Novello's diplomacy to date could have given him small cause for alarm. But the impetuous young man was proving a liability at close quarters. Gone now were the hints of glittering lordships; Novello was offered a poverty-stricken 'kingdom' ruled from a half-ruinous castle in the Piedmontese hills. He accepted; even a poor mountain fief was better than the assassin's knife he had undoubtedly earned.

With his departure Giangaleazzo could at last feel that his first major operation had been brought to a tidy end. Not four years had passed since the May morning when he had ridden out to gamble everything upon one swift blow; now he, the erstwhile simple lord of Pavia, could claim that throughout Lombardy his wish was law. In all that expanse only Mantua and Ferrara retained independence under the Gonzaghi and the Este respectively; but Francesco Gonzaga had long since been bound to him by curiously strong ties of loyalty and the young marquis d'Este looked upon him as a hero. Venice alone closed the eastward vista, and though the Republic was beginning to wonder just what it was that had been unleashed in Lombardy, Serenissima and signore at the moment were sharing the spoils with every outward appearance of amicability.

V: THE COURT

DEPARTURE OF VALENTINA

In the spring of 1388 an uncertain peace had settled again upon the plain of Lombardy. The cities now were less crowded as, the threat of sudden attack removed, the dwellers of the *contadi* returned to their suburbs, villas and farms. There was hunger but, for the first time in two years, a promise that the harvests would be brought in. Plague was rumoured to be again rampant in the south, but in Milan and Pavia, in Piacenza, Como, Bergamo and the score of cities of the State the air was clean so that it was possible to pick up the threads of normal life, disrupted by two years of war. The citizens of the Milanese State had suffered less than their enemies for the war had been fought, by mercenaries, at a distance from them. But they too had known the burden of increased taxes and the ever-present fear that a mercenary company might break its leash and rend them for ransom; the burden and the fear were, briefly, suspended. Milan went back to its primary function as foreign merchants again appeared in the city, and trains of packhorses replaced the warhorses on the roads of the plain.

In the June of that year Valentina, daughter of the Count, began a two weeks' round of festivities in Milan as prelude to her departure from Italy. The long-drawn-out negotiations between her father and the Valois had been finally brought to a conclusion with the solemn transferring of 200,000 florins to her agents and those of her proxy husband. There was still a quarter of a million florins outstanding, but that was to be paid in instalments and Valentina was at last permitted to emerge from her ambiguous position of the past two years and appear before the Milanese as duchess of Touraine. She was then nineteen years of age and, among her contemporaries, must have seemed destined to remain unmarried. The legal age of nubility was twelve and a girl not married by her early teens was usually the victim of her father's poverty or meanness. The fantastic increase in the cost of dowries — an increase of over 700 per cent over the last century — ensured that the bestowal of a girl remained entirely in her father's keeping. Valentina's dower differed only in size, not in principle, even as her father shared with his humblest subject the right of disposing of his daughter as he chose. The daughter of a shoemaker or the daughter of the lord of Milan were alike bound by the iron custom of the dower, and not until the great weight of gold was locked in a chest with four keys was Valentina free to enjoy the brief prestige of the betrothed maiden. On June 22nd she returned to Pavia to take final farewell of her childhood home before leaving for France. Her father was absent. 'My lord of Milan left Pavia without speaking to his daughter and this was because he could not take leave of her without bursting into tears.'[105] Or so says Monstrelet, giving no hint of his source for a statement so uncharacteristic of the controlled lord of Milan. But Giangaleazzo was neither ill at that time nor was his presence required elsewhere on urgent matters of state; his decision to avoid his daughter during her last hours at Pavia must in truth have arisen from some such fear of breakdown, rare indication of the man behind the cold public mask. Her marriage was the climax of two years' complex negotiations, but although it crowned a political ambition it also severed him for ever from the person whom he seems to have held most dear. No one knew better than he the instability of political alliances; at this moment the French court was preparing to

[105] Collas, p. 48.

welcome his daughter and her 200,000 florins with every appearance of eagerness, but it needed only a slight change in the political wind to turn that court into a bitter enemy and hence, by inescapable logic, turning his daughter into an opponent.

The tragedy which Valentina unwittingly brought upon her country was such that, four centuries later Giulini could dismiss her with his remark that 'the wars which Lombardy suffered because of her has made her name odious among us'. The Lombards knew only the nineteen-year-old girl who was the no passive instrument of her father's policy; far different was her reputation in the adopted country which saw her full development. 'She loves God, is herself loved by all. In her own country she was regretted and in that which she now lives she keeps herself unsullied and pure. Injustice she hates; compassion attends her'[106] — so the courtier poet Eustache Deschamps who came to know her well both in the days of her brief triumph and the long personal tragedy which ended only with her death. Giangaleazzo's influence on his daughter's education bore fruit during those years when, exiled from Paris, she established her own small cultural centre, earning the respect and admiration of accomplished poets and scholars in a court whose ethos was in striking contrast with that presided over by her cousin the queen of France. As a child Valentina had benefited from the atmosphere of Pavia with its positive approach to learning. Among most of the great families of Italy it was considered amply sufficient if a girl's reading was restricted to religious works; a generation before and Barberino could say flatly that reading led to a maiden's corruption and was therefore better avoided.[107] The ability to read and write

---

[106] Ibid., p. 21.
[107] Del Reggimento e dei costumi delle donne, p. 49.

was doubtless a useful accomplishment for a merchant's wife who might be called upon to superintend his business during his long absences, but the marital value of a daughter of a great house lay in her name, her accomplishments mere garnishes. The elaborate etiquette of the Renaissance still lay a generation ahead and it was sufficient for a girl to be taught the basic elements of the social decencies. Dancing ranked high, for though in Lombardy state banquets were rarely graced by the presence of women, the ball was as recognized a form of entertainment as the tournament. Singing went with dancing and, in the privacy of her family, skill with lute or harp. Valentina possessed all the feminine accomplishments deemed necessary but added to them a rare learning. Among the mass of treasure which she took with her to France was her own harp, but also included in that treasure were books. Apart from her mother's French the girl was fluent in German and Latin; the great library of Pavia contained not only solid treatises and the discovered classics of antiquity but more frivolous works, some of them those French romances which had aroused Barberino's disgust. With access to that library, familiar with some of the most learned men of the day who appeared at her father's court as guests or officials of the state, the girl at nineteen probably possessed a grounding in culture wider than her father had possessed at a similar age. One of the two miniatures of her which survive show her, significantly, as a patron of the arts accepting from Honoré Bonnet his 'L'apparacion de maistre Jehan de Meung' dedicated to her as duchess of Orléans. Both miniatures are by the unknown but considerable master who illuminated Bonnet's work, their freshness and energy transcending the usual formal representation and so creating one of the rare authentic portraits of a Visconti. The women of the family tended to the striking rather than the beautiful, but in Valentina the florid colouring and heavy build was fined down by the grace inherited from her Valois mother. In the first miniature she is shown seated wearing a long, low-necked robe with narrow sleeves, a rich mantle and the small golden crown of her rank. Black eyes half closed she leans forward with a gracious gesture of acceptance to Bonnet offering his book. The second miniature shows her standing in conversation with her physician, an attitude which more clearly shows her tall, slender stature; the chestnut hair is caught up by the crown and allowed to fall in two plaits on either side. She appears genuinely interested in her companion and the subject under discussion. The face is alive, framed by the plaits of chestnut hair; a straight nose slightly tilted, small delicate mouth, light colouring — all together a figure combining unstudied dignity with considerable personal charm.

Valentina left Pavia for ever on June 24th. Her father was still in his country retreat but, as lord of Milan, he had arranged the most impressive departure for her. An escort of some 1300 knights, under the command of the Count's personal friend Francesco Gonzaga of Mantua, left Pavia with her. All the neighbouring states had been invited to send representatives. Venice alone was lukewarm, the Senate debating for four days whether to so honour their suddenly powerful neighbour, and the eventual vote in favour was carried by the narrowest majority. The smaller courts were glad enough to be identified with the rising star of Milan and the journey across Lombardy took on the nature of a triumphant procession, the cities en route providing lavish hospitality and replacing those members of the escort who dropped out as the distance from Pavia lengthened. Valentina was under the care of her great-uncle Amadeus of Savoy and the dowry money itself was in the charge of Bertrand Guasco, the Count's governor of Vertus. In addition to the great mass of gold to be guarded, was Valentina's trousseau; the dowry money was provided by the state of Milan, but the trousseau belonged to the Visconti, indication of the family's astonishing personal wealth. Corio found the inventory and in order 'to perpetuate the memory of such unheard-of splendour' detailed the items for six close-packed pages.[108] Valentina's personal taste reflected the current taste for the gaudy and the expensive; one of her dresses was a green robe embroidered with 2500 large pearls and liberally sprinkled with diamonds; a headdress of pure white brocade was embroidered with large golden birds. Among her personal ornaments was a necklace of eight pendant golden doves, the centre drop consisting of a single white dove in golden rays and the motto 'a bon droit', the same device which Petrarch had devised for her father when he was a boy and which became in turn her most treasured device. The trousseau consisted not only of items of personal use but also the complete furnishings for bedroom and chapel, as though Visconti feared that civilization ceased at the Alps and his beloved daughter would find herself naked in a barbaric land. Diamonds, pearls, sapphires, some made into rings and tiaras, others loose or embroidered into fabrics; dining sets of silver, ornaments of gold for table and boudoir; a table of jasper, a bed with hangings of cloth of gold — the mass of treasure was a temptation for the hordes of wandering semi-bandits called mercenaries and the escort was as much for its protection as in Valentina's honour. The cavalcade passed through Piedmont, following much the same route that her mother had taken into Italy on her journey twenty-eight years before; Alessandria, Susa, over the pass of Mont Cenis, on to Chambéry, her

---

[108] Corio, III, 7, pp. 349-355.

grandmother's childhood home, and so at last to Mâcon after a five-week journey, where Amadeus of Savoy handed over his charge to servants of the duke of Orléans. At Dijon Philip the Bold welcomed his niece with Burgundian splendour and brought her to Melun, where she met her bridegroom for the first time. There, on August 17th, the marriage which was to have such fatal consequences for her country at last took place.

CATERINA

The great castle of Pavia housed an unusually small family, for, with the departure of Valentina, the Count's immediate kin consisted only of his wife Caterina and her baby son now seven months old. His sister and mother were both dead. Violante had not long survived the deeply painful situation in which Giangaleazzo's success had placed her. There was probably little love between her and the third husband imposed upon her by Bernabò; Lodovico had been a coarse and violent man, yet his imprisonment by her brother in the May of 1386 robbed her of a normal life. She returned to the family home for the third time but lived on wanly for only a few months more, dying in November 1386. 'This lady Violante had evil fortune in her time even though she was a good and pious lady', de' Mussi recorded with grave sympathy. 'Neither great nor little people, alas! can escape their evil fortune. When she died this lady was not more than thirty-two years old.'[109] Her mother's end was more fortunate. Throughout her married life Bianca had been overshadowed by the flamboyant and vital Regina della Scala, even as her husband had been overshadowed by Bernabò. Nevertheless, the approval and support she gave Giangaleazzo before the crucial moment of his challenge to Bernabò indicated a more

---

[109] de' Mussi, p. 546.

courageous and firmer nature than was readily apparent from the role she preferred to play. After her husband's death she retired from the great castle to her own palace of the Corte Nuova and there pursued her gentle ways, unaffected by the increasing splendour of her son. The Pavese adored her; pious and humble, she was accessible to the meanest citizen, playing a vital enough role by acting as intermediary between the virtually disfranchised citizens and the ultimate authority which was her son. She was a staunch defender of the clergy against him when need be. Giangaleazzo from the beginning had made it very clear that he was master in his own state, that he would tax or not tax the clergy as he pleased and, in general, order the secular side of their lives as best suited the state. The very beds in the castle were paid for by the clergy of Novara. He was in his legal rights, but a discreet word from Bianca on at least one occasion drew his attention to a grievance which, uninvestigated, could have led to an explosive situation. Much of the Count's character can be attributed to the gentle but pervading influence of his mother; certainly she had controlled her husband and through him their naturally timid only son. Bianca had made herself responsible for the upbringing of the orphaned Valentina; the girl's proxy marriage had been celebrated not in her father's castle but in her grandmother's palace of the Corte Nuova. Only a few days after that marriage the Lady of Pavia died at the early age of forty-eight.

The closeness between grandmother and granddaughter underlined the isolation of Caterina, the Count's second wife. There is no record of the slightest act of affection offered her by Giangaleazzo during the twenty-two years of their life together. Significantly, not one of the writers or poets of the court, of all people the most alert to nuances, thought it worth while to write even a formal praise of her. She was ignored by

142

them as she was by her husband. The shock of the early death of Isabella and the circumstances under which he had been obliged to marry Caterina probably account for the unyielding coldness of his attitude. Caterina had been introduced into his household as a spy and it must have been long before he was able to place trust in her. In the first weeks of their marriage he made over certain territories to her, even dispossessing his mother of her castle at Monza to do so. These first gifts were obvious bribes, an attempt to win her over from her father. Caterina however, understandably enough, preferred to be the first lady of Pavia rather than the least of Bernabò's daughters and from beginning to end she remained utterly loyal to her husband, accepting the imprisonment of her father and brothers in silence, making no plea for mercy, as she later accepted her subordinate role in silence. But even after the motive of bribery had passed, Giangaleazzo still from time to time ceded considerable territories to her, for, like her mother before her, Caterina proved a remarkably capable administrator. Once indeed something of her mother's imperious nature showed itself and, overstepping her position, she suffered a reprimand from her husband and the humiliation of retreat. But Giangaleazzo's faith in her ability did not diminish and after obtaining Vicenza by fraud from Carrara he made it over to her. His reasons were political, for it was through her mother that he established legal claim to Vicenza, but the ceding of such an important city to Caterina speaks much for her competence.

Caterina was some four years younger than her husband. Commonly spoken of as the most beautiful of the daughters of Bernabò, fair of face and majestic of bearing, her portrait yet shows her as a rather heavy-faced, solemn woman, handsome enough but sharing too many of the male Visconti features to be deemed beautiful. Throughout Giangaleazzo's life she remained in the background and it was only with his death that her dormant qualities awoke. Then, with the state crumbling around her, she proved that she possessed in abundance that courage which no Visconti ever lacked; defying the mob in person, rallying her late husband's supporters, engaged in complex political manoeuvring, for eighteen months she dominated the chaotic, murderous situation. Then, too, flowered the strange, pathetic love of her life when she, a woman in her late forties and already crippled by gout, could at last openly declare her affection for Francesco Barbavara, her husband's most powerful servant. From her activities in those tumultuous days Caterina's character can be clearly perceived. Faced by violent and immediate danger she could react with vigour and intelligence, but she lacked the ability to pursue a steady course of intrigue, was unable to exact vengeance when politically desirable and so ultimately died at the hands of the bestial son whose inheritance she had saved. For though the papal dispensation granted to them on their marriage saved Giangaleazzo and Caterina from papal displeasure, it could not cleanse from their blood the taint which consanguinity turned into madness for their children.

Giovanni Maria, the elder, was born at the full tide of his father's career when Visconti arms were sweeping across Lombardy in the autumn of 1388. Verona had fallen and the capture of Padua only six weeks away when, on September 7th, Caterina wrote to her husband that 'God, the Giver of all gifts... has given us a son which, with felicity, we have brought to the light.'[110] Plague was raging throughout Lombardy; in Parma, Reggio, Pavia, Padua, Verona, the dead increased daily in the streets. Giangaleazzo had retired deep into the country

---

[110] Corio, III, 7.

and Caterina herself went to Abbiategrasso, where she remained after the birth of the boy until the following April. The Pavese held for tier little of the affection that they had held for the late lady of Pavia, and after deliberating to give Caterina 5000 florins as a birth gift they thriftily reduced it to 1000. So soon as the plague had sufficiently abated, Giangaleazzo ordered the Grand Council of Milan to meet and choose deputies, and shortly after they swore allegiance afresh to himself and his new born son, formally excluding the heirs of Bernabò for ever from the succession. The birth of Giovanni Maria had finally closed the dangerously open question of the succession. One more child was born to Caterina four years later and was christened Fillipo Maria. Both survived and even as Giovanni inherited the insane violence of one side of the Visconti character so Fillipo inherited, to an extreme degree, the timidity of the other, both sons displaying in the last years of the dynasty a case history of the results of consanguinity.

Caterina had fulfilled her prime function but received in return barely the honours of her position. Indeed, in the very hour of her husband's supreme triumph seven years later, when Milan was paying homage to him as its first duke, she was forced to share her reflected glory with his favourite mistress, Agnese Mantegazza. Agnese was installed in the palace of her lover's late mother, the Corte Nuova in Pavia, and there, in a sedate enough household, provided him with his true home. The records show in addition that honours were to be paid to a certain 'Lusotta, mistress of the Count of Virtue' and in his will he asked that provision should be made for Antonio, a son by an unidentified peasant woman. Certainly in comparison with his father the Count enjoyed licence enough, yet Giovio's considered statement that 'he was not distracted... by the delights of women' comes nearer to the truth than 'Minerbetti's' wild accusation that 'he had many women wherewith to commit adulteries'.[111] Few princes sought to equal the late Bernabò Visconti with his dozen or more establishments, yet there were fewer again who did not make honourable and open provision for the women who shared their emotional lives. The courtesan who modelled herself upon the Greek 'companion', allying wit and learning with elegance and beauty, was still a century in the future; the Count found his mistresses, as did his fellows, among women of his own class. Yet that curiously uncharacteristic liaison with a peasant woman showed that in this, as in certain other aspects of his character, he shared rather more of the nature of his uncle than his father. Behind the affable manners and the cold mind there was an emotionalism which, usually restrained, sometimes broke its bonds. A man who feared breaking down in public on his daughter's departure, who could remember a peasant's bastard when at the point of death, was not altogether the political machine he appeared to be.

THE CASTLE OF PAVIA

Giangaleazzo's personal life was rooted deep in Pavia. Politically, his presence there was an affirmation that the lord of the Milanese State was superior to any one city, affixing his residence where he pleased. But the home of his childhood remained the home of his manhood because it touched that chord in him which was responsive to solitude and order, both lacking in the tumult of Milan. The deep and abiding love for country life was a common trait with an Italian wealthy enough to indulge in it, to provide himself with a villa with a few acres of orchards and vineyards and a handful of hard-working

---

[111] 'Minerbetti', XIV, A. 1402.

peasants to run it while he made his living in the city. Urban though he was to the core, yet still there came the recurring hunger for clean air and green trees, pure water and silence. 'While every other possession causes work and danger, fear and disappointment, the villa brings a great and honourable advantage; if you dwell in it at the right time and with love it will not only satisfy you but add reward to reward. In spring the green trees will make you joyful and hopeful; in autumn a moderate exertion will bring forth fruit a hundredfold. The villa is the spot where good and honest men love to congregate. Hasten hither and fly away from the pride of the rich, the dishonour of the bad.'[112] And all who could, did so hasten away from the exciting but treacherous, profitable but dangerous life of the cities to seek — and occasionally find — a living memory of the Golden Age. This love of country life had little connection with the sweat of farming, but neither had it yet become the play-acting of bored sophisticates; the possession of land was still the ultimate security and it was no dishonour for the most nobly born to be able to talk knowledgeably of vines and wheat and pigs.

Giangaleazzo's favourite 'villa' was an enormous castle girt round with walls and moats and guarded by the pick of Milanese soldiers, but it enabled him to attend to affairs of state while enjoying rural peace. The castle was physically within the city of Pavia, its northern face actually displacing part of the wall of the city, but it looked out upon a great garden which itself gave on to a park so large as to constitute open country. 'There was no home like it in Italy,'[113] Decembrio remarked, but such praise was too modest for Corio. 'It was the first palace in the universe,'[114] was his

[112] Pandolfini, Trattato del Governo della Famiglia, p. 84.
[113] Vita Phillipi Mariae Viceco metis XLIX, p. 25.

opinion. The perfectly square, rose-red building summed up the contradictions, the sense of transition, which was the fourteenth century. The deep moat fed by the waters of the Carona, the battlemented walls, the drawbridges, the ubiquitous soldiery, represented the need of security in a turbulent age, the last reminder of the feudal spirit. It could and did withstand siege. But let into those same massive walls were over a hundred large and beautiful windows which illuminated rooms of elegant proportions and beautiful decoration. The original cost of the castle was reckoned at half a million florins, the greater part of which the commune paid either by direct taxation or by the provision of labour. Long after the building was in occupation, taxes and compulsory labour were still contributing to it; Piacenza was taxed in order to extend the moat and Novara was ordered to send 400 workers, including master carpenters, on alternate months for similar improvements. Galeazzo had designed upon a pharaonic scale but with an attention to detail which turned a castle into a home. There were some forty rooms upon each of the floors but each was individual, taking its name from some dominant feature within it; the Red room, the room of the Leopard, of the Clock, of Arms. Many were decorated with glowing murals, some historical, some personal, as that which commemorated the infant Giangaleazzo with Petrarch. One room was a scintillating jewel, the sunlight from the great windows illuminating a ceiling of coloured glass and floor of mosaic, and here Giangaleazzo's most precious personal possessions were housed. The four towers were utilized as much for administration as for defence, many edicts and letters being dated from 'the room of the tower facing the garden'; it was here that the final agreement for Valentina's marriage was

[114] Corio, III, p. 466.

made. In one of these tower rooms the priceless library was housed. The Visconti had always collected books, but under Petrarch's expert direction the haphazard collection began to take the form of a library. Book collecting had impoverished many a too-enthusiastic scholar, but Petrarch's position among the Visconti gave him a unique opportunity to tap some of their wealth for a laudable end. The library was freely open to all accredited scholars and proved indeed a lodestone for the kind of man Giangaleazzo was desirous of attracting to Pavia. He continued to expand it both by purchase and conquest; after its fall Padua yielded up a number of Petrarch's own books which had been housed there after his death. In recognition of the great scholar, Giangaleazzo later went to considerable trouble to obtain that Virgil manuscript which had been Petrarch's most treasured possession and upon whose flyleaf he had set down 'a record of the cruel events, not without a bitter sweetness in the remembrance of them' — a record which included the death of Laura. The tower library housed only Giangaleazzo's personal collection; the mass of state archives whose order so impressed Giovio were preserved elsewhere in the castle, under the eye of the signore but removed from his personal life. Two contrasting apartments summed up the two functions of the building. On the first floor was a huge room with a very large window which gave access to a balcony projecting over the moat. Here, during the heat of summer, Giangaleazzo could dine alone or in company, refreshed by the sight and sound of nearby water and with a view of the green park and garden. A few vertical yards away, at the bottom of the eastern tower, was a dungeon which had for its centre a cage of wicker; the 'lunga dimora' was its common name, the long residence for certain important prisoners.

The castle's park was fully in keeping with the overall scale. Its creation entailed the construction of a wall thirteen miles in circumference, moated and furnished with drawbridges, enclosing a living cross-section of Lombardy, for it took in not only woods and streams and vineyards but hamlets, churches and farms. Galeazzo's land-hunger had led him to dispossess many small farmers with a brutality worthy of Bernabò's, and, in keeping with his policy of clemency, Giangaleazzo paid generous recompense to those who had been so despoiled. The agricultural lands within the wall were not wasted, for those who could pay rent were allowed to farm and, in spite of the difficulties created by the swarms of sacrosanct game and the damage of frequent hunts, the privilege was much sought after. Harvests were excellent, for the already high fertility of the land was increased by the great irrigation canal, the Naviglio Grande, which Galeazzo constructed between Milan and Pavia. The park's produce was exempt from the usual customs duties at the city gates and the tenants, classed as servants of the signore, enjoyed a considerable reduction in the general taxes. Giangaleazzo shared with his father a deep interest in natural history: an excellent botanical garden was maintained in the park together with a rudimentary zoo consisting for the most part of bears, ostriches and lions. An ornithological collection was housed in the castle, the gamekeepers being ordered to embalm the best specimen of each bird taken in the hunt.

Hunting was the single passion which Giangaleazzo shared to the full with all the Visconti. Pavia itself probably saw little of him during his residence, for when not in the castle he was in the heavily guarded park. The plan which Francesco Novello evolved to assassinate him was based on the regularity of his life, and took into account the extraordinary guard which accompanied him. 'The Count goes hunting on Thursdays in great state; his servants and officers with dogs, hawks and all the implements of the chase ride first; next the ladies of the court, next the Count himself with one of the ladies of the family on the crupper or on a palfrey at his side; next the gentlemen of the court and the family, and finally 300 horsemen of whom fifty are in steel corselets.'[115] In the heat of the Lombard summer the Count and a few chosen associates might remain for some days within the park, living in the beautiful little summer palace which Galeazzo had constructed. Normally when hunting he was incommunicado, Pasquino Capelli dealing with any pressing matters of state, but occasionally, when anxious to propitiate an ally, or deal personally with some immediate problem, ambassadors would be brought to him and an impromptu conference held in the field. Although continually moving from one to the other of his country palaces, sometimes in quest of sport, sometimes for reasons of health, very rarely did he visit the cities of the state.

His presence in judgement was not necessary, for the *podestà* of each city was competent to try all criminal cases; even an attempted assassination of himself was tried by the *podestà* of the city in which it occurred. Yet, though absent, he was in constant communication with the most remote areas of the state through the excellent system of post-horses which he early developed as a necessity of his kind of remote-control rule. Little went on in the state of which he was not aware: each city had a species of passport office which recorded the movements of all entering and leaving, hotel owners being obliged to report the names of guests. The returns, forwarded to a central office, gave a clear picture of movements both

---

[115] Gatari, p. 361.

within the state and, more important, of foreigners. This, allied with a censorship of letters, enabled the signor to keep a very close watch on any potential conspirators. Visconti agents were present in every major state of Italy. The employment of merchants as eyes of their government was a commonplace, but Giangaleazzo developed a corps of what can only be called *agents-provocateur* in every city where the controlling power was at once anti-Visconti and insecure. Some were paid Milanese, but most were citizens of the coveted city who, on promise of political reward, were prepared to betray their government. A great part of the multitudinous reports from within and without the state came direct to Giangaleazzo, for behind the manifold activities of his officials was his single, co-ordinating brain. But his senior staff enjoyed wide freedom of action within the overall framework of his policy. Ambassadors were frequently given only the main objective towards which they were to work, the methods and details being left to their own specialized judgement. Many of them were less his employees than his colleagues, jurists who had already reached the height of their profession elsewhere and were now utilizing the power of Milan to bring about the changes they themselves desired.

BUILDING OF THE CATHEDRAL

In the second year of Giangaleazzo's reign, work began on Milan's greatest monument which was still uncompleted six centuries later. The cathedral was essentially a creation of the Milanese people, the very last they were free to make, yet, from the earliest days, the honour was given to Giangaleazzo. Giovanni di Bonis, a contemporary poet, praised him for its initiation in indifferent verse fifty years afterwards, and the Annalist of Milan stated with considerable circumspection that he had laid the first stone. Once recorded, the error — if error it were — grew in detail, successive Milanese historians all repeating the story and producing further alleged evidence. It reached a climax of uncritical reporting in 1674 with the affirmation that work had already commenced when, on May 23rd 1385, the Count ordered its destruction because he was displeased with what had been done and instructed the architects to start afresh. On that day Giangaleazzo had been in possession of Milan for barely three weeks and could have had neither time nor inclination to indulge in aesthetic criticism. The original error of ascribing the foundation to him may have risen innocently, but its continuation through three centuries was almost certainly a deliberate manipulation of the truth by writers desirous of flattering a succession of princes. The fact that Milan's principal glory was a creation of the people and not of the prince was something to be glossed over. In 1392 Giangaleazzo formally banned the use of the word 'Popolo' as a rallying cry, the identity of the People itself joining the oblivion of Guelph and Ghibelline. After a century beneath a despotic family the Milanese were almost completely tamed, but occasionally the intangible but real phenomenon of the popular will broke through the restraints placed upon them by the signore. Between 1386 and the end of the century Milan witnessed a manifestation of the phenomenon, channelled into the building of the cathedral and rendered tangible, a distasteful memory to the Sforza and their successors.

The motive commonly given to Giangaleazzo was that the cathedral was erected in the honouring of a vow. A mysterious malady affected all Milanese women which prevented them giving birth to male children and the Count therefore swore that, should Caterina produce an heir, all his male descendants would bear the name Maria and a temple to the Mother of God be erected in gratitude. His sons did in fact bear the name

Maria, testimony to the probability of such a vow, but it was Antonio da Saluzzo, the archbishop of Milan, who provided the final impulse for the building of the cathedral. Antonio's action itself merely placed in definite form the intentions of two generations of Milanese. The existing cathedral was ruinous; attempts had been made to repair and enlarge it and, thirty years before, Archbishop Giovanni had even contemplated building a magnificent new one. But none of the plans came to fruition and Santa Maria Maggiore mouldered on, a shabby building unworthy of the growing city, while elsewhere in Italy the great new cathedrals of the republics were beginning to break the skyline. Antonio must have been assured of the active support of the head of the State when, a year after Giangaleazzo's succession, he published an episcopal letter urging the faithful to contribute towards the colossal undertaking. During Bernabò's rule the archbishop was too much occupied in retaining his position, under a signore who was predictable only in his dislike of the clergy, to attempt a work which would channel away so much potential revenue. The accession of Giangaleazzo infused a new spirit into the State and, almost as a by-product, the great cathedral came into being.

From the beginning of the construction the Deputies of the Fabric relied not only on popular financial offerings but also voluntary labour drawn from all levels of society. The Guild of Armourers was the first to demonstrate the close identification of the Milanese with their cathedral, presenting themselves at the site in a body to undertake unskilled labour. The Drapers followed, then the local government officials, and the movement then spread upwards. On October 30th 1387, the highest officials of the Commune — the *podestà* and his court accompanied by the colleges of advocates and notaries —

appeared on the site and, having made the customary financial donations, set to work at the lowliest of tasks, transporting rubble in baskets. The nobles of the city followed their example a month later, and thereafter the cathedral never lacked voluntary labour. The raising of money was made in the same spirit. The natural groups within the city vied with each other in the collecting of goods or kind; the citizens of Porta Orientale presented an ass worth 50 lire and put in a day's work on the excavations; those of Porta Vercellina gave a calf worth three times as much. Groups of Milanese children dressed all in white went singing throughout Lombardy, collecting alms from cities many miles distant for the glorification of Milan. Daily, streams of people made their way to the temporary altar on the site to deposit their offerings. The clerks stationed beside the altar recorded each donation as it was made, their unadorned book-keeping giving a vivid picture of the widespread enthusiasm which the project raised. Here, among the ruins of the old cathedral and on the foundations of the new, the will of the people was made concrete in their gifts. Caterina da Abbiategrasso, penniless, placed her shawl upon the altar and it was immediately redeemed for many times its worth by Emmanuel Zuperenio, who returned it to her. A courtier joined the queue bearing the purse of a stranger who had suddenly died in the city. A young woman deposited all the money she had with her; asked her name for the register she responded 'Raffalda, prostitute.' The clerk recorded her gift 'oblatio per donalam dictam Raffaldam meretricem lire 3 soldi 4' and immediately followed that entry with another for 160 lire. The donor was listed as Antonino da Figno, secretary to the duchess of Touraine, better known to the citizens of Milan as Valentina dei Visconti. In a few consecutive entries duchess and prostitute, courtier and peasant meet briefly on common ground.[116]

Giangaleazzo appears mostly in the role of benign observer, doubtless approving of the harmless channelling of a potentially disruptive force. The Deputies many times turned to him with requests for contributions in his personal capacity or for aid as head of the State. He granted them a subsidy of 500 florins per month, allowed them to mine the pure marble of Candoglia without charge or tax. A tradition holds that, at the outset of the work, he despatched a group of nobles to examine all the monuments of Christendom and to choose that form which would make the noblest cathedral. The tradition is unsubstantiated; the first plans for the cathedral were drawn up in the same impulsive and haphazard method as the collection of money and the allocation of labour and were the work of a committee with all its particular faults. Characteristically, the names of the primary architects were first recorded during the course of the public enquiry instituted to allay apprehensions that the work on the cathedral was not only going badly, but constituted a public danger. Giangaleazzo appointed his vicar-general, Faustino da Lantini, to preside over the court which sat on March 20th 1388. Marco and Giacomo da Campione and Simone da Orsenigo arose one after the other to defend their work and so earned a place in the Annals of the Fabric. They were exonerated of any blame and work went on at so great a pace that by 1392 the great pillars of the nave were completed. In a little over six years from its foundation the Milanese saw the walls already dominating their surroundings and it would have seemed a reasonable hope that the next generation would see the cathedral complete. But after the heady period of Giangaleazzo's first two years of rule, the end

[116] Romussi, V2, p. 384.

of which saw the Viper standard waving over most of Lombardy, the impetus died within the state. As Giangaleazzo's ambitions grew greater, creating ever greater dangers from threatened powers, so revenues were needed to feed the ambitions and avoid the dangers. Money grew scarce, the queues of donors at the temporary altar grew shorter. Seeking money where he could, the Count was first obliged to suspend the special privileges he had granted the Deputies and finally actually to lay hands on the money raised, enforcing a tax upon legacies for the building. The same astonishing burst of popular energy which had initiated the work created a morass of conflicting ideas in which the enthusiasms became lost and there was neither time nor money to spare to extricate them. The cathedral no less than the populace paid the price of the glory which the Count brought to Milan.

VI: THE CLASH WITH FLORENCE

Looking back over the momentous years which concluded the fourteenth century and seeking the point which marked the break-up of the old world, Goro Dati coincided it with the fall of Padua. Generations of Italians had accepted the fragmentation of the peninsula as an inescapable fact of life; national adventures were to be left to foreigners with high-sounding titles and shadowy rights, and the duty of Florentine was to fight Sienese, Pisan to subdue Lucchese, Bolognese to resist Milanese. But with Padua's fall and the emergence of the Visconti multi-city state the parochial concepts of despots and republicans alike were abruptly outdated. Some found the new spirit exhilarating; the poets who hailed the Count of Virtue as the new king who, Italian, might bring peace to Italy were not necessarily timeserving, and Dati's own History was an expression of the same spirit of *italianita*. The reactions of most, however, was shock followed by fear. For the Florentines particularly 'that war was as a stroke of lightning so sudden... that they were incapable of deciding what to do in so difficult a situation. Even the Venetians who were affected more nearly than the Florentines made no preparation for their defence... not being able to believe that the intentions of the Count went even further.' Dati erred in assuming that Giangaleazzo was already planning a peninsula-wide onslaught, but it was an error in which all Florentines and most Italians shared. Two great and independent cities had fallen the sudden prey of a hitherto undistinguished young man, 'and certainly from the sign he carried... a serpent which swallows a man' it was logical to prepare for the worst.[117] So at least thought the

Florentines after recovering from the shock, and prepared to take up again their self-appointed role of guardian of Italian liberty.

Leonardo Bruni's description of his city where he likens it to a castle and a shield perfectly reflected the opinions of his fellow citizens.[118] Impervious to the jibes of lesser people who did not necessarily equate Italian with Florentine good, indignant indeed at such blindness, the Florentines saw their city as the last citadel of reason and liberty, a shield for the defence of weaker brethren against the despot. But behind the façade of a calm and ordered beauty was a turbulent community which only a near autocratic power kept in subjection. In 1378 the city had been engulfed in its most violent revolution when the Ciompi, the voteless, despised bottom layer of society whom Florentine propagandists conveniently forgot, surged in rebellion, their forces unleashed by a too-liberal Medici. They established a genuinely popular government but soon fell easy prey to the experienced statecraft of the class they had temporarily dispossessed. The *nobili popolani* returned; 'nobles of the people' in the city which had disfranchised the aristocracy, dedicated to the principles of pure, undefiled Guelphism, they had lost ground during the war with the Church, the fount of Guelphism. Now, under the leadership of Maso degli Albizzi, the *Parte Guelfa* was restored, the work of proscriptions and exiles began anew, and Florence was turned aside from the dangerous course of pure democracy. Tension remained between the great families, but the Florentine genius for self-government was just stronger than the Italian genius for self-destruction. The constitution was framed precisely to allow the practice, while controlling

[117] Dati, pp. 18, 19.
[118] Bruni, *Le vere lodi...* I, p. 14.

the results, of ambition. 'Nothing in this state is ill proportioned, nothing left vague; everything occupies its proper place which is not only clearly defined but also in the right relation to all others.'[119] The remarkably brief tenures of office — sometimes as little as two months, rarely longer than six — ensured that no one man could retain power long enough for it to become subtly his right. But the prime requisite for a state whose government renewed its parts every few weeks was a permanent and incorruptible body which could continue the daily task of administration without regard to politics. Florence had perfected such a body and was particularly fortunate in that, at the time when the state entered upon its most critical period, the head of that body was Coluccio Salutati.

Salutati was appointed to the office of Chancellor in 1375; primarily because of his legal qualifications as notary he remained in office until his death in 1406. The holding of such an appointment for thirty-two years, in a city where hatred of the single ruler was elevated into a political principle, speaks much for his skill and probity as a civil servant. But the Florentine merchants who approved his re-elections were interested less in his honesty and common legal qualifications than in the ever-developing power of his pen. Salutati may have earned the right of citizenship for humanist scholarship, but the Florentines had no intention of merely adorning their government with a literary figure; they were investing their hard-won florins in a new weapon, the scholar propagandist. That he and his fellows brought a new glory to Florence was gratifying but incidental. Salutati's prime purpose was to convince Italian states of the wisdom and strength of Florentine policy and in such a manner did the new learning

---

[119] Ibid., III, p. 53.

make its debut in Italy. That scholarship which had been universal and abstract in the hands of Petrarch's generation was now local and specific, less concerned with the ethics of government in ancient Rome than with the pressing need to secure allies in modern Italy. And Salutati discharged his duties ably through the medium of a superb Latin prose. 'Princes praised it without measure, for like a well-adjusted instrument of war which protects its friends and injures enemies it supported both the proposals and replies of the Florentines with serious philosophies and completely broke down the reasoning of the maladjusted.'[120] He became the voice of Florence, transmuting the mixed motives of his fellow citizens into a constant idealism. Giangaleazzo recognized his ability, ruefully remarked that a letter of Salutati's did him more damage than 1000 Florentine horsemen, and paid him the compliment of attempting to traduce him. 'He caused a letter counterfeiting the hand of Coluccio and containing many treasonable expressions to be laid before the Signoria. This letter was shown to Salutati in the presence of a highly excited senate and he was asked in whose hand it was written. He read it through without a change of countenance and replied boldly, without a tremor in his voice, "The handwriting is indeed mine but I never wrote the letter." And this answer — such is the power of a well-established reputation — freed him completely from all suspicion and from the very thought, not to mention the execution of so unworthy a purpose.'[121] The ability to satisfy a suspicious Florentine committee with a simple denial must rank as one of Salutati's higher achievements.

The presence of two such men as Maso degli Albizzi and Coluccio Salutati in the upper levels of Florentine society gave

---

[120] Emerton, p. 44.
[121] Ibid.

evidence of the split personality which the Republic developed as it drew ahead of its immediate neighbours. Within the city's walls Salutati and his fellows created the beginning of an astonishing republic of letters, composed of men striving to form a new concept of life in which the word 'liberty' was not a hollow catchphrase but an essential component. But within those walls were also the merchants who had created the city's power and to whom, trammelled still by the limited concept of the city-state, elimination of the freedom of neighbouring cities was an equally essential component of life. The two groups counted many of the same men; those merchants who had elected Salutati were aware of the power of scholarship, for they were themselves no mean scholars. But primarily they were Florentines for whom the dominance of their city was sacred axiom, and secondarily they were merchants who must needs find outlet for their goods — if necessary at the expense of their neighbours. Florence as the leader of a national rebellion could rise to remarkable heights of self-sacrifice, but Florence as the major merchant republic of central Italy could also descend to extreme depths to weaken commercial rivals. Of the dozen or so Tuscan cities which had entered the century as sovereign states, three only retained a real degree of independence — Florence herself, Siena, and Pisa, and the constant feature of Tuscan politics was a three-cornered struggle between them for possession of the rest as preliminary to total dominance. Florentine wealth enabled the city to employ mercenaries on a scale equalled only by Milan; Pisa and Siena, Ghibelline, turning naturally to the Ghibelline Visconti to redress the balance, created a means of entry into Tuscany for them. Bernabò had exploited the situation with conspicuous success and the Florentine Signoria professed themselves unable to believe that Giangaleazzo would not do the same. 'To tell the truth the Sienese were already in accord with the Count of Virtue to act against the Florentines who were certain that the Visconti wanted war between the two Tuscan cities so that, when exhausted, he could take to himself the lordship of Tuscany.'[122] The Sienese, smarting under the aggressiveness of their rivals, had in fact made overtures to Giangaleazzo but, occupied with his wars in Lombardy, he had been obliged to refuse them. 'Nevertheless, they continued to say what shame and damage the Florentines did them. In order to revenge themselves they would give themselves to the devil if that was the only way to break the arrogance of the Florentines.'[123]

On the testimony of the ambassadorial records of the powers involved, Giangaleazzo's activities before the inevitable clash seem to be unplanned reactions in the approved style; building pressure here in response to pressure there, countering threat with threat, backing down when room for manoeuvre was lacking — city-state politics at its most complex and sterile. The records were a true indication of the parochial world which Italy was leaving. But in addition to these ephemerae is the work of three Florentine writers who, both charting and reflecting the substantive changes through which Italy was passing, placed Giangaleazzo in the perspective of Italian rather than civic history. The chronicle of 'Minerbetti' and the histories of Dati and Bruni[124] were products not only of different generations but of three separate stages of Italian historiography, the last two themselves the product of the crisis to which Giangaleazzo subjected Italy in the closing years of the century. 'Minerbetti' was sixty years old

---

[122] 'Minerbetti', VI, A. 1389.
[123] Ibid.
[124] Dati, Goro, *Istoria di Firenze*; Bruni, Leonardo, *Istoria fiorentina*.

when he began his chronicle in 1385, Dati was forty in the crucial year of 1402 when only Giangaleazzo's sudden death saved Florence, and Bruni was writing with the detachment of the scholar twenty years after that death closed the chapter. Each has his obvious defects. The 'Minerbetti' work is that of the old-fashioned chronicler, vivid and immediate but rambling and non-selective; Dati, struggling with both a new form and a new idea, frequently becomes incoherent or carried away by a tumbling enthusiasm, while Bruni, better equipped than either to examine the true causes of the events, has the humanist's love of rhetoric. But, sharing the same heritage while separated by time, they form an invaluable sequence of successive Italian reactions to the same phenomenon. For 'Minerbetti' the Count of Virtue was merely the most recent, if the most formidable, of a series of enemies over whom Florence had managed to triumph in the past; the struggle was still essentially a struggle between city-states; Dati accurately judged that it was a clash of ideologies but, having taken part in it in person, found objectivity difficult. Bruni placed the struggle in its historic perspective and drew a moral for Italian posterity. Between them, the three Florentines better plotted the Milanese progress towards hegemony than the most dedicated Visconti apologist. Their viewpoints ranging from the hostile to the objective, their conclusions yet agreed. Giangaleazzo, in posing a national threat, forced Italians to think in national terms.

There can be little doubt that, after his Lombard successes had proved his technique, the Count was moving towards a definite goal — the elimination of Florence and some form of sovereignty over all north Italy. The one followed naturally from the other, for, even though he were to accept the prevailing city-state ethos and destroy Florence in order that Milan might live, the removal of the Tuscan republic would create a vacuum which only Milan could fill. And he and Milan were synonymous. Only the dynamic survived and therefore, the Lombard affair tidily concluded, he prepared to accept the Sienese offer which would allow a legal infiltration into the heart of Italy. Bologna was his immediate aim, but before it could be taken Florence itself must be neutralized by fear or siege. Yet still he did not wish an immediately open clash with the Tuscan Republic, and when Pietro Gambacorta, lord of Pisa, began frantic attempts to make peace Giangaleazzo gave all the appearance of reasonable attention. Apart from the Count himself, Gambacorta alone seems to have been aware of the nature and scale of the looming war. His motives were a most rare altruism; for over a decade he had managed to create between his city and Florence a rapport which most Pisans privately considered to be against nature, but his genuine nobility earned him sufficient support to pursue his unique experiment in co-operation. Now the first gusts of a peninsular war threatened the feeble light he had kindled. Florence lent a grudging ear to his persuasions, reluctantly took part in a series of conferences which broke up under new tensions. The last was held in the Count's own city of Pavia, when an attempt was made to establish lines of demarcation beyond which neither party would interfere in the affairs of the other. But only the most sanguine could have hoped that discussion would have resolved the deep-rooted antagonisms. Florence was publicly humiliated; not only did her ambassadors, Luigi Guicciardini and Giovanni Ricci, fail in their tasks, but they were so completely outwitted that their government was forced to disown them publicly and retract their disastrous concessions. The ambassadors sent to replace them were no more successful, the Florentine preference for the amateur proving its inherent weakness when opposed to Giangaleazzo's system of professionals.

The conference of Pavia dragged to its close in the May of 1389; from thenceforward it was clear that the steadily increasing tension could be broken only by war. In Bologna a pro-Visconti conspiracy was put down bloodily; Giangaleazzo in return expelled all Bolognese and Florentine citizens from the state of Milan. Rumour arose in Pavia that one of the Florentine ambassadors had attempted to poison the Count; in Florence a plot to corrupt a leading citizen was exposed. Giovanni Ubaldini was sent down into Tuscany with 200 lances to guard the Sienese against the ravages of mercenaries well known to be in the official pay of Florence. Ubaldini cherished a deep hatred for the Republic, for he was of those Ghibelline nobility of the Apennines whom Florence had dispossessed; his Tuscan connections were wide and varied and he vigorously set about creating a ring of enemies around Florence. The city itself belied that atmosphere of calm and resolute preparation of which its citizens later boasted. The antagonism of the great families resulted in a deep division of policy, in turn creating a ludicrous vacillation of purpose. As one crisis increased so war fervour mounted, fanned by the members of the *Parte Guelfa*, as it diminished 'it was the council of the wise that one should not spend money to buy trouble',[125] and the city, momentarily under the control of the moderates, again backed from the brink. None suffered more from that indecision than Francesco Carrara who, at Florentine invitation, had arrived in the city in April after a dramatic escape. Throughout the dangers of his journey he had been buoyed up by the hope that Florence had at last recognized the danger from the Count and intended to declare war. But on his

---

[125] Dati, p. 18.

arrival he discovered that a temporary accord had been patched up and his presence was an embarrassment. The Signoria coldly ignored him and he left after a brief stay to go off on a long European tour in search of allies. Throughout the following year he again and again received specific instructions and encouragements from the allies: he even concluded an alliance with the duke of Bavaria upon their behalf, but on each occasion as danger temporarily receded he was again disowned. The Signoria displayed the same pusillanimity towards their main military hope, John Hawkwood. The Englishman, as a son-in-law of the dead Bernabò, had a vested interest in the destruction of the Count of Virtue. In the *Processus* against Bernabò, Giangaleazzo had gone out of his way to impugn the legitimacy of Hawkwood's wife, fearing just such a situation as the Signoria could now exploit. But, irritated by the Florentine lack of decision, Hawkwood had taken himself off on a free-lance tour, ignoring the messengers who came to urge him that 'the event which he had long desired would soon happen and if he stayed in this country good would accrue to himself and his friends'. Ghino di Roberto reported back to his government that Hawkwood had retorted 'In the affairs of Lombardy one must act and not merely make a show. (In truth he spoke wisely.)'[126]

It was the disgraced ambassador Giovanni Ricci who finally brought the matter into the open, repeating in a public speech those fears placed in the records of the secret debates. His speech was an outright attack on the Count as the instigator of all troubles in Lombardy and Tuscany and beyond. 'This man makes many signs. If he was interested only in Lombardy then we should have no fear, but he wishes to mix in with the Sienese our neighbours who are already angry with us, he

---

[126] Temple-Leader, pp. 218, 219.

interferes in Lucca and Pisa... From the beginning his signoria was ample enough, but not content with his father's dominions he desired that of messer Bernabò's and those also he obtained with great art. And not remaining content with the state already so increased he joined to it that of Verona and Vicenza... and still not quietened with these gains he turned to the enterprise of Padua and all the state of the Paduans. And even this was not the end of his insatiable cupidity... Already he drools after Bologna as though it were his heritage. Already his hopes, the Apennines passed, reaches out to the Sienese and the Lucchese. Therefore seeing these things, O citizens, we must raise ourselves and look to the defence of our liberty because it is unbelievable that he should desire Siena and Lucca and not lust after the city of Florence. Bologna must be aided immediately because if that city should fall into the hands of our enemies we should find ourselves in the gravest peril.'[127] Ricci's speech earned for him a place in the annals of Florence, but it also caused him to be marked down in Milan. Giangaleazzo was incensed; he protested to the Signoria that such an attack should be made upon him in public debates of an ostensibly friendly city. The protest included an accusation that it had been Ricci who, during the period of his ambassade to Pavia, had attempted to poison him. The Signoria ignored the protest and rejected the accusation; the Florentines did not settle their problems in that manner. But the situation had now gone beyond recall. In the spring of 1390 Boniface 'acting as a good pastor' sent the Cardinal of Bologna to Florence and then to Pisa to confer with Milanese representatives, but after hearing both sides he came to the heavy conclusion that war was inevitable. The Venetians also sent envoys to both Pavia and Florence. They met afterwards at Ferrara and after

---

[127] Bruni, Istoria X, p. 508.

exchanging experiences came to the same conclusion as the Cardinal.

On April 28th 1390 Pasquino Capelli put his signature to a mildly worded document — a defiance by definition, but one carefully worded to appeal to a large section of the Florentine community. The Count had sought by all means to preserve peace so that Italy, wearied by long war, 'for at least one period in our time should possess herself in peace'. But all in vain, the councils of malign men have prevailed. Nevertheless, it is not against the commune of Florence, whom he respects, that he moves 'but against that rabble of archguelfs who, under pretext of liberty, have oppressed that flourishing republic as tyrants more swift to choose peace than war... We desire that upon them and not upon the other lovers of peace, upon their heads and not upon their victims', shall punishment fall.'[128] Milanese heralds delivered the declaration of war simultaneously in Bologna and Florence on May 1st. The Bolognese contented themselves with the reply that they looked forward to the day when Judith would triumph over Holofernes, but in Florence the 'archguelf' jibe struck home. In a heated reply Salutati denied that there was any such division in the city, warned the Count that if he proceeded on that assumption it would be at his peril. Then, in a manifesto addressed to all Italians, he sounded the first note of that appeal to nationalism which was to be the leitmotiv of Italian polemics until Giangaleazzo's death. 'Italians! At last the Viper is leaving his insidious hiding-place. Now it is very clear what the Serpent has been attempting with his flatteries. The great secret which he masked with a stupefying hypocrisy, the secret for which he killed his father-in-law, deceived brothers, took with subterfuge Padua, Verona and Vicenza and the Tuscan and Piedmontese

---

[128] Annales Mediolanenses CLII, col. 815.

cities, is at length revealed. He wants the crown of Italy to give a colour of respectability to his title of tyranny. But we that are the true Italy, by defending our very existence, shall defend all Italians from falling into servitude.'[129]

The call to arms was Florentine, but Bologna was the Count's prime objective and on the outbreak of war the bulk of the Milanese force under his senior general, Jacopo dal Verme, was hurled against the city. But the attack ground to a stop, for Florence too was acutely aware of Bologna's value and had denuded herself of troops for its defence, placing them under the command of John Hawkwood. The Count was able to place 15,000 horse and 5000 foot in the field; Florence was surrounded by pro-Visconti powers with Bologna her only contact with the outside world. But the very wideness of Giangaleazzo's alliances proved an embarrassment to him. His allies' motives for supporting him were varied but they had one common need — troops or the money with which to pay them. Giovanni Ubaldini was stiffening the Sienese with 1000 lances; further south Paolo Savelli was in command of a large contingent in Perugia, and each of the smaller lords of Romagna and the Marches had to be supplied with Milanese troops under the command of professional Milanese generals. Montefeltro of Urbino, Manfredi of Faenza, Malatesta of Rimini, the lords of Forlì and Imola, each was theoretically a threat to Florence but each took his toll of the total fighting force which the Count would have preferred to direct against Bologna. After the first bloody opening the war swiftly degenerated into local triumphs and defeats, and there indeed it might have ended in stalemate had it not been for the young man whom friends and enemies alike had dismissed as a nonentity. On June 19th, while the professional soldiers were

---

[129] Valeri, p. 258.

still manoeuvring for position, the amateur Francesco Novello retook his city of Padua with a skeleton force. Florence had declined to supply troops for what was reasonably considered to be an impossible enterprise. Troops were needed for the defence of Bologna; the re-taking of Padua, many miles behind the Milanese frontier, came a very poor second. Aid was coming from Bavaria; let the impetuous young man wait until it arrived. But the same blind optimism which had led Carrara to confide his state to an enemy's general, and to triumph over the bitter disappointments caused by Florentine vacillation, now stood him in good stead. It was impossible for Padua to be re-taken and therefore Florence had made no plans for such a contingency. But neither had Giangaleazzo. One additional factor, without which even Carrara's optimism would have been useless, was the growing suspicion which Venice held for Visconti. At no point would the Serenissima consider open warfare, but they had adjusted their marvellously elastic neutrality in favour of the allies, allowing troops to cross Venetian territory. Carrara took advantage and with a force hastily collected crossed into the Paduan state.

Eighteen months earlier Francesco Novello had left his home with the execrations of the Paduans ringing in his ears. No sooner had he gone, while he was still in fact legally the lord of Padua, his subjects had hailed the Count of Virtue as deliverer and consigned their city into his hands. For the few there had been the rewards of some minor posts while for the many was the hope that their inclusion in the Milanese state would bring about that peace and prosperity which had been so sadly lacking under the Carraresi. Now, in June 1390, the same populace which had jeered father and son into exile flocked to Novello's banner, welcoming him back into the state with an almost hysterical joy. The intervening eighteen months had taught them the bitter lesson that a captured capital city becomes a provincial town within a greater state. The Count's attitude towards Padua had been no less, if no more, liberal than towards any of the other cities subject to him. But Padua's adoption within the Milanese state coincided with the period of his most urgent need for money. The tax concessions with which he had introduced his rule had been forced to give way to the reality of empire. Valentina's marriage and two successive wars had severely strained even the wealthy Milanese State and Padua was immediately forced to pay its share. It was an intolerable burden for a people with a recent memory of independence, for though the reign of the Carraresi was harsh enough the family had naturally identified itself closely with the city. The citizens found themselves grievously taxed to support the ambitions of a foreign lord, to contribute towards the ever-increasing glory of the foreign city on the other side of Lombardy. The presence of a Milanese garrison and the lack of any natural leader among the Paduans had prevented any outburst of coherent resentment, but the appearance of the standard of the Car immediately acted as a catalyst. Hundreds flocked to join Carrara; most were undisciplined peasants and had Giangaleazzo acted immediately the rebellion would have been smashed in open country. But Carrara was able to approach Padua itself and, aided by the disillusioned citizens of the capital, secretly entered during the night. Once within the confines of the walls, an armed crowd bred in the tradition of street fighting was as effective as a professional army. By the morning of June 21st the Milanese garrison was sealed within its citadel in Padua and ten other cities of the Paduan State had thrown out their own garrisons and declared for their legal ruler.

Giangaleazzo's fatal delay may have been partly due to his knowledge that the garrison in Padua could hold out indefinitely and the fact that the only troops immediately available were those sieging Bologna. The opposing forces there were too equally balanced to permit the withdrawal of a detachment without a drastic reversal of his strategy, entailing the abandonment of the siege. But, military considerations apart, that flaw in his character which Corio divined, that 'timidity in adversity', probably accounted for the lack of action during the vital hours before and after the fall of Padua. It was his first great failure for which a string of brilliant successes had left him unprepared. And while he hesitated in his distant castle and his commanders waited for orders the situation was irretrievably lost, dal Verme was at length ordered to withdraw from Bologna and detach a column under Ugolotto Biancardo for the relief of the garrison in Padua; the machine was again moving and thereafter it was the ability of the Milanese commanders to make tactical decisions on the spot which contained the local failure, preventing it from becoming widespread disaster. For news of Padua's success ran swiftly through the Milanese State, a heady draught for people becoming already weary with the expenses of war. Two days after Carrara's success Verona rose in arms. Under the sudden, fierce assault of the united citizens the Milanese garrison there retreated to the citadel, but then the impetus of rebellion became lost in a partisan quarrel. For the first time in a generation Verona was free and a section of the populace — 'good and wise men' 'Minerbetti' inevitably calls them — wanted to declare a republic while others wished to restore the Scaligieri. After milling around the citadel 'they abandoned the piazzas and each went to his home, having no regard whatsoever for their fortunes'.[130] But while the citizens were engrossed in a constitutional debate, the column detached from Bologna under the command of Ugolotto Biancardo was approaching the Po. Biancardo heard of the new rebellion, made a swift decision and instead of continuing on to Padua turned aside to Verona, the 'good and wise' republicans conniving at his entry under cover of darkness.[131] 'Minerbetti' fails to make clear what the republicans thought they stood to gain by the introduction of Milanese soldiers; the self-destroying jealousy of city faction was probably explanation enough for him. Biancardo's mercenaries and the revengeful garrison found a sleeping city at their mercy 'and with fire and with sword brought the unhappy city again under the yoke of the Visconti'. Corio, detached Milanese historian though he was, confessed himself appalled at the vengeance which struck the Veronese. 'The populace, deprived of every hope, retreated to the river Adige, the victors not pursuing them because of the darkness, and later, profiting by that darkness, they fled. It was a thing most dolorous and worthy of compassion to see the calamity of so noble and ancient a city, presenting to the eye an indescribable spectacle of misery because of the merciless slaughter of many citizens. The most noble matrons, virgins, widows and even little children dragged from every corner, their laments rising to the heavens... prisoners oppressed by new tortures for ransoms... temples profaned... citizens exiled.'[132] Biancardo's main object was to suppress the rebellion with the maximum speed, for ahead of him still lay the task for which he had turned aside to deal with Verona. But though the massacre of that night was his undoubted responsibility, the wholesale exiles which followed could only

---

[130] Gatari, p. 424.
[131] 'Minerbetti', XXXVI, A. 1390.
[132] Corio, III, 7.

have been executed on direct orders from Pavia. Both Corio and 'Minerbetti' maintain that Verona remained virtually uninhabited for many months afterwards, mute witness to the policy of calculated revenge to which Giangaleazzo subjected the entire population. Padua's success had established a dangerous precedent, for it had been a political secession instead of the usual tumult arising from tax grievances. Verona's attempt to follow was doubly dangerous for, unlike Padua, the city could be shown to be the legal possession of the Visconti, bound by the same ties as that which bound the oldest cities of the Milanese state. Corio's considered phrase that the massacre of Verona 'was truly the re-establishment of the Milanese empire' was exactly true, for it demonstrated that, though a city might enter the state of its own free will, once in it could not contract out. But Verona's agony was Padua's salvation. Biancardo hastened on to his goal, but the brief delay had enabled Novello to establish himself. Now that he had succeeded he was overwhelmed with assistance; the Bavarians arrived with 6000 horse, Florence despatched a hastily collected group and Biancardo, having entered the Paduan citadel, wisely retreated, taking with him the garrison and the Paduan renegades. By the middle of August, Padua was totally lost to Giangaleazzo and the entire balance of the war upset by the mere force of desire of one obstinate and not particularly intelligent young man. The Count's eastward frontier was torn open; instead of a suspicious but passive Venice upon his flank he now had the impetuous Novello, burning to revenge himself upon his betrayer. Reinforced by the Florentines, Novello swept westward on to the territories of Ferrara and after a brief campaign Este deserted his hero and ally. There was much face-saving talk about the 'treacheries and deceits of the Count of Virtue' and whether by accident or design Este managed to spin out the negotiations by nearly a month, gaining some respite for the Count. But by October Ferrara was detached and the roads between Lombardy and Tuscany were again open.

After five months of warfare the Count's position was grave; Padua and Ferrara lost, Verona demanding a disproportionately large garrison, Siena dispirited by plague and dissension, Mantua dejected, it would seem that the wealth of Milan had been dissipated to no purpose. Yet the unity of his enemies was more apparent than real, Francesco Novello's vigorous activities masking an apprehension which Bologna at last voiced. Giangaleazzo had already sensed that the city was the most vulnerable political point of the coalition and discreetly offered a separate peace. The offer was taken sufficiently seriously for an embassy to be sent to Florence to discuss the matter. The Signoria received them with dismay 'for it appeared to them that here began the destruction of the foundation of things'. The burden of their reply was that he who loses liberty loses all, for everything falls into the hands of the victor. They politely disagreed that Bologna could not afford to carry on 'because with a city so blessed with natural resources it is reasonable to suppose that it should be abundant of riches'. True, it was hard for the mob who lacked foresight, but the government should be like a good doctor who gives present pain for future good. They should spend something of what they had now in order to protect the whole. Admittedly Bologna was in the forefront of the battle, but with some craft the Signoria suggested that this was because Visconti looked upon it as his own lost heritage. As regards the requested loan they pointed out that Florence had borne, alone, the expenses of the war in Tuscany 'and in Lombardy everyone knows how intolerable has been our expenses. But let the people of

176

Bologna take heart, for things are improving — Padua retaken, the Germans present, our armies now upon the Po and France is expected to send a large army.'[133]

It was this last rather than the airy generalizations which gave comfort to the Bolognese. For the sake of immediate interests Florence had again invoked the ancient curse of Italy, again appealing to the non-italic races beyond the Alps whose coming ended always in Italian tragedy. The Republic claimed to be acting on behalf of all free Italians, but some of her allies were beginning to wonder if such a price were justified. Pier Paolo Vergierio, Carrara's secretary, protested: 'There is no place for the barbarian in Italy. If Italy must become enslaved she shall be enslaved only by Italians.'[134] But the young scholar enjoyed no influence outside Padua and his colleagues in the Florentine chancery were gripped too firmly by war fever to forgo French help for the sake of an embryonic nationalism. The tarnished instrument of their policy was Carlo, dispossessed son of Bernabò, whose wanderings in search of a champion had taken him to Florence in 1388. He had met a similar reception to that of Francesco Novello's but, thicker-skinned, was content to wait until somebody did something for him, accepting a small pension from the Signoria and nominally joining Hawkwood's brigade. 'A stupid, low kind of fellow'[135] was the general Florentine opinion, but his value increased on the outbreak of war. His wife, Beatrice d'Armagnac, had returned home, stirring up her brother 'to defend her against that tyrant the Count of Vertus who had disinherited her without the smallest reason'.[136] Of all those to

---

[133] Bruni, Istoria X, pp. 529, 531.

[134] Valeri, *Le Signorie.*

[135] 'Minerbetti', III, A. 1388.

[136] Froissart, Bk. IV, Chap. XXVI.

whom the heirs of Bernabò appealed the twenty-four-year-old Comte d'Armagnac was the only one to be moved by a genuine sense of justice, and Florentine ambassadors, backed by Florentine gold, found no difficulty in persuading him to join the common cause. The Armagnac alliance secured on October 16th, the Signoria hastened to disembarrass themselves of Carlo, particularly as another and more attractive pretender to Milan, Luchino Visconti, Giangaleazzo's half-brother, had come upon the scene. 'Respecting messer Carlo,' they wrote to their commissioner at Padua, 'we must beg you to urge Sir John Hawkwood to try by all means to dissuade Carlo from joining him (in Padua), for within the last few days certain persons have come from Milan secretly to us, telling us plainly that if messer Luchino goes with the brigade the Milanese will let him enter, but if messer Carlo goes they will not turn but will keep steadfast to the Count.'[137] So ardent was their desire to dispense with Carlo that he was offered a regular salary, payable on the strict condition that he cut his link with the army. Florentine hopes of a rising in Milan in favour of Luchino Visconti recurred regularly. Forty years had passed since Luchino had fled the city, but every Florentine plan for an attack upon the Visconti was garnished with a plot to restore him. The identity of the 'certain persons from Milan' was kept a close secret, but whoever they were they enjoyed neither influence nor power in Milan, the Count never troubled to root them out and from first to last the cherished rebellion was a figment of the vivid Florentine imagination.

Throughout the autumn and winter of 1390 a great build-up of Florentine arms proceeded with Padua as base. The plan of campaign was similar to that which had menaced the Visconti twenty years before when two armies had entered the state

---

[137] Temple-Leader, p. 238.

from east and west with the intention of meeting in its heart. Exact timing was vital and again and again Florentine envoys were sent into France, urging Armagnac to hasten, to avoid all private fights on the road to Lombardy. The attempts of Giangaleazzo's supporters in France to bribe Armagnac had proved unsuccessful, but the negotiations all occasioned delay. Salutati joined his golden pen to the urgent solicitation of the ambassadors in a letter which, intended to sound a trumpet call to action, nevertheless struck an almost hysterical note. Patriotic fervour seems to have blinded the scholar's objectivity. The twenty-four-year-old Frenchman was to be the new saviour of Italy, earning such a glory as no man had ever seen before. 'But glorious though it is to triumph in arms, far more glorious is it to throw down arrogance, confound iniquity... to destroy the Count of nonvirtue, this enemy of the entire human species — unfaithful, cruel as Jugurtha, perfidious as Philip of Macedon, libidinous as Heliogabalus, arrogant and vain as Xerxes, impious as Julian the Apostate... Come, come swiftly most excellent prince, all Italy is rising against the tyrant, companions in arms await you.'[138] The letter is in decided contrast not only to Giangaleazzo's dignified letters to his enemy but to Salutati's own private opinion of the tyrant. But Armagnac's delay was beginning to threaten the grand strategy, and if fulsome compliment was needed to hasten him, then Salutati was willing to provide that stimulus even at some slight cost to his reputation. The army of the League, under the command of Hawkwood, had taken the field in May. Little opposition was met for most of the Milanese army was in Piedmont under dal Verme, awaiting the coming of the French. By the end of June Hawkwood had reached a point barely sixteen miles from Milan, but there the initiative

---

[138] Annales Mediolanenses CLIII, col. 818.

was taken from him, for further advance would have forced a pitched battle where, miles from his base, even victory would have been costly. Everything now depended upon the swift arrival of the Armagnacs. But the French, 'ferocious by their nature, were most quick to place themselves in every peril… and thus the extraordinary endeavours and almost infinite expense of the Florentines were rendered vain'.[139] In spite of the protests of the Florentine commissioners guiding the army, time was lost in a series of pointless actions and Giangaleazzo, balancing the hazards, deemed it opportune to force the issue. He had been poised in an agonizing indecision for nearly three weeks, aware that an attack upon either Hawkwood in the east or Armagnac in the west would have allowed the other to sweep down upon his capital. Padua had taught him that indecision could be as costly as a wrong decision and he therefore withdrew dal Verme from Piedmont and sent him against the nearer enemy. Hawkwood raised camp; short of supplies, outnumbered and deep in enemy country, there was nothing else he could do. Neither commander desired a pitched battle and dal Verme followed his enemy only as far as the riverine frontier of the Adige; there his pioneers destroyed the dykes, flooded the plain and eliminated the army as a fighting force. He then hastened back and established himself in Alessandria after, an action so swift that the Florentines were still worrying how to keep Hawkwood in the field when the bedraggled army was actually in Padua. The commissioners with Armagnac continued to urge him on, quite unaware that there was now no army to reinforce. Even now, when the combined offensive had failed, the presence of Armagnac's 10,000 veteran horse could still have turned the scales, whether he chose to fight a pitched battle or withdraw to the south and

---

[139] Bruni, Istoria X, p. 535.

attack in concert with the reorganized army, dal Verme in Alessandria and Giangaleazzo in Milan could do nothing but wait until the Frenchman had made his decision.

Milan saw nothing of its lord, for he had withdrawn to the castle, shutting himself away from the public gaze, waiting. The thirty-six hours which followed after dal Verme had established himself in Alessandria must have subjected one of his nature to an almost intolerable degree of strain. Earlier there had been reports that he wept for fear, but now gossip was stilled for it had nothing to feed on; for thirty-six hours the Count of Virtue might have been dead for all that his people knew as, alone, he endured the ultimate loneliness of the prince. There had been that other critical moment seven years before when his very life hung in the balance, but the attack upon Bernabò outside Milan had been throughout under his direct control. But now, for the first time in his life, his fate lay in the hands of another man, his general dal Verme. During the tense days leading up to the attack upon Hawkwood he had been able to deploy his troops in his preferred manner, using them as instruments of threat and encouragement. But, once having committed dal Verme to the east, the actual shock of battle became unavoidable for the Armagnacs were scarcely a day's march away. Time and space had alike run out; in place of diplomacy and strategy there loomed the test of power, the clash between two groups of armed men. dal Verme alone could decide whether to fight or retreat when Armagnac attacked; either decision, it seemed, must result in disaster, for his force was half the size of the French. 'But the Supreme Creator, wishing to make known his favour in regard to the Lombards, permitted that the Count of Armagnac, already sieging Castelazzo, should decide to attack Alessandria at the same time.'[140] The love of knightly glory at the expense of military efficiency now doomed the Armagnacs and saved the Count of Virtue. The French attack on Alessandria was in the nature of a joust, for, leaving a leaderless army to continue the siege of Castelazzo, Armagnac took with him only his peers. Outside Alessandria, 'more bold than wise, more ardent than experienced in Italian ways', they taunted dal Verme, rattling their lances upon the gates crying 'Come out, come out, most vile Lombards.'[141] dal Verme came out. It was the hottest hour of a day of great heat and the French, dismounted to receive dal Verme's charge, were weighed down and sweltering within the heavy armour they favoured. They might still have withstood the kind of swift charge in which they themselves excelled, but dal Verme instead dismounted his more lightly armoured men. The tormented knights fought with incredible gallantry, but heat and thirst incapacitated almost as many as were killed or wounded. By mid-afternoon all 500 were dead or captured and dal Verme, despatching a hasty report to his master, continued on to Castelazzo. In a second report, written during the small hours of the following day, he stated that barely 1200 men accompanied him, 'but by the third hour all your enemies were destroyed or captured'.[142] The massive army at Castelazzo, leaderless and surprised at nightfall, fell easy prey to men fighting on familiar ground. Some few were captured but the majority fled only to be cut down by peasants revenging themselves on the now helpless French for their own hardships of war. Giangaleazzo was eager to establish good relations with France and therefore the French captives who fell into his hands found quick release for small ransom. But the Florentines were less fortunate: one of the two

---

[140] Corio, III, 7.
[141] Ibid.
[142] Giulini, Vol. III.

commissioners was Giovanni Ricci, who, suffering from a head wound, was brought to Milan; for him the Count felt a deep and personal hatred. He deserved death, Pasquino Capelli informed him; nevertheless the generosity of the Count extended even to Giovanni Ricci, his would-be murderer, and Ricci could hope for a ransom — at some time in the future.

The battle of Alessandria was the effective end of a war which, opening as a Florentine crusade, was ending with Florentine policy totally discredited, dal Verme's action had not only snatched victory from certain defeat but enabled Giangaleazzo to appear as the defender of *italianita* against the foreigner, and in a letter to the Roman pope written the day after the battle, he made great play with the fact that the hosts of France were defeated 'by my captain with only my Italian people'. It was an argument which Milanese writers were to develop to its fullest extent, but the Count's immediate task was to grasp the fruits which dal Verme had presented him. For the first time since the loss of Padua the initiative was again in his hands; neither he nor his enemy could summon much more reserves, both were reluctantly moving towards an armistice, but desiring to negotiate from strength the Count despatched dal Verme to Tuscany. Pisa was available as a base, for though Pietro Gambacorta still held faith with the Florentines while believing that goodwill and conferences could solve all, his secretary Jacopo Appiano was openly the Count's supporter. In spite of Florentine warnings Gambacorta continued to repose confidence in the man who had served him for over fifty years, accepting Appiano's assurances that the toleration of Milanese troops was essential for Pisan neutrality. But though dal Verme had a base his burdens were great, for winter was approaching, famine was abroad and he was fighting on the enemy's ground. Hawkwood had re-formed his army and for five months the two conducted a superbly executed campaign. They had fought with or against each other for the better part of thirty years and each knew the other's strengths and weaknesses as well as he knew his own, and their campaign was a kind of military chess played among the Tuscan hills, dal Verme appealed for troops, money, provisions, but received little more than encouraging words; Hawkwood was forced to employ peasant militia, and while the exhausted, starving armies fought for the routes into Florence their masters were forced on to an imposed peace. There were no possible grounds for negotiation for the attitude of both had hardened into final form; but, urged on by their war-weary allies, the Count and the Florentine Signoria agreed that the proposed conference should take the form of arbitration with the Doge of Genoa and the Grand Master of Rhodes as arbitrators. It was the only thing to which they did agree; from September to January 1391 a bitter argument as to the milieu dragged on even before a tentative agenda was reached. Genoa was at length chosen although the Florentines protested that its Doge, Antoniotto Adorno, was an open supporter of the Count's and his judgement would be a foregone conclusion. Or so 'Minerbetti' implied but, in spite of himself, the account he gives of his fellow citizens at Genoa is that of a group of obstinate, querulous men following private goals regardless of the needs of the conference.[143] Led by Tommaso di Neri the delegates opened their case with a lengthy discourse on the deceits and falsities of the Count of Virtue. Adorno cut them short, saying that it seemed best to leave such general accusations and that each party should put its case 'with courteous words' a justified rebuke which earned for him the malice of the delegates and probably the later

---

[143] 'Minerbetti', XXXVII, A. 1391.

accusations of partiality. The main issue of the conference very swiftly became apparent — who owned Padua? All other details were ancillary, for Padua, the Count's major single contribution to the glory of Milan, was the hinge of his policy. It belonged to him by right of conquest, Bevilacqua claimed, 'because when the war began it was already his'. The demand was totally rejected by Neri and his colleagues. Padua was a sovereign state which the Count had gained through trickery; it was unthinkable that Francesco Novello should again be dispossessed — and incidentally lose a bridgehead for Florence. Neither side would give way and Adorno, pointing out that peace could never be made without some sort of compromise, asked both to refer back to their principals. The measure was quite unsuccessful; both Bologna and Florence backed up their ambassadors, while Bevilacqua returned from Pavia to say that his master refused any treaty beforehand which did not include the return of Padua. The conference was on the point of breaking up when Adorno and the Grand Master, using their powers as arbitrators, forced through a compromise under threat of heavy fine. Francesco Novello's right to Padua was recognized on condition that he paid a yearly tribute of 10,000 florins for fifty years. No formal decision was made in regard to his father, still languishing in the dungeons of Monza castle, and an attempt to obtain the release of Giovanni Ricci ended inconclusively. For the rest the *status quo* was accepted — each to remain in possession of that which he had at the moment of arbitration and neither party was to interfere in the affairs of the other. It was an unhappy, cobbled solution, its long-term value adequately shown by Neri's reaction. Cutting short a discussion as to guarantees he rose and said: 'Our guarantee shall be the sword, because Giovanni Galeazzo has had experience of our forces and we have proved his.'[144] With the exception of the ever-optimistic Pietro Gambacorta, all involved in the Treaty of Genoa realized that it was little more than a respite to allow the fatigued combatants to regain their strength. Even while the ambassadors were arguing in Genoa, Florence was engaged in drawing up plans for another grouping against the Count. Three months later, in April 1392, the League of Bologna came into being. Ironically, its creation enabled Giangaleazzo to achieve the summit of Italian ambitions and create an alliance with France.

---

[144] Bruni, Istoria, X, 540.

VII: DUKE OF MILAN

THE KINGDOM OF ADRIA

There was a certain poignancy in Giangaleazzo's personal and political relations with the French monarchy. The hatred and fear he inspired among fellow Italians was sincere token to his supremacy in his chosen field; in Italy he dealt with social equals, veteran politicians who, sprung from a common source, were well aware of the dangerous game they were playing. He therefore led; the amorality of his enemies gave him extra weapons against them for he was capable always of adding another twist to a plot, of deceiving a deceiver, of raising stakes always higher knowing the precise maximum to which they could be raised. A politician who could use the Venetians, the most accomplished tricksters in Europe, had nothing to learn of his trade. But in dealing with France the equality dropped, for the Valois was a leading house of Europe and he but an elected official of an Italian city, his sole personal title held of the king of France. It must have been exceedingly galling for him to compare those territories of his, carved out and held together by his single will, with the vast potential which accident had given the Valois. For behind the appearance of the Count of Virtue suing the king of France was the reality of a veteran statesman of forty attempting to negotiate with a romantic youth of twenty and his even more irresponsible eighteen-year-old brother. Charles VI of France had come to the throne as a boy of twelve in 1380 and for eight years had remained under the regency of his four uncles, the dukes of Berry, Burgundy, Anjou and Bourbon. Anjou died during the Neapolitan expedition of 1384 and the regency was largely in the hands of Burgundy until Charles, urged on by his brother, declared himself emancipated and summarily dismissed his uncles. The Well-Beloved his people called him, and his beauty and humanity made of him the young Christian king of all romances. Yet there was already in him an indication of that basic mental instability which became madness. His prodigality was fantastic; the ending of the regency saw also an ending of financial and moral restraint, so that the court of France became a shame in Europe. Supporting Charles in his extravagances was that brother Louis, now son-in-law to the Count of Virtue, sharing the same physical beauty and intelligence but lacking the high sense of duty which Charles could bring to his office. He was no longer styled duke of Touraine but of Orléans, having persuaded his brother to break their father's promise to the Orléanaise that their city would never be an appanage; Touraine lacked that splendour which Louis desired even at some cost to a dead man's honour. In marrying his only daughter to this attractive, hedonistic Valois prince, Giangaleazzo had hoped to gain an ally who might, in some degree, fill the place of an adult son. Louis proved a broken staff, his political ambitions just a little less powerful than his physical desires.

In the summer of 1390 French ambassadors had arrived at Pavia to obtain the Count's support for a projected expedition into Italy. Designed to eliminate the Schism by a forcible deposition of the Roman pope, the expedition would also present an opportunity for yet another Angevin attempt upon Naples and therefore it received wide support in France. The need for an Italian ally was paramount and Giangaleazzo's personal connections with the French throne made him an obvious candidate for the role. He declined the honour. The ambassadors could not have approached him at a more inopportune moment, for he was too deeply involved with the problems attending the sudden loss of Padua to pay much attention to them. He was not only preoccupied, the ambassadors reported, but he was also distinctly cold; the Florentine attempts to enlist the Armagnacs in France had not passed unnoticed by him. A further embassy proving fruitless, Louis of Orléans decided to exert his personal influence. He had a strong additional incentive to make the long journey to Pavia; the first instalment of Valentina's dowry had fallen due but had not yet been paid, and deep though his hands were in his brother's coffers, he required ever more gold for his ever greater extravagances. Someone made the wise decision that the duke of Burgundy should accompany him. Philip the Bold had much in common with Giangaleazzo; older by nine years, he too was engaged in constructing a state from many fragments and had coldly manipulated his regency to that end. Giangaleazzo had gone to considerable trouble to establish and maintain contact with this premier duke of France, exchanging gifts and even making loans, and though Philip was without Italian ambitions he was aware of the value of this link in his European network. But his influence proved of little use on this occasion. He and Louis arrived in Pavia in March 1391 and though the Count welcomed them warmly, he firmly refused to support the expedition. His attitude was reasonable. In the matter of the Schism he had granted complete freedom of choice to his subjects and they were, as were most Italians, fervent supporters of the Roman pope. He was being asked to sow dissension among his own people during the course of a bitter war at the very time when his Florentine enemies were themselves awaiting French aid. He would go no further than to make a strictly private statement that he, personally, considered Clement of Avignon to be the true pope, but not even the hinted promise of a Lombard crown would make him publish his statement. Louis obtained, for his part, only 16,000 of the outstanding 100,000 florins instalment, and after a few days' lavish entertainment in Pavia the French dukes returned home empty-handed. The episode had proved fruitless for the French but it opened a new path for the Count. Shortly afterwards the League of Bologna came into being and garbled news of its object came to Clement; it was to include Giangaleazzo himself and was formed for the defence of the Roman pope, Boniface IX. Both Clement and Boniface contacted the Count, the former praying him to do nothing which would prejudice France, the latter urging him not to fear, for European powers were moving in his favour. The information of both popes was totally inaccurate; the sole object of the League of Bologna was the destruction of Giangaleazzo with only an incidental interest in the defence of Boniface. Nevertheless, at no cost to himself, Giangaleazzo was able to appear as the valuable friend of France. He acted swiftly, despatching Niccolo Spinelli to Paris in the spring of 1392 to commence negotiations.

The Count could not have chosen a better instrument for his purpose; indeed, in some sense, he was himself the instrument which the great jurist used to forward his own most dear ambition — the severance of the spiritual power of the Papacy from the temporal. No living man better understood the machinery of Papal power than Niccolo Spinelli or was better able to find his way through the tangle of Neapolitan, Angevin, and Avignonese interests which was throttling Italy. A Neapolitan by birth, he entered the service of the Church under Egidio Albornoz, the Spanish Legate, who had single-handed subdued the rebellious States of the Church. They became close friends, corresponding daily when Spinelli was himself transferred to Avignon, where, helpless, he witnessed the Spaniard's final humiliation at the hands of Avignonese place-hunters. Spinelli returned to Italy as Apostolic Delegate, became Chancellor of Naples under the wretched Giovanna, then Siniscalco of Provence, and filially entered the ungrateful service of the Angevin court. He returned again to Italy on a mission in 1387 and passed through Milan. There the world-weary old man, himself used to the highest authority, sensed as others had done that the young lord of Milan had the ability to bring some kind of peace to the peninsula. And, sensing, he abandoned his mission and stayed, wholeheartedly entering the Count's service. At the age of seventy he agreed to go back into France to plunge once more into the tortuous world of Papal politics.

Giangaleazzo's formal instructions to him were an ingenious admixture of truth and adapted truth. At the request of Charles, acting on behalf of Clement, he had not joined the League of Bologna but now, thanks to his devotion to French interests, he found himself isolated among enemies. Spinelli was therefore to beg Charles to take his master under direct protection, accepting the Count's enemies as his own; if the imperial dignity should be conferred upon Charles or upon any other French prince, then it was hoped that Charles would remember that earlier hint made to the Count that he should be granted some title which would place him in the ranks of hereditary princes. For his part the Count in return would wholeheartedly support any French expedition into Italy. Spinelli's reception in Paris was at first cool, but he found a strong supporter in Clement who, hearing in Avignon of his mission, despatched an envoy to help him. Giangaleazzo's abandonment of his role of defender of *italianita* passed unnoticed. It was expedient and that was sufficient reason, but his refusal to declare openly for Clement was another matter. Charles accepted all that Spinelli had argued, promised to grant the French arms to the Count and to confer upon him the desired title if it were ever in his power to do so. But he nevertheless reminded Spinelli of the confidences made by his master to both Louis and Burgundy on their visit to Pavia; even before that, at the time of Valentina's marriage, he had let it be known privately that he was a Clementist. But when would he come into the open? Spinelli again outlined the Count's position. He did indeed accept Clement but, isolated as he was, it would be courting disaster to declare his allegiance openly. There was, however, a way of obtaining a result advantageous to all parties.

Spinelli had been speaking as an ambassador of the lord of Milan but now, at the crux of the conference, he departed from his brief to develop that plan for which he, an old man, had made the arduous journey to Paris. He argued for the creation of a kingdom out of the Papal states. Other Italians had seen that the possession of these states earned hatred for the Papacy, had known the same shame that the spiritual splendour of the Church should be debased by temporal ambitions. 'It is now more than a thousand years since these territories and cities were given to the priests and ever since then the most violent wars have been waged upon their account and yet the priests neither now possess them in peace nor ever will be able to possess them. It were better in truth before God's eyes and the world that these pastors should entirely renounce the temporal dominium... the source of inquietude and a burden for body and soul not only for themselves but for all Christians and especially for Italians.'[145] Spinelli echoed the lament. 'The temporal dominium resulted

---

[145] de' Mussi, col. 528.

in an offence to God, a ruin for the peoples and a shame to the Church',[146] he declared. But if these states were infeudated to a French prince, preferably Louis of Orléans, the Papacy would not only enjoy the support of French arms in Italy when Clement came to take his seat in Rome, but would be free of the burden of temporal politics. In raising his project of the 'kingdom of Adria' Spinelli was speaking essentially as an Italian Christian, but his plan exactly coincided with Giangaleazzo's needs, the creation of a friendly state in central Italy. The kingdom of Adria, under the rule of his son-in-law, would hem in his inveterate enemy Florence and provide for him a secure base for operations south of the Apennines. Spinelli carried the conference with him. In January 1393 Guy de Tremouille prepared to go to Pavia to make the Count officially cognizant of the deliberations, while Enguerrand de Coucy was ordered to Avignon to persuade Clement to prepare the bull of infeudation. But then, when it seemed that all was concluded save for formalities, Charles VI suffered a severe recurrence of his madness, delaying the departure of Tremouille and de Coucy for five months. The delay proved fatal for Spinelli's ideal. By the time the king had recovered, French opinion had swung away from the always repugnant idea of Boniface's forcible deposition; talk now was of the voluntary abdication of both the Roman and Avignonese popes. Clement himself, receiving de Coucy on May 26th, had obviously become alarmed at the responsibility of virtually liquidating the Papal states. He claimed he could do nothing without his cardinals' consent; demanded again the impossible condition that Giangaleazzo should declare openly for him. With his death in September and the accession of the less sanguine Benedict XIII, the kingdom of Adria passed into the

---

[146] ASN XXVI, pp. 479-496.

limbo of history. But Giangaleazzo was still determined to forge a French alliance, Louis of Orléans still ambitious to carve for himself an Italian kingdom, and Spinelli went back to his role of Milanese diplomat, adapting the workable residue of his plan to another project, the establishment of Louis of Orléans in Genoa. In February 1392 Genoese exiles had appealed to Charles, offering him the sovereignty of their city in exchange for help. Such a move would entail the reversal of nearly a century of Visconti policy for which Genoa was as vital as Bologna. Nevertheless, the prospect of establishing his son-in-law in Liguria was attractive enough to Giangaleazzo to counterbalance the loss of the port and Andreolo Arese was hastened to Paris to support Spinelli.

Giangaleazzo had failed to take into account the instability of Louis of Orléans. Spinelli's devoted work at length produced the desired results; in September 1394 Enguerrand de Coucy arrived to commence military operations against Savona as a preliminary to an attack upon Genoa and received all possible aid from the Count; in November Genoa was formally dedicated to Louis. The Count gained nothing but a simple declaration of mutual interests with general promises of alliance, but even this anticlimax to the high hopes of two years earlier was not the end. Three months after the formal dedication, Louis ceded his rights over Genoa to his brother for 300,000 francs; instead of a docile son-in-law as neighbour and supporter, the Count now had the French monarchy itself, a monarchy rapidly falling under the control of his most bitter enemy, Isabella of Bavaria.

THE LEAGUE OF BOLOGNA

The pressure of war had forced the Count of Virtue to abandon or modify many of his aims, but that same pressure had also forced Florence from her original position. The League of Bologna, spearhead of republican liberty against the despot, counted but two republics among its signatories, Florence and Bologna. The rest were the lords of Ferrara, Faenza, Imola, Padua, Ravenna. Salutati issued no ringing proclamation on its formation, for the League was no crusade but a band of frightened men desirous of clinging to their own autocratic power and so allying themselves with the enemy of a greater autocrat. But even their ignoble reasons were less of a blow to Florentine pride than the fact that the very existence of the League was due to the tacit approval of Venice. The Serenissima had observed the steady rise of Visconti with an increasing suspicion which led to a gradual alteration of policy. At the end of the war their fear of Milan was just slightly stronger than their dislike of involvement in the peninsula; but it was not yet strong enough to make them abandon formal neutrality. They approved the formation of the League but would sign no articles, would commit themselves to nothing, reserving to themselves a godlike freedom of action. The Florentine Signoria attempted many times to draw them directly into the League, even hinting that it might be necessary for themselves and the Bolognese to make common cause with the Visconti to combat the mercenaries. But the Serenissima were not to be trapped. Their sole aim was to avoid an accidental war with the Count due to a miscalculation on his part, and their public support of the League was to make it clear to him that any further advance in eastern Lombardy would earn their active displeasure. Giangaleazzo temporarily accepted the position and under Venetian protection the 'little lords' of Lombardy and Romagna felt secure enough to defy Milan. Only Francesco Gonzaga of Mantua kept faith and he was linked by such ties to the Count that his seduction seemed improbable.

The Gonzaghi had climbed to power in Mantua by similar means and at about the same time as the Visconti had seized Milan. But where Milan was already a considerable city, the natural geographic centre of a growing state, Mantua was confined in a marsh which, though affording excellent defence, limited its growth. A tacit recognition of limitations had developed between the two families, the Gonzaghi prudently did not interfere with their powerful neighbours, while the Visconti, aware that the overcoming of Mantua's natural defences would need a greater effort than the city's value warranted, were content to leave the Gonzaghi in quiet possession. Bernabò had made a series of spirited attacks but had ultimately preferred to bind the family to him in his usual manner by imposing a daughter, Agnese, upon Francesco. A cordial relationship had existed between the courts of Pavia and Mantua and when Francesco came into his inheritance, some two years after Giangaleazzo, the two young men continued the relationship of their fathers. During the years of Bernabò's dominance the vulnerability of their individual positions probably did much to draw them together, and when at length Giangaleazzo overthrew his uncle, the one certain ally he had was Mantua. Gonzaga seems to have been moved throughout by a genuine admiration for Giangaleazzo as well as by a vivid awareness of Mantua's proximity to Milan. Throughout the recent war he was under continual pressure from the allies, eager to secure a foothold in central Lombardy, but even through the tense days when the coming of the Armagnacs seemed to spell doom for the Count he remained loyal.

But the female heirs of Bernabò possessed a spirit conspicuously lacking in the male. Agnese from the beginning cherished a hatred for her father's usurper. 'The Count of all-Filth' she referred to him habitually in place of his accepted title; on news of the loss of Padua she rejoiced publicly and her husband, apprehensive for his reputation with the Count, beat her for it. Nevertheless she continued in her open contempt until, in the winter of 1390, certain letters were found in her room as a result of which she was beheaded by her husband. Gonzaga, a moody, suspicious man, kept his reasons secret and gossip ran wild. The pro-Visconti writers assumed that Gonzaga was seeking a way out of his commitments and that Agnese was his innocent victim. 'The reason why this was done is not well known,' de' Mussi wrote, 'but it is believed that it was done to disgrace the Count of Virtue.'[147] The Tuscan chroniclers as automatically assumed that the whole thing was the work of the Count anxious to eliminate Agnese and secure Gonzaga. Their version was adopted by later pro-Florentine writers anxious to place one more crime to Visconti's score. The one consistent factor appearing in garbled form in the Tuscan writers relates to the letters found in her room. In Sozomeno's story[148] they were adulterous, whereas 'Minerbetti' believed them to have been treasonable correspondence between Agnese and her brother Carlo. Both writers agree that they were planted upon the unfortunate girl by Visconti agents, 'Minerbetti' stating that 'the Count of Virtue did this thinking that the lord of Mantua would never consider making concord with the League'[149] — the exact opposite of de' Mussi's conjecture. It is difficult to see exactly what Giangaleazzo was supposed to have gained by traducing Agnese, considering that her attitude towards him was already

---

[147] de' Mussi, A. 1392.
[148] Sozomeno, Specimen Historic RIS XVI.
[149] 'Minerbetti', XLIX, A. 1390.

well known to Gonzaga, nor how Gonzaga thought that her execution would 'disgrace the Count of Virtue'. Agnese was in fact executed for adultery, she and her lover confessing their guilt to a secret but legal court presided over by the *podestà* of Mantua. The Count therefore could have had nothing to do with her execution, but Gonzaga's later violent reaction against him could have arisen only from a bitter sense of personal betrayal, a belief that, in some fashion, the Count was responsible. Such is the received version, enshrined by Sisimondi. 'The infernal intrigues were discovered and, tormented by remorse, Gonzaga thought of nothing but revenge on he who had led his spouse to the gallows.'[150] This was precisely what the Florentines required; in September 1392 Gonzaga, the last of the 'little lords' to remain faithful to the Count, deserted him and enrolled in the League of Bologna. The probability is that both Gonzaga and Visconti were victims of a Florentine conspiracy;[151] significantly, only the Tuscan chroniclers mention the letters which were supposed to be proof successively of Agnese's and Giangaleazzo's guilt. His defection caused Giangaleazzo considerable personal distress 'because he had confided in him and loved him more than any other signore of the world and always honoured him in his court above all…'[152] but the personal distress was as nothing compared to the sudden upset of the balance in Lombardy. Mantua now formed the apex of a triangle aimed at Milan with the allied cities of Bologna, Padua, and Ferrara forming the

---

[150] Sismondi, T. VII, p. 343.

[151] The Florentines had no masters in the art of character assassination. A decade later they planned and executed a plot against the Count which involved at least a score of people in three countries and yet was kept a close secret. See pp. 301-503.

[152] Gatari, p. 451.

base. The great barrier of the Po bisected the triangle, cutting off Bologna from the other two cities, but the creators of the League had already planned a grandiose engineering project in anticipation of Gonzaga's defection. A bridge was to be built across the river at Borgoforte in the Mantuan territory establishing in actuality the political significance of Gonzaga's act. Troops of the League would be able to march into the heart of Lombardy before striking a blow.

Giangaleazzo accepted his political defeat with resignation if not equanimity. The network of his intrigues now encompassed Florence; somewhere along it a situation must develop which would cancel out the loss of Mantua. That cancellation came with the murder of Pietro Gambacorta, an act of violence of which the Count probably disapproved but which brought Pisa within his control. Gambacorta had governed Pisa for over thirty years and, though an idealist, was an experienced politician, well aware of the Visconti system of infiltration. But though alert to all moves from Giangaleazzo he remained singularly blind to the activities of his secretary, Jacopo Appiano. It was not an unnatural blindness. Appiano's father had served his own and had lost his life for his loyalty, and in recognition Pietro Gambacorta had taken Jacopo under his protection on becoming ruler of Pisa in 1366. Master and man had worked in perfect harmony for a generation; Gambacorta was pro-Florentine, but he realized the need for remaining on good terms with Milan and Appiano's predilection for Visconti created a valuable balance in the state.

Or so Gambacorta must have thought and made no protest even when Appiano sent one of his sons to fight with the Milanese in Tuscany. The son was captured by the English mercenaries and, as a singular mark of favour, Giangaleazzo handed over the wretched Giovanni Ricci to be used in exchange. The Signoria redoubled their warnings to Gambacorta, but he ignored them still. He and Appiano were both in their seventies and it was unthinkable that his secretary would be contemplating treachery at the close of a long and loyal career. But the bait of absolute power proved too strong for Appiano. Backed by those Pisans who deplored Gambacorta's pro-Florentine policy, he fell upon his friend and master during the course of a city riot, slew him and all his children, and in the succeeding confusion proclaimed himself Doge of Pisa. His first act was to place himself under the Count's protection and Giangaleazzo promptly sent a Milanese force. 'Never since Judas was there a greater treachery, because messer Piero was the best man in the world... and of a little man had made a great one... and in Florence there was great sorrow partly for a dear friend lost, and partly for an abominable and iniquitous act, but most for the ominous signs of future evil.'[153] Dati did not err in divining presages. Both Florence and the Count were careful to keep within the letter of the Treaty of Genoa, husbanding their resources; yet each knew that the respite was temporary, that the deep-seated antagonisms between despot and republic could be eliminated only by the destruction of one or the other. Each therefore interpreted the Treaty to a point just short of open war, jockeying for position. The Florentines began to develop their Mantuan potential by building the bridge at Borgoforte and the Count responded by ordering the construction of a gigantic dam upon the Mincio which, when drained, would leave Mantua naked and stifling in acres of mud. Dati was fascinated by the scale of the rival operations, the enormous expense and organization necessary to bring about a military advantage; here, upon the great river of Lombardy, was made concrete the

---

[153] Dati, p. 40.

clash of ideologies. It preceded, fittingly, the supreme symbol of the clash, the creation of the dukedom of Milan.

THE GAINING OF THE CROWN

The Florentine Signoria, working still within the accepted frame of city-state politics, had not yet learned to plan sufficiently far ahead. There were not lacking rumours to mark Giangaleazzo's path towards a crown nor did he attempt to deny them, so indifferent now was he to Milanese opinion. Indeed, at the time of the fall of della Scala he openly told the Florentine ambassadors who came to congratulate him on Verona's capture 'that he had the intention to change name and abandon altogether the style of tyrant, but he would not say what name he wished to take, but on other occasions he used to say that he wished to take the name of king of Lombardy'.[154] Such ambitions provided the Florentines with excellent material for attacks upon the overweening arrogance of the despot, but it was not only Milanese propagandists who believed that Italian hopes resided in a crowned Italian in the north. Nearly eighty years before John XXII had sent two envoys from Avignon to enquire into the state of Italy. The envoys were as French as their master, their verdict disinterested. 'Lombardy,' they considered, 'shall never have peace until it has its own king who is not of the barbaric nations and whose reign continues with natural successors.'[155] As the ancient dream of the Empire faded so began to dawn the first pale indications of nationalism. Cola di Rienzi's hope of an Italian federation centred on Rome was six centuries too early; the anointed king alone was the natural expression of nationhood. For many that king was found when, heralded by

[154] 'Minerbetti', XXXIV, A. 1387.
[155] ASL XVIII.

the fall of Padua, the young Count of Virtue stepped on to the Italian stage. Politicians spoke loudly of treachery, urging their peoples to group against the rising tyrant, but some few poets and scholars, some indeed of the same politicians in their role of scholar, pondered a different interpretation. The earliest to voice that new awareness was the Paduan, Francesco Vanozzo. He had been a friend of Petrarch and shared with him and with Dante the passionate desire for a king in Italy. But where they looked to the foreigner, Vanozzo, reflecting the changes of the past half-century, sought an Italian and, on news of the capture of Verona, identified him with the Count of Virtue in a sonnet sequence of considerable beauty.[156] Others swiftly joined Vanozzo's chorus.

Antonio Loschi, the rising young scholar from Vicenza whose career was shattered by the fall of della Scala, prayed that the Count's generals would join together the dismembered parts of Italy and that the new lord in Lombardy would bring peace to the tortured land. An anonymous poet addresses the Count in the name of Rome, calling upon the new Caesar come to cover her nakedness with his own mantle. Antonio Beccaria joins the images of Imperial eagle and Visconti viper together in metaphor as they were to be joined together in reality upon the ducal arms. That eagle, falling from heaven, dwelt first with the Trojans, then with Rome, then Germany, and finding no worthy welcome had turned at last to the house of the Viper

'*as to my most faithful servant*
Last refuge of my endless flight'.

Saviozzo da Siena compares him to Caesar camped on the

---

[156] ASI V, 25.

Rubicon before the final throw.[157] Vanozzo and Loschi, Beccaria and Saviozzo, these were poets not worthy to be placed in the same scale as Dante and Petrarch, yet they were capable, in a few verses of indifferent quality, of voicing that which more nearly touched the desires of Italians than the lofty ideal of the two Tuscans. The coming of the Emperor invariably signified bloodshed; the creation of the king might bring peace. The small court poets were men of froth, but they were the froth of deep moving waters; the Count's attainment of his personal ambition was itself a result of that current which, rising from anarchy, swept down inexorably to monarchy.

The possibility that Charles VI of France might some day be in a position to grant him an hereditary title had formed a constant factor in the Count's French negotiations during 1392. But as the hopes from France grew weaker the Count turned, as a last resort, to that source which theoretically alone could grant such a title, the Emperor. Wenceslaus had cherished a bitter hatred for Giangaleazzo ever since the marriage between Valentina and his half-brother had been unceremoniously broken off. Giangaleazzo had attempted to lay the blame elsewhere, particularly in his challenge to Antonio della Scala, whom he accused of 'rendering vain the negotiations for marriage between us and the princes of Germany'. But Wenceslaus had not been fooled and all contacts between the courts of Prague and Pavia were ended. Nevertheless, the Emperor was in no position to play offended majesty. The son of Charles IV and the grandson of Henry VII, Wenceslaus possessed no trace of the realism of the one or the nobility of the other. He was a drunkard, incapable of working in the morning because of the debauches of the night

---

[157] ASL XVIII.

before; the Empire forgot him, while at home his capricious rule created a host of enemies. His father had sacrificed the majesty of Empire to be Bohemian king; Wenceslaus sacrificed both for personal indulgence. He had never even troubled to go to Italy for a formal coronation until, in 1394, the few supporters he still possessed urged him to secure even that shadowy authority in order to strengthen his domestic position. But, as ever, in order that the king of the Romans could obtain his crown, money was needed for the journey; he made tentative overtures to the League of Bologna offering his services in their fight against the tyrant of Milan in exchange for a subsidy. Venice was unimpressed; money would be forthcoming 'when he came'. Florence, remembering her role of Guelph champion, refused outright. The time was ripe for Giangaleazzo to act, yet, pressing though was Wenceslaus' need for money, there was still the memory of the insult to his house to be expunged. The Count's negotiator would therefore require less the legal qualifications of a Spinelli than those reserves of tact and flattery which he himself could call forth when needed. But again he was able to choose from among his councillors precisely the right kind of man for the specific task.

The ambassador appointed to represent him at the court of Prague was Pietro Filargo, then bishop of Novara, one of the small but influential band of men who had identified themselves with the Count of Virtue when he was still the simple lord of Pavia. Filargo was a Cretan by birth, deeply learned in the Greek which, his mother tongue, became a priceless asset in Italy. Gaining his baccalaureat in Oxford, lecturing in Paris, he had already won a European reputation for a great and multiform culture when he came to Pavia in 1381. The Count appointed him *professore in sacra pagina* to the University and Filargo's subsequent career amply vindicated his decision to join the court of an unknown young man, his successive bishoprics of Piacenza, Vicenza and Novara the first stages of an ascent which led to the Papal throne as Alexander V. The Count had already found him of particular value in negotiating with Florence where his genuine love of scholarship made an immediate contact with Salutati and his fellows, easing the process of otherwise acrimonious negotiations. But though possessed of a keen and subtle intellect, Filargo was also an easy-going, jovial, and worldly man, and it was this aspect of his character which fitted him for the task of smoothing Wenceslaus' ruffled feelings preparatory to extracting the desired concession from him. Florentine ambassadors were at Prague when Filargo arrived in the middle of December 1394, the Signoria having apparently changed their minds on news of his mission. They were no match for the Cretan and the promise of immediate gold. In return for 100,000 florins Wenceslaus promised to create the Count duke of Milan with dominance over twenty-five cities, the style and title to pass to his male descendants. So swiftly and well did Filargo work that he was able to inform Giangaleazzo privately of certain success a few days after arriving in Prague and, anticipating the diploma, the Count issued an edict on January 4th that henceforth the Viper was to be quartered with the Imperial Eagle on all Visconti arms. Formal confirmation came on May 11th and the Count ordered preparations for his coronation in September on a scale fitting for the new glory brought to the Milanese State.

The city of Milan paid immediately and literally for that new glory. Throughout the year taxes increased; in February the price of salt shot up, in March a forced loan of 19,000 florins was imposed on the richer citizens, in July an extraordinary tax of 36,500 florins was levied on the property assessment. In accordance with his custom of granting minor concessions to sweeten heavy increases, Giangaleazzo ceded back to the city the taxes on brothels. Doubtless the cynicism was accidental, but it was an unfortunate coincidence that, in that same month of July, four delegates in the name of Milan should swear fealty to him for the first time as duke. On the 21st of the month the four men, dressed all in white, knelt before him and with a few brief words brought to an end the free city of Milan, the citizens receiving in apparent exchange for their liberty the tax levied on whores.

Shortly after 11 o'clock on the morning of Sunday September 5th 1395, Giangaleazzo left the Castle of Porta Giovia for the last time as simple Count of Virtue. Accompanying him, in formal procession, was a large crowd of ambassadors and court officials, while behind them tumbled, incongruous in the solemnity, a company of players and clowns. The procession moved through the decorated streets towards the square in front of Milan's mother church, the ancient basilica of Sant'Ambrogio. The square was thronged with foreigners and citizens, among the latter being two men, Giorgio Azzannello and Annovello da Imbonate, who in different media and for different reasons were recording this unique moment in Milanese history. Azzannello was a private citizen, come to note all the details for the information of his friend Andreolo Arese, the Count's chancellor, who was absent from Milan. Azzannello's letter,[158] written five days afterwards, showed accurately enough the average Milanese reaction to a ceremony which turned them into subjects. Its theme was an unqualified — an unthinking — pride in the glory which had come to Milan; even the heavy expense was a matter for self-congratulation although the money for the rich robes, the

---

[158] Verga, pp. 124-126.

banquet and the gifts necessary for the honour of the prince came from the pockets of the people. Imbonate was probably one of the illuminators permanently at work in the library of Pavia and he was present in the square in an official capacity. Giangaleazzo intended to present to this same basilica of Sant' Ambrogio an illuminated missal which would combine both a pious thank-offering and a rich record of his day of splendour. In the missal, pride of place was given to the actual moment of coronation, Imbonate devoting a whole page to it with a wealth of gold and crimson. In the borders around the miniature were displayed those arms in which Giangaleazzo took the greatest pride, the coronet of the Count and the serpent of the Visconti guarding those arms of France and Empire which now were also his. But dominating these grand ensigns was the simple device of the dove in rays which Petrarch had created for him long ago and which his daughter now bore in France.

Imbonate's portraits are formal — the figures of Giangaleazzo and the Imperial delegate tower like giants among pigmies — but his eye for movement and detail was sharp and human. A notary sits among the illustrious, dictating the official record to a young amanuensis, a pilgrim pauses to admire, the banners flutter and the trumpets move up in salutation. Between them, he and Azzannello give a vivid citizen's-eye view of the moment when the dukedom of Milan came into being. A huge wooden platform, hung with purple cloth, had been erected in the square and a palisade surrounded it to keep back the pressing mob. A short distance from the platform were two compact groups of veteran soldiers, the one commanded by Paolo Savelli, the other by Ugolotto Biancardo. Upon the platform itself Benasio Cumsinich, the imperial lieutenant, attended by barons of the Empire, awaited the coming of the procession. On his right floated the imperial standard held by a Bohemian knight; on his left the new Milanese standard with the Eagle and Viper was carried by Ottone da Mandello, one of the men who had been with Giangaleazzo on the morning of May 6th 1385. Drums thundered, trumpets shrilled as the procession, dominated by the Count's burly figure dressed in vivid scarlet, entered the square and halted at the foot of the platform. Giangaleazzo ascended the steps alone to stand before Cumsinich. The lieutenant 'welcomed him benignantly' and began to read from a parchment handed to him. 'Wenceslaus Dei gratia Romanorum Rex semper Augustus, et Bohemia Rex' — by the merits of Visconti and the loyalty of his ancestors, with the consent and counsel of the princes, barons, nobles and magnates of the Empire, by Wenceslaus' own motives and not at the instance of Visconti, deigned to transfer the Count of Virtue from servant and official of the Empire to hereditary duke. Visconti knelt and Benasio placed a fur-lined mantle over his shoulders — a garment worth at least 2000 florins, the impressed Azzannello informed his friend — and the ducal biretta upon his head. That done, Benasio cried out with a creditable appearance of spontaneity, 'Happy, happy, happy Lombardy who, having been so long oppressed by the most grave calamities, at last hast gained thy desired duke and son.' Pietro Filargo enlarged upon the Lombard felicity with a more studied oration; he had earned his privileged place upon the dais. Mass heard, the company moved on to the ancient palace of the Commune for a banquet whose splendour was curiously touched with vulgarity. It discharged a dual purpose; it was an inescapable ceremonial to mark the occasion, but the presence or absence of invited guests provided the new duke with a useful indication of his standing in Italy. Dati says that 'all the world was there — save only the Florentines',[159] but he was given the lie by his own compatriot 'Minerbetti' who, as desirous of praising Florentine integrity, nevertheless gave the name of three Florentines who were present, among them Maso degli Albizzi.[160] They were in good company; every major power in Italy had prudently sent representatives — except one. Francesco Gonzaga, still nursing his hatred, had declined to witness the triumph of his late friend and ally. In Mantua the insignia of the Visconti, which had for many years been quartered with that of the Gonzaghi, was torn down. In Padua Francesco Novello temporized; no less steadfast in his hatred of Visconti, declining to come in person, he yet deemed it prudent to send his two young sons. According to Gatari they received signal honours from the new duke during the festivities. He sat beside them, gave them his biretta, informed them that it was his intention to make over to them the tribute which their father paid him. 'I give these to you for I wish you to be my dearest sons.'[161] But either Gatari misinterpreted the duke's famous affability or Giangaleazzo thought better of the offer, for though the two boys kept the biretta their father continued to pay his tribute. The festivities continued in Milan for three days with an indifference to cost before the great crowd dispersed, some to plot the destruction of the new duke, others to reassess their basic thinking.

The granting of the title was the major weapon used by the Electors to depose Wenceslaus five years later, their indictment accusing him of the 'serious and damnable dismemberment of the Empire by the corrupt promotion to ducal rank of the Milanese servant and official of the Holy Empire'.[162] But in

---

[159] Dati, p. 52.

[160] 'Minerbetti', A. 1395.

[161] Gatari, p. 450.

Italy, Dati alone held that 'with deceit and fraud he (Visconti) acquired a dishonest and iniquitous privilege... and this was that from the Emperor he received a blank sheet of parchment with the seal attached, empowering him to write thereon what he wished'.[163] It is not clear from Dati's tumbling style whether his 'carta bianca' is intended as metaphor or a reality in which he personally believed, but in either case he was alone in his opinion. Even 'Minerbetti', avid for weapons against the Count, did not deny Wenceslaus' right, nor the legitimacy of the new dignity. It was only later, when the full significance of the dukedom became apparent, that the Florentines joined the Germans in impugning it. But then it was too late. The inability of the Florentine ambassadors to block Filargo was at the time merely a tactical failure, but once created the title could not be extinguished; the first hereditary dukedom had been created in Italy. Once the principle had been established others were swift to copy, the rulers of Urbino and Savoy, of Mantua, Ferrara and Modena and finally Florence herself following the ruler of Milan.

There were ample indications of the logical end of Italian city-state politics; already, in this last century of the free cities, certain men had begun to forge those principles which Machiavelli polished in the century of the princes. The new men came first from Lombardy, nurtured in the Lombard ethos of the single ruler, but they spread at last to Tuscany and when, finally, they entered Florence the end of republican ideals was in sight for all Italy. And by a supreme irony their most able spokesman was the Chancellor of the Florentine Republic. Those who, like Loschi and Giovanni Conversino, owed their careers to the despot were naturally suspect, but

---

[162] Emerton.

[163] Dati, p. 57.

Salutati's defence of the 'tyrant' was wrung unwilling from him. Many had sought to define the tyrant, no longer content with the assumption of the virtuous that the single ruler must at all times and under all circumstances be an evil thing. Salutati's apologia was begun as a by-product of propaganda warfare and developed into a major study. Attacked by Loschi on behalf of the new duke, he was forced to delve deeper into the nature of political authority, to discover just what it was that he was defending. Long after the urgent need of war had passed, the struggle continued in the rarefied atmosphere of humanist debate. The discovery of Cicero had opened the first true vision into the empire of the Caesars, and from there the long controversy swept down to engulf the sacred Florentine Dante who had thrust the patriots Brutus and Cassius into the very mouth of Lucifer whilst placing Caesar in Limbo. 'Are we to believe that Dante, the most learned man of his age, did not know in what manner Caesar had achieved dominion — that he did not know of the rape of liberty, the abject fear of the people when Mark Anthony placed the crown upon Caesar's head.'[164] Dante could not be wrong, therefore Caesar must be justified, and if Caesar be justified then so also must the modern 'tyrant'.

So, inexorably, Salutati was driven to defend, if only by implication, the first duke of Milan. Florence was free and would remain so for another century but, even as the shadow of the future was thrown by the new duke in the north, her principal republican was preparing the ground for the Medici.

The years had dealt kindly with Giangaleazzo. It is from this period, in his mid-forties, that his surviving portraits date. They show a stout man whose heavy face under the new ducal biretta appeared more that of a prosperous merchant than a

---

[164] Baron, p. 39.

prince, an appearance which probably did not belie the mind behind it, for the new duke showed little interest in the pomp of power. When necessary he could organize a public festival in keeping with his honour, but such displays lacked any personal touch and were mere rituals marked, indeed, by that curious lack of taste which seemed inherent in the Visconti. The splendour of his banquets depended upon the vast quantities of food and ostentatious richness of presents with little care expended upon ancillary entertainment. Something of the intellectualism of the young lord of Pavia seems to have become lost in the middle-aged duke of Milan, suppressed by or diverted to the care of government. Giangaleazzo had taken only that of the new culture which would serve his political ends; soldiers and lawyers of merit could count upon lucrative employment with him, but painters and poets were rarities at his court. In maturity he was seen to share more of the better qualities of Bernabò than of his father, for in his private life his conservatism bordered on the old-fashioned. Politically he was a daring innovator, going always just one step further than his enemies were prepared to go, exploiting the blind parochial jealousies of the city-states in a system which antedated Machiavelli's by a century. But even while he moved politically in the Renaissance he was accepting afresh concepts which were already being questioned. The fact that he relied openly and explicitly upon the predictions of astrologers was perhaps surprising only in one of his otherwise clear intellect, for the practice of the art, having lain dormant for centuries, was again powerful in influence throughout Italy. Governments as a matter of course turned to the astrologer to determine the propitious moment for inaugurating policy; even the habitually sceptical Florentines practised it, once nearly losing a vital battle in consequence. The humanists attacked the practice but with little effect. Petrarch loathed them; Pico della Mirandola took the trouble to check their weather forecasts and found that three-quarters were inaccurate; Guicciardini ironically remarked upon that which everyone must have observed: 'How happy are the astrologers who are believed if they tell one truth to a hundred lies while other people lose all credit if they tell one lie to a hundred truths.'[165] Horoscopes continued to be cast at the birth of children of great families and the astrologer with his decorative charts and tables appeared at every important function. Giangaleazzo habitually employed two; one of them, Gusperto da Maltraversi, was his personal physician and a man of considerable skill in his legitimate profession, but he enjoyed more fame practising his occult works. It is difficult to see how Giangaleazzo could reconcile his own deeply experienced knowledge of the measures which had to be taken for a particular political conclusion and the possibly contradictory advice of his non-political astrologer. Presumably, if Maltraversi was misguided enough to give a too divergent opinion, his own common sense would override. Certainly he was never the slave of his astrologers and their function seems for the most part to have been limited to choosing dates for comparatively unimportant social events or confirming the dates he had himself chosen for important political moves. But his employment of them at all was a contradiction in the character of a man 'who was wont to say that in the affairs of the world there was nothing like order'. An even more curious manifestation of his personality was the considerable trouble he took to resurrect the mythical county of Angera as appanage for his eldest son. The fable which sought to prove that the Visconti were the descendants of the Counts of Angera, who were themselves descendants of the

---

[165] Burckhardt, p. 517.

family of Aeneas, had long been in deserved obscurity. In the dukedom of Milan there were a score of ancient and honourable cities which could have provided a fitting title for Giangaleazzo's son, yet the duke chose to erect this demonstrably absurd tale of Trojan descent into a formal title. The choice was made at the very time when the Italian republics were beginning to examine their origins, rejecting at last those myths which had been hitherto accepted without question. In Lombardy, the Count of Angera reappeared to make a mockery of the newfound love of antiquity. Giangaleazzo may have had little interest in the outward pomp of power, but he shared in full the Visconti need to be permanently demonstrating legality of tenure. The whole world knew that the new dukedom of Milan was founded not on blood or steel but upon gold, but though the corruptibility of the Emperor was one of the facts of life it did not thereby became more palatable for those who benefited from it. The title of Count of Angera gave a patina to the too-bright newness of the ducal crown, even though its origins were questionable to the most mildly sceptical eye. Yet, side by side with his unquestioning acceptance of astrologers and fable-merchants went a coolness towards religion which seemed to amount to scepticism. It was natural that he should share in the prevailing anti-clericalism, but some believed that he went beyond the bounds of the permissible. 'He had little faith in Christ and little believed and sought all that he could to overturn the Christian faith'[166] was 'Minerbetti's' charge. Froissart was convinced that the appalling disaster of Nicopolis arose from his apostasy, reporting as proof an alleged conversation between Bajacet and the king of Babylon in which the former claimed that he had been closely informed of

---

[166] 'Minerbetti'.

French intentions by Visconti. 'What Bajacet told the king of Babylon respecting this information he had received from the lord of Milan must surprise everyone. It was supposed that he was baptized and regenerated in our Faith and yet he sought the friendship and alliance of an infidel king, an enemy of our religion.'[167] 'Minerbetti' was an avowed enemy of the duke's and Froissart's promise to substantiate his astounding accusation is later discharged only with a feeble explanation that the supposed alliance 'was to spite the king of France'. The Florentine and the Frenchman nevertheless seem to have touched upon a basic truth regarding Giangaleazzo. He was probably indifferent, rather than hostile, to religion. In moments of national triumph or disaster he invariably ordained religious processions of thanksgiving or intercession, but the one helped to bruit his fame abroad, the other to weld his people together. He allowed his subjects to follow which pope they chose, for neutrality was a matter of political profit to him; he himself never did declare which, if either, pope he held to be the true one even after such declaration could have done him no harm. More telling than the gossip of chroniclers or his own political manipulations was the manner of his death. Bernabò, the brutal enemy of the Church, died a contrite Christian; Giangaleazzo spent his last hours making detailed arrangements for the transference of his State to his heir.

Giangaleazzo's new status as duke was swiftly made apparent in Milan. Five months after the coronation, the revision of the statutes which was begun in 1385 was finally completed. The new laws took from the hands of the populace the power of electing its officers, for the *podestà*, the last link with the republican past, together with the Twelve of Provisions, became an appointment of the duke's. Giangaleazzo approved

---

[167] Froissart, LXXIV, p. 604.

the revision and on January 13th 1396 the new laws were published, to the sound of bells and trumpets, in the presence of the *podestà*, his officers, and all those inhabitants of Milan, no longer citizens but subjects, who could crowd into the narrow confines of the Broletto piazza. The revision of the statutes had commenced ten years before Wenceslaus granted his diploma of dukedom and yet the new laws exactly framed the new status of Milan. Even the autocratic Bernabò had never contemplated such a drastic break with the past, but from the very earliest days Giangaleazzo must have been so certain of eventual success that he anticipated the basic changes wrought by his coronation. So clearly did he envisage the ramifications of the dukedom which succeeded 1000 years of republican history that the statutes he approved lasted virtually without change into the eighteenth century, 400 years beyond the climacteric century.

Wenceslaus had alienated many both in Italy and Germany by his creation of a dukedom but, as though to bind at least one person more firmly to himself, he followed the creation with yet more grandiloquent titles. Giangaleazzo even obtained from him the long-desired style of duke of Lombardy, but wisely he never adopted the title, even though it was limited to those places which he held as duke of Milan. Such an aggrandizement would have been a standing challenge to the states still remaining independent in Lombardy, and he preferred the reality to an appearance which would have entailed endless profitless quarrels. He was probably never invested with the dignity, but nevertheless successive Emperors confirmed it first upon his eldest son and then upon the Sforza. He obtained a more personal satisfaction than either the mythical County of Angera or dukedom of Lombardy could give with the erection of his own beloved city of Pavia into a County for his son. The Pavese themselves were jubilant, for it restored something of the prestige they had lost when their city was incorporated into the State, yielding precedence, as did all others, to Milan. But for those statesmen with longer sight it argued a retrograde step, a return to that fragmentation of the State which was an incentive to civil discord. It was no impulsive move of Giangaleazzo's, for his later will, while recognizing Giovanni Maria as heir to the dukedom, specifically assigned the County of Pavia to Fillipo Maria. It would seem that the duke already saw in his elder son those qualities which, a decade later, assumed Neronic proportions. Both his legitimate children were disappointments and there was small wonder that he preferred his illegitimate son by Agnese Mantegazza even to the extent of legitimizing him and making him lord of Pisa in his will. Throughout his career the duke had been haunted by the problem of an heir and it was peculiarly ironical that he, of all the Visconti, should have no adult sons to share the burden of power and be trained into the inheritance. Perforce he accepted the situation and, while making provision to ensure some limitation upon Giovanni Maria, he began to groom the boy for his future role. The family continued to live in Pavia, but a household was established for the heir in Milan and he began to be associated with his father in public ceremonials.

The problem of controlling the Milanese State from close quarters forced the Count to spend even less time in Pavia. The city of his childhood was, and would remain, his true home but, as others had found before him, it was not possible to ignore the currents set up by the capital city. As affairs of state drew him back ever more frequently to Milan so the cramped, comfortless conditions of his castle at Porta Giovia became intolerable. Giovia was one of the six main gates of the city which, massively built, had evolved into small fortresses over the centuries. Bernabò had developed that of Porta Romana as his own seat and in self-defence his brother had commenced to enlarge Giovia. But Galeazzo had never intended it to be other than a military garrison which would protect his rights over his half of Milan while he was absent in Pavia. It proved inadequate to house a permanent court. In 1392, therefore, the Count had ordered the Twelve of Provisions to develop Porta Vercellina to house the garrison, and when work was completed there and the garrison transferred, the builders turned their attention to Giovia. Galeazzo had developed his castle within the walls but now it began to push its way out of the northern perimeter, destroying the city's symmetry, becoming, like its lord, independent of Milan.

The Count's edict ensured that the fabled castle of Pavia would remain only a country seat and Pavia itself a minor city within the shadow of Milan. But while the masons were still busy upon Porta Giovia, erecting the fortress of the duke of Milan, just outside Pavia other workers were engaged upon a monument to the Visconti which became Pavia's greatest glory. The Certosa of Pavia came into being as a result of a vow made by Caterina in 1390. Presumably it was made during the course of a difficult pregnancy, for it was 'in form of testament' and with the added request that, should she die in childbed, her husband would undertake its honouring.[168] The child, if any, must have been stillborn for there was no record of baptism, Caterina herself recovered and the matter remained undecided. But although it had been his wife's vow, it fitted well enough with Giangaleazzo's own desire 'to have a castle for his habitation, a garden for his disport and a chapel for his

---

[168] Corio, III, 7.

devotion'[169] all within the vicinity of his favoured city. Six years passed between the first suggestion and the beginning of work, six years during which every economic fibre of Milan was strained to its utmost. Pietro Filargo pressed his master many times on the matter and, in December 1393, Giangaleazzo took the first definite steps with the granting of essential lands and revenues. By then the concept had become considerably grander than the simple monastery of Carthusians with twelve brothers which Caterina had envisaged for, writing on other matters to the Sienese in 1394, Giangaleazzo informed them in passing that he intended to build a charterhouse 'non erit in orbe simile'. In that same year he had set in motion the process of obtaining the diploma from Wenceslaus and it probably seemed fitting to him that the foundations of the Visconti monument should be laid in the year which would witness the Visconti apotheosis.

The Certosa of Pavia, like the cathedral of Milan, was the product, not of an architect, but of a committee, enjoying the considerable advantage of having a single, impatient mind behind that committee. Giangaleazzo was creating a physical witness to the glory of his family, not of his city, and did not hesitate to rob the cathedral of able workers when required. He had an extremely able man already working on the Castle of Pavia in the person of Bernardo da Venezia. Bernardo had taken part in the controversy over the stability of the cathedral's foundations for, under the simple title of 'engineer' in which he figures in the account books, he practised several arts with skill — architect, woodcarver, sculptor, painter, turning his hand to each with equal facility. Therefore when Giangaleazzo required a 'generalis inzignierius' for the work at Pavia it was Bernardo who was appointed and prepared the

---

[169] Beltrami, p. 18.

ground. The problems of logistics which faced him were considerable for, where the cathedral was rising in the centre of a populous city, it was planned to build the Certosa some five miles from Pavia in open country. Shelter and provisions for over 300 workers had to be arranged, together with transport for the thousands of tons of materials required. He was helped in the latter by the great water-road of the Naviglio which connected Milan to Pavia, and a secondary canal was constructed to connect it to the site. In July 1395 work was begun, clearing the area of its thick woods, and by August trenches for the foundations were being excavated. It was then that Bernardo called in his colleagues from Milan for a preliminary discussion. The enormous cathedral was attracting architects from all over Europe and Pavia gained by it, for there was considerable interchange between the two sites. Ultimately almost all the master craftsmen at work on the cathedral put in some time on the Certosa, occasioning frequent complaints from the cathedral committee to the Duke. They were particularly annoyed with Giacomo da Campione who had been working on the cathedral since its foundation but who, as soon as work began on the Certosa, spent less and less time in Milan. The committee received little encouragement from the duke and thereafter Giacomo devoted himself almost exclusively to the Certosa. It would indeed have been unthinkable for any great work of Lombard architecture to proceed without the presence of a man from Campione. This or that great lord might decree the erection of a stupendous building and take the historical credit for it, but the work was done by the masons of Campione. They had laboured for a hundred years under the Visconti, transforming Milan, and now that Giangaleazzo had decided to follow the lead of his ancestors and perpetuate his glory in stone, it was inevitable that the Campionese should make their way to Pavia. It was into the hands of Giacomo da Campione therefore that the day-to-day work on the Certosa fell.

On the morning of the 27th of August the duke, accompanied by his legitimate and illegitimate sons, rode from Pavia for the ceremony of the foundation; Caterina, who could justly have claimed to be the founder of the Certosa, was again not present at a major ceremony. Domenico da Campione had prepared four stones for the act of foundation and they were laid one after the other, the duke first laying his, followed by Giovanni Maria, then by the illegitimate Gabriele Maria, and finally Francesco Barbavara laid the fourth stone in the name of the infant Fillipo Maria. It was a moment of high personal triumph for Giangaleazzo, the foundation of the princely building setting a seal on his status as prince.[170] Yet he did not stay for the elaborate celebrations which followed; presumably affairs of state were too pressing to allow even a few hours' absence. For, as though to underline the fact that, duke or no, he yet retained power only by his own exertions, three weeks

---

[170] The later history of the Certosa was a model of the history of the Milanese State. Giangaleazzo's express desire that he should be buried there was only carried out seventy-two years after his death, and then at the instruction of the Sforza. Another generation passed before his request that his first wife Isabella should be buried with him was honoured, and this was done by the second power to claim Milan as a descendant of the Visconti, Louis XII of France. Thereafter, as the transalpine nations sought their fortune in Italy so the Certosa suffered. And when at length the foreigner was driven from Italy and the building passed into national care, the first act was to disturb the bones of the founder and his wife, in casual curiosity, to find that nothing remained of the treasures buried with them except a broken sword, a spur, fragments of a prayer book and a crude earthenware vessel with the sign of the Viper upon it.

after the ceremony his inveterate enemy Florence signed an alliance with his kinsman and ally, Charles VI of France, and his daughter Valentina was driven in ignominy from Paris. The Certosa remained unfinished while he fought for the reality of power. The great monument to the Visconti was destined to be completed by the usurping Sforza who enjoyed the fruits of his work.

ISABELLA AND VALENTINA

The statecraft which, for fifteen years, had guided the Count of Virtue through the shoals of Italian politics proved useless in France, mocking his pretensions to European status, so that he was defeated at his own preferred game by a twenty-five-year-old woman who had only recently made her debut into politics. There was, however, no precedent to guide him in a situation of which the chief compounds were madness and lust, the madness squalid, the lust itself coldly directed towards political ends. But it was a situation which precisely suited Isabella of Bavaria.

The marriage between Charles VI and Isabella took place in July 1385. The fact that Isabella was the granddaughter of Bernabò was quite incidental to French policy, ominous though it was for Giangaleazzo. Isabella, indeed, became queen of France with a degree of casualness which must have been humiliating to her imperious nature. French policy required an alliance with any German house to counteract the threat from England; Charles agreed that the search for a wife might as well be extended to include the Bavarian house of Wittelsbach, but it was the duke of Burgundy, primarily interested in protecting his own growing territories, who finally engineered the marriage. Isabella was fifteen years of age when she became queen of France, and in the first seven years of her reign she occupied herself exclusively with those frivolous pleasures of the Valois court which passed swiftly into debauchery. In this she was at first merely following the example set by her husband and his brother, romantic young men suddenly freed from the restraints of regency. Nevertheless, dedicated to pleasure though he was, Charles's innate sense of duty placed a rein upon the court's more extreme activities until the summer of 1392 when he suffered the onset of his malady. Thereafter, the king of France was, for all practical purposes, a madman and in the resultant scramble for power Isabella fought her way to the top, free now to indulge both her insatiable eroticism and her equally insatiable desire for revenge, using the one to advance the other.

There was little of the Visconti or even of the Italian in Isabella — save perhaps for her steady and passionate desire for vengeance on the man who had overthrown her grandfather, disinheriting the Wittelsbach. Intellectually, she could not compare with her cousin Valentina. Her grasp of French was never complete and she spoke with a thick and gutteral accent to the end of her days. Her preferred reading was the Bavarian epics which exalted the history of her family; her more innocent pleasures the tending of birds and flowers and the running of a model farm. Pride in her family took precedence over all her affections. The Wittelsbach were at least as old as the Valois but the family policy of dividing the inheritance had resulted in a diversity and a poverty, and Isabella saw her mission as the reestablishment of the family in all its antique glory. Giangaleazzo had robbed them and he must therefore be made to repay. Her father, Stephen of Bavaria, had shown a regrettable lack of a sense of mission in 1390 when, enlisted by the Florentines against the Count of Virtue, he had betrayed his allies and his family by accepting a bribe from the usurper. But Isabella more than compensated for her feckless father and in her ambitions she was ably supported by the brother she adored. Lewis of Bavaria, *condottiere* by profession and intriguer by aptitude, came to France in 1392 to share in his sister's fortune, plunging his hand in his turn into the coffers of France, amassing his own fortune as a by-product of the crusade to bring about the downfall of the lord of Milan.

In the first years of her reign Isabella had been too young, and French hopes of Milanese alliance too strong, to allow of any open move against Giangaleazzo. Charles dreamed still of the glory of deposing the Roman pope; Louis of Orléans still hoped to establish himself in an Italian kingdom; the house of Anjou continued to need an Italian ally for their eternal designs upon Naples — the support of the lord of Milan for all these projects was vital until the French acquisition of Genoa in 1395. Even the duke of Burgundy, to whom Isabella looked as protector and ally, had received many little aids and loans from the Count of Virtue. Additionally, the daughter of her enemy was in high favour at court and his son-in-law was the beloved brother of the king; before Isabella could move both would have to be eliminated. But while she waited she could make discreet arrangements with the Italian enemies of her enemy, the Florentines. It was they indeed who made the first move. Fillipo Corsini, having failed to create a Florentine alliance with Charles in 1386, nevertheless divined the attitude of the queen and told his government on his return and from thenceforward Florentine ambassadors played steady court to Isabella. Shrewdly, the Signoria seized upon that aspect of her character which was as developed as her hatred for Visconti — her active pride in the Wittelsbach. Fillipo Cavvicuili was charged to obtain private audience with her, ask her to use her influence to obtain Charles's alliance and, if she refused, to say that Florence would be forced to accept the friendship of Wenceslaus, open enemy of the Wittelsbach. Isabella needed no such threat but there was nothing she could do at that moment; Paris was even then awaiting the arrival of Valentina and Milanese stock stood high. Nevertheless, she bore the mission in mind and the malady which struck Charles opened the path to her.

Louis of Orléans naturally found a place on the council of regency which took charge during the king's 'absences' as Charles's periodic fits were diplomatically called. Louis still supported his father-in-law, but as his hopes of an Italian kingdom receded, to be replaced by increased power in France, his championship became rather less spirited. Nevertheless, all his policies were in opposition to Isabella's; he either had to be won over to her or eliminated. Exactly when he and Isabella became lovers is open to doubt; his passiveness during the attack on Valentina argues that, at least by 1396, Isabella exercised control over him even though she was leagued with his enemy's wife, the duchess of Burgundy, to destroy his own wife. For the elimination of Valentina, Giangaleazzo's most constant friend at court, was Isabella's penultimate motive.

The attack on Valentina was essentially feminine, a skilled campaign of whispers and rumours. Sorcery was to be the charge — and a suspicion of something graver. It was whispered that her father had arranged her marriage with a view to her eventually occupying the throne itself. 'Adieu, my daughter, I shall not see you again until you are queen of France,'[171] he was supposed to have said to her when she left Pavia. The rumours were vague, contradictory in detail, yet agreeing in their main charge; that the madness of the king

---

[171] Monstrelet, Lib. I, XXXIX.

coincided with her presence because she used poison or witchcraft. 'Their suspicions were founded on this — that in Lombardy, which was the country of the duchess, they make use of witchcraft and poisons more than in any other land.'[172] The rumours found their way to Milan and Giangaleazzo sent an embassy to investigate the matter and deny it to the king, a champion offering single combat to whosoever should seek to maintain it. But the rumours continued without abate, spreading, as they were intended to, outside the court. Charles was immensely popular with the mob; Valentina, beloved though she was by intimates, was an Italian, the very emblem of her house an indication of its nature. Through the spring of 1396 the rumours ran wild in Paris and the mob marched upon her residence, crying out for her punishment; in April the young duchess bent to the storm and went into exile. She never returned. The informed were perfectly well aware that the charges were a fabrication. 'For my part I reject entirely the vulgar accusations of sorcery brought against her by extravagant people. That this generous duchess had committed such a great crime no person ever had the slightest proof and no one had the right to defame her on the subject.' So maintained the chronicler of St Denis from first-hand knowledge of the persons involved.[173] Nevertheless, Valentina remained in exile for the rest of her life. She retained the affections of all those who had ever been her allies and enjoyed all the privileges of her high rank — save for the vital privilege of being present at court. Yet Isabella did not immediately trust Louis and during the negotiations which were immediately set in train between herself and the Florentine ambassadors Louis was carefully excluded. The treaty of alliance was arranged

---

[172] *Religieux de Saint-Denis*, T. II, p. 91.
[173] Ibid., p. 29.

largely between Buonaccorso Pitti and Isabella herself, who ensured that the document went to Charles for signature during one of his bouts of madness. On September 29th 1396 the Florentine hope was translated into fact and the Tuscan Republic and the French monarchy were as one against the Milanese tyrant. In December Pitti was authorized to recruit troops in France for the expedition designed to overthrow the duke of Milan.

VIII: SPREAD OF THE VIPER

THE MANTUAN WAR

'So we see again how your pretended constancy and Roman fortitude are used to defend a mockery of liberty which you twist to suit your needs. Beautiful liberty is yours in whose name you oppress your immediate neighbours under a yoke of intolerable servitude! Splendid new Romans who do not hesitate to implore the help of the French, suggesting to them that at last the time has come to dominate Italy hand in hand with the Papacy! And you think that only by Florentine hands can peace be made throughout the peninsula, tumults suppressed, the affairs of Italy composed into a tranquillity it has never before known. Fools! Ever you act against your own and Italy's true good in opposing the duke of Milan, against good council, against peace, against your country's state and rest.'[174]

The salvo which Antonio Loschi fired off at the opening of the third clash between the duke and Florence marked both the dismissal of Milanese hopes for a French alliance and the explicit claiming of the role of Italian champion against the foreigner. Giangaleazzo had claimed that role after the defeat of the Armagnacs, only to discard it during Spinelli's lengthy negotiations, but from henceforth, as Isabella drove the wedge between himself and France ever further, it was the single consistent note of Milanese propaganda. In the hands of Loschi and his colleagues the political defeat in France was skilfully turned into a potent appeal to nationalism in Italy. No

---

[174] Valeri, p. 262.

matter that Giangaleazzo had also wooed the French; it was Florence yet again who had summoned them. No matter that Loschi himself had urged Wenceslaus to enter Italy as Messiah; it was Florence who, claiming to be the true heir of the Roman republic, was opening the gates of Italy to the northern barbarians. Salutati's reply has all the weakness of the *tu quoque*. 'That which we defend is truly liberty and that which you call our tyranny is only the curb of necessity without which liberty itself becomes corrupt.' The Florentine Chancellor now was speaking less to Italians than to Florentines, stirring in them their ever-present hatred of the signore, spurring them on to another costly, bloody struggle. 'Liberty is properly obedient to the laws while tyranny is obedient to one single man who governs everything according to his caprices. Tyranny equals fear; fear of the signore, of his suspicions, of his fickle motives, of his humours... This is the destiny that awaits every people that Giangaleazzo succeeds in conquering. Therefore in the same act that we Florentines defend that precious thing which is our liberty, at the same time we defend the common cause of Italian liberty which, if we are conquered, shall become irremediably servant to him.'[175]

But France failed Florence even as she had failed Visconti. Pitti was still engaged in organizing the expedition when news came to Paris, on the Christmas Eve of 1396, of the battle of Nicopolis. The French dead lay in their thousands before the Muslim spears, victims of that terrifying French assurance which had already resulted in Crécy, Poitiers and Alessandria and now added the name of Nicopolis, the battle which was to have held and smashed the Saracen but instead plunged all France in mourning. Under the pressing need to raise the enormous ransoms for the few remaining prisoners, the

---

[175] Ibid.

French court totally ignored the Lombard expedition and Florence was again alone with her uncertain allies, having bartered her reputation for nothing. Still there was formal peace between the Republic and the duke, but while Pitti and Spinelli and Albizzi were feeling their way through the maze of the French court, in Italy the political manoeuvres again became the movements of armed men. 'Minerbetti' and his fellow chroniclers spoke of three separate wars, but Bruni and Dati, surveying the whole field many years later, saw those three wars as but one, a twelve-year conflict opening with the war of 1390 and closing only with Giangaleazzo's death. Nevertheless Florentines though they were they did not fall into the obvious error of laying the blame exclusively on Visconti for the open war which succeeded the false peace. 'Both sides gathered men at arms and each had suspicion that the other would not be found wanting. But finally it would perhaps be difficult to find proof of who first broke the peace.'[176] Giangaleazzo's commitments in Tuscany had increased, for Pisa was now added to that number of allies who must needs be encouraged and protected and supplied. Yet still there was that formal 'peace' to be honoured and the campaign in Tuscany was conducted by his favoured method of remote control. Alberico Barbiano, the Italian *condottiere* who had done more than any other to raise the prestige of Italian arms, was unofficially engaged to ravage the Florentine borders, but the activities in Tuscany were comparative skirmishes, pin-pricks which enraged more than they wounded. It was in Lombardy that Giangaleazzo's greatest danger lay — specifically in Mantua where armed enemies were gathering, pouring across the bridge at Borgoforte, awaiting only the official declaration of war to launch themselves at the heart of Milan. The great

---

[176] Dati, p. 41.

dam which was to have eliminated Mantua had proved too complex an operation and a military operation alone could remove the military danger. It was at Mantua that, without warning, Visconti struck in March 1397.

The peculiar physical advantages enjoyed by the marshland city demanded military preparations more approximating to naval warfare than the land warfare in which Milan excelled, and it was now that Pavia came into its own. The Pavese understood the handling of river craft better as instruments of trade than of war, but under pressure of need the shipyards launched a high proportion of the 300 vessels assembled for the attack upon Mantua. The armada was placed under the control of dal Verme whose prime object was the destruction of the bridge at Borgoforte. But dal Verme was a soldier and not a sailor and the potentialities of the fleet were wasted in a supporting role. The defenders held the bridge for many days until a change in the wind enabled dal Verme to employ a more certain weapon than the ships inexpertly handled by landsmen. Fire ships were hastily prepared and sent down against the target. A thousand men perished on the bridge by fire or by drowning and Francesco Gonzaga, who had been personally leading the defenders, was forced to retreat to Mantua. There he was trapped. To the east a group from Verona under Biancardo assailed the fortress on the Mincio, while in the south dal Verme assembled a pontoon bridge across the Po and marched into the Mantuan *serraglio*, the rich plain which lay between Mincio and Po, and ravaged up to the very gates of Mantua. The city's natural defences had proved useless and by August the bridgehead into Lombardy was almost gone.

The Florentines were well aware that the collapse of Mantua would reduce them yet again to the defensive. Carlo Malatesta, relative and one-time guardian of the young Gonzaga, was detached from Tuscany with 3000 horse and sent hastening to Lombardy. But the Florentines were a land power, unprepared for the peculiar problems which the relief of Mantua presented; the 3000 horse were useless until the Po was crossed and the nearest route across the Po was in the hands of dal Verme. Naval assistance was needed and the only sea power capable of providing that assistance with the necessary speed was Venice, who hitherto had declined to take an active part. Francesco Carrara went in person to the Serenissima 'and showed them that, if the lord of Mantua were overcome, in process of time both he and the lord of Ferrara too would be destroyed and if this should happen it would turn to their harm, for without fail the duke of Milan would attack them; and therefore he urged the Signoria to open their eyes and give aid to the lord of Mantua, who was his dear friend.'[177] Carrara's logic was unassailable. The fall of Mantua would indeed start a chain reaction across Lombardy and ultimately the Milanese frontier would again touch the Venetian as it had touched a decade before. Then the lord of Milan had been the young Count of Virtue, desirous of pleasing the formidable maritime republic; but the duke of Milan — there was no knowing that in his new confidence he might attempt the unthinkable and actually violate Venetian territory. The Serenissima agreed to send help but still they refused a formal commitment, the war vessels they contributed being hired out as though it were a commercial undertaking. But they were manned by veteran Venetian seamen, commanded by Francesco Bembo. News of open Venetian action acted as a tonic to dispirited hopes. Along the great river road of the Po the riverine cities stirred themselves to help Mantua and so protect themselves,

---

[177] Gatari, p. 455.

contributing men and ships. Ambassadors of Florence, Venice, Bologna, Ferrara, Padua and Lucca met in Bologna and decided to give the greatest possible aid in concert, the land forces to be under the command of Carlo Malatesta. In mid-August a massive army gathered near Ferrara and commenced moving eastward, while accompanying them the armada of the League sailed slowly on the Po. And somewhere near the confluence of Mincio and Po the ships met the Milanese fleet.

dal Verme failed to grasp the nature of the element in which he was expected to fight, but it was a blindness which he shared with the Lombard and Florentine chroniclers. Friends and enemies alike saw the fleets as little more than elaborate ferries designed to neutralize an irritating natural barrier. Sercambi alone was intrigued by the curious nature of a naval battle fought over 100 miles from the sea.[178] As far as he was concerned the entire operation was a Venetian campaign from start to finish. The Venetian craft were not river vessels hastily adapted but war galleys of the kind which were sweeping the Mediterranean clean of rivals, fast, manoeuvrable professionals that tore into the lumbering Milanese amateurs with a deadly precision. Corio claimed that the Milanese craft were not only undermanned but their crews were 'oppressed by the new climate', possibly a reference to the unhealthy marshland environment, a burden to men accustomed to the clean heat of the central plain.[179] Nevertheless they fought well, the battle continuing throughout afternoon and evening, and even when night fell they had no respite for the Venetians illuminated ship and followed up their advantage. By dawn the Milanese fleet was routed, dal Verme was still in the *serraglio* on the northern bank of the river and in order to avoid being marooned he

---

[178] Sercambi, CCCCXCV.
[179] Corio, IV, 1.

hurriedly retired across the pontoon bridge while it was still intact. His retreat became a rout, a desperate scurry to get the more valuable materials and men across the bridge before the victorious fleet could swoop down upon it, but 6000 men were left behind together with 100 of the new bombards, and equipment to the value of 200,000 florins. It was a Venetian triumph; the captains of the galleys were knighted by Gonzaga and the captured Milanese standards, the proud new standards with the Viper and the Eagle, were sent to Venice to be ritually dragged through the canals. In Florence hopes ran high, as much from the triumph of bringing the Venetians into the open as at the open defeat of the duke. 'Now we have brought the Venetians to what we wish because thus manifestly… they have shamed the arms of the duke of Milan.'[180] But Florentine self-congratulation was previous.

In one swift battle Giangaleazzo had lost the advantage of all the war, dissipated the savings of five years. The expenses of the previous war with Florence and the expenses of his coronation had drained the surplus of income and to finance the attack on Mantua — to build the ships and hire the mercenaries — taxes had been heavily increased throughout the state. And as taxes grew higher resistance to paying increased and some of the evils of the older system returned. 'Many poor families were reduced to extremity and it was a cruel thing to see the extortion of his ministers.'[181] Now, in September, the enormous sacrifices of his subjects were made a mockery; now, not only were they impoverished and tormented by the never ceasing demands of the collectors, but daily they were expecting an enemy army to erupt into the state and exact vengeance. 'And there was sorrow and terror without

---

[180] Sercambi, CCCCXCVI.
[181] Corio, IV, 1, p. 409.

measure and never before or since had the Count greater fear for his state.'[182] The confusion entered even the quiet court of the duke. He, the cold and calculating man who used all men as his instruments, was himself used during the fear-stricken days of early autumn. Or so it would seem when the news broke that Pasquino Capelli, his chancellor and his father's chancellor before him, Pasquino, the aged Cremonese 'who knew all the secrets of the Count', who had worked with and for him since the days of Pavia, had died an atrocious death at his master's hand. The castle of Pavia kept its secrets for long and the manner and reason for his death were garbled as they sped from mouth to mouth, but they were linked with dal Verme's sudden and disastrous retreat from Mantua. It was said that the commander had received a letter ordering him to report to Pavia shortly before the naval clash; that he had done so, only to find on his arrival that it was a ruse and, hastening back to Mantua, was too late to stay the rout. Capelli alone had the power to issue such a letter and, traced, he suffered the penalty. Some said that he was sewn up, naked and living, in the still warm belly of an ox; others, and this the more probable, that he had gone to the 'long residence', the dungeon at the foot of the eastern tower in whose upper room he had signed so many of his florid letters. Later, Gonzaga confessed to having forged the letter and, though Giangaleazzo was distrait with grief, it was then too late, the old man having expired of his privations. Or so the gossips said, to be duly recorded by Corio and the Annalist.[183] But dal Verme's retreat needed no forged letter to hasten it. Capelli fell as the result of a palace revolution, a disquieting enough event in those tense days when solidarity was being tested to the utmost. Shortly

---

[182] Dati, p. 48.
[183] Corio, IV, 1, p. 15; Annales Mediolanenses CLX, col. 81.

afterwards his official position was taken over by Francesco Barbavara, the plebeian who had worked his way up from the lowest levels of society through Giangaleazzo's policy of encouraging merit whatever its origins. Barbavara now was second only to the duke's family in rank as well as power, for Giangaleazzo had conferred lands and titles upon him. But as Barbavara broke through the ranks of palace servants so another, younger man began to make his presence known, the ambitious young Antonio Loschi whose name was appearing ever more frequently in the spirited exchanges between Milan and Florence. Loschi had held a minor position in the court of Antonio della Scala and, after his fall, migrated like so many others to the court of Giangaleazzo. His position there was at first obscure, one of the many minor clerks in the Chancery, but his command of Latin brought him more and more into the foreground. Some twenty years Salutati's junior, he had nevertheless studied with the Florentine scholar under the great Greek teacher Manuel Chrysoloras and, until the outbreak of the Mantuan war, Salutati maintained a friendly if cool correspondence with him, urging him to complete a translation of Homer, reproving him for solecisms of speech, acting in general as a father towards a brilliant but morally dubious son. It may have been a coincidence that Giangaleazzo, recognizing the value of his Ciceronian scholarship, should have promoted him to be the mouthpiece of Milan after the death of Capelli. But it was a coincidence which struck Salutati, mourning the death of his friend 'our Pasquino' and remarking on the fact that 'our Loschi, before our eyes' should take his place so swiftly.[184] There were no more friendly little letters despatched from Florence to Pavia thereafterwards; Loschi might not have assisted Barbavara to

[184] Salutati, Epist. XXN, vol. 3.

bring about Capelli's downfall, but he certainly profited from it.

But though a scapegoat had been found, none involved in the events of that summer night upon the Po could be held entirely blameless. The undermanned ships, the undefended bridge, the armies of Biancardo and dal Verme separated by the lagoon and so unable to provide mutual support, all these were indications of a lack of planning by the general staff, of a curious disharmony in the normally smooth-running court. The field commanders were apparently working without plan, dal Verme had ample warning of the approach of the Venetian fleet and could have retreated to the southern bank of the Po in good order long before the Milanese fleet was destroyed. Presumably he had not realized the great discrepancy between professional and amateur, believing that the numerically superior Milanese would be able to hold the attackers. Biancardo spent too much time attempting to reduce the fortress at Governolo on the Mincio and failed to work in closely enough with dal Verme. But these tactical errors were as nothing compared with Giangaleazzo's own miscalculation which brought about that which every Italian power feared. Venice was openly in arms against him and with the broad Po now free almost to the walls of Pavia, the danger was great indeed. Nevertheless, no fleet of galleys appeared before Pavia, no armies crossed the Mincio to take advantage of the seething discontents and fears of the populace. 'And certainly if the Florentines had gone on towards Milan they would have taken it. And the reason why they did not go, they say, was because some of those princes who were defending Mantua... did not wish the Florentines to have so much glory.'[185] Carlo Malatesta, who had hastened to the aid of his relative, had no intention of

---

[185] Dati, pp. 47, 48.

becoming involved in an aggressive war against Milan. And as for the Venetians, 'they wished that the forces should remain in equilibrium... not wishing that the Florentines should remain victors, as we shall see in the sequel'.[186] Venetian troops and vessels had the strictest orders not to go beyond Mantuan territory. Not for the first time the Florentines found that their allies did not necessarily share their view that war with Milan was tantamount to crusade; in danger the allies could present a united front, but victory, no matter how transient, immediately brought the old rivalries out into the open again. Giangaleazzo was able to mount another massive attack upon Mantua in the late autumn, Milanese troops again penetrating into the *serraglio*; in the spring of 1398 allied arms again forced them back, but yet again the Venetians temporized, refusing to follow beyond the Mantuan frontier. For the Serenissima had no desire to see the balance upset in Lombardy, to aid a Tuscan power to establish itself in a region vital to their interests. And so soon as their true intentions were displayed, the martial ardour of the smaller members of the League abated, the Lombard situation swiftly becoming a stalemate. It suited Giangaleazzo; the Mantuan war had been born of the need to destroy an enemy bridgehead, and that purpose accomplished he was free to prosecute his aims elsewhere now that he was certain that Venice would move no further westward. He turned his attention again to Tuscany, for the time was ripe to bring Pisa under direct Milanese control — or so he was informed by his agents.

THE TUSCAN BRIDGEHEAD

Appiano's establishment in Pisa had followed the classic pattern by which the Visconti had gained control of most of

---

[186] Dati, p. 49.

their cities; first the corruption of an ambitious man who arranged for the presence of Milanese troops, then his seizing of high office, and finally open Visconti dominance with the puppet granted a sinecure or swept away if necessary. The formal transformation of Pisa into an integral part of the dukedom of Milan should have proceeded almost automatically, for it was merely the last stage of a process which had been perfected over generations. Jacopo Appiano had dared to make his attempt upon Gambacorta only with the knowledge that Milanese lances were at call and he kept his position only with that continuing support. Arms and men which Giangaleazzo badly needed elsewhere had to be detached to protect his *protégé* from enemies both within and without the state, and in return the duke did not even have a garrison within the city. His intentions towards Appiano were both mild and reasonable. Appiano was an old man; the son upon whom he had counted to succeed him had died in the October of 1397 and his other sons were useless, 'men of little'. Something had to be done to regularize the position and protect Milan's investment, for if the Pisans did not decide to take matters in their own hands then the Florentines would. Giangaleazzo was working on familiar ground and with familiar tools, but for once his normally sure touch was clumsy and though the blame for the affair in Pisa in January 1398 was immediately traceable to his agent in the city, the responsibility was his. The disruptive element in his court, which had contributed to Pasquino's fall and the Mantuan debacle, was still operating.

The duke began in his usual cautious manner, basing his action on the reports of Niccolo Diversi, his agent in Pisa. Diversi was a typical example of the duke's staff of political generals. He was by birth a Lucchese and had later served

Florence as a captain of militia, but tiring of arms and finding little hopes of political advancement in a city naturally hostile to any subject of Pisa, he took the road to Milan. His intimate knowledge of Florentine affairs made him particularly valuable to the Count of Virtue and he further took the trouble to maintain a cordial friendship with the powerful men in the Florentine Signoria. His relationship with Salutati was that of a personal friend and the bonds remained unbroken even by Diversi's adoption of Milanese citizenship. War finally shattered them and after 1390 his name appeared no more in Florentine records save as that of a man most zealous for the Count of Virtue. But though the Florentines accepted, amiably enough, the fact that he had become a confidant of the Count, the city of his birth pursued him with implacable hatred, the *podestà* of Lucca condemning him to be hanged, drawn and decapitated should he ever fall into Lucchese hands. His journeys to Pisa placed him in considerable danger, but he specialized in Pisan affairs. Hitherto his advice to his master had been sound, but whether the fiasco was totally due to misjudgement on his part or to an unpredictable move on the part of Appiano the result was the same.

After the death of his son Vanni, Appiano had despaired publicly of being able to maintain power within the city on account of his age and ill-health. Diversi seems to have based his subsequent actions not on direct information from Appiano himself but from a certain messer Tiglio, a Pisan citizen who scented rich rewards in a new constitution. Together Diversi and Tiglio went to Pavia and assured the duke that Appiano was prepared to sell the city. It was precisely what Giangaleazzo both hoped and expected and, without query, he ordered Paolo Savelli to return with them to Pisa and hasten the matter. On arrival in Pisa, Diversi and

Savelli sought audience with Appiano, but in the interim he had changed his mind. Such a feeble excuse would have been unacceptable to their master and they therefore sent to Pavia asking that a squadron of cavalry should be immediately despatched to Pavia. Giangaleazzo, depending upon their first-hand knowledge of the situation, sent Niccolo Pallavicino with the necessary troops.

The three men then waited upon Appiano on January 3rd. They pointed out that their master, having poured out so much money in his defence, was naturally anxious to know what was going to happen in the near future. Appiano tried to evade the point by asking for time during which he could send a personal representative to Giangaleazzo, but Savelli 'speaking haughtily' told him that he must reply without delay. Appiano thereupon insisted that he could make no decision until he had consulted the Pisan Anziani and promised to give their reply in the morning. Pisa was still theoretically a republic and Appiano's action was therefore justified, but the Milanese seem to have been remarkably trusting. Even Sercambi, who professed himself surprised by the degree of power exercised by Appiano, an elected official, was scornful of the Milanese. 'O messer Niccolo Diversi… how could you think that messer Jacopo could act so like a boy that he had need to take council of his inferiors. For certain, the delay was for no other reason than to do harm to you and the others.'[187] Appiano made a formal statement to the Anziani during the evening, discovered what he expected — that the Pisans would resist any attempt to sell them — and put into motion that upon which he had already decided. During the night his son Gerardo, at the head of a troop of armed Pisans, arrested every Milanese agent in the city. Savelli suspected such a move and was prepared, but

---

[187] Sercambi, DXXXIV.

in a sharp skirmish he was wounded and captured while Diversi and Pallavicino, taken utterly unawares, were dragged from their beds. Other minor members of the 'conspiracy' were arrested, including messer Tiglio, a friar and a citizen of Lucca, and the troop of Milanese cavalry expelled from the city. Two weeks later Appiano instituted a form of trial in which Diversi was tortured and condemned to death, Savelli sentenced to imprisonment and the others fined. Savelli was released after a few days and Diversi's death sentence was thriftily changed to a fine of 50,000 florins.

Such is Sercambi's account of the curious affair at Pisa. His method of telling the story by mingling straight narrative with apostrophes to the parties concerned results in a contradiction. In the narrative, Appiano found that he could command no support for the suggested transference of power and therefore, identifying himself with the champions of Pisan liberty, attacked the Milanese. But in the apostrophes Sercambi appears to be convinced that the whole incident was a ruse on the part of the wily lord of Pisa. Why else was Savelli released, Sercambi demands. Again, even though Pallavicino was not sentenced he too was imprisoned; is it likely that Appiano would have dared to affront a rich and powerful man with many friends unless there had been prior agreement? And finally, if the Milanese suggestion were displeasing to Appiano, why was it that throughout there was a great number of Milanese soldiers quartered in Pisa. 'It was all a deceit, *gusmini*, to test the opinions of the communes and lords of Italy.'[188] In Florence, 'Minerbetti' gave a substantially similar version of the events leading up to the arrests, but he believed that the trial which followed was based on the discovery of a murder plot.[189]

---

[188] Sercambi, DLXIII.
[189] 'Minerbetti', XXXV, A. 1397.

A servant of Savelli's allegedly confessed to having been ordered to kill Appiano, which plot was known to a messer Malpiglio (Sercambi's messer Tiglio), Gino Rapondi of Lucca and certain others all of whom had been promised, not merely cash, but actual lands to be carved out of the Pisan state. They were all fined. The gravity of their supposed crime was hardly consistent with a mere fine as punishment, even though Appiano preferred florins to flesh as Sercambi pointed out, and the mildness of the punishment adds some weight to his charge that there was connivance between Appiano and the Milanese. Nevertheless the probability was that the Milanese on this occasion were more fools than knaves; Giangaleazzo's subsequent action shows that he certainly thought so. Appiano at the beginning was ready to lay down the burden of office in return for substantial reward but, finding that the Pisans were against him and fearing the swift vengeance which would follow an unsuccessful attempt to sell them, he saved himself at the expense of the Milanese envoys. His first moves were instinctive reactions to a sudden danger, but with the agents in prison he proceeded to make capital of the situation, posing as a friend of liberty in Pisa while increasing his value in the eyes of Giangaleazzo and Florence. Forgetting the fine words uttered when Appiano had scrambled to power over the corpse of Gambacorta, the Florentine Signoria immediately extended the hand of friendship to him, seeing the opportunity of again opening the road to the sea.

But Giangaleazzo moved before them. True to his policy of abandoning the indefensible, no punitive squadron rode down to Pisa to exact vengeance for the ill-treatment of important Milanese officials. Instead, Antonio Porro, a member of his inner council, came in humility, instructed to do anything to retain the Milanese outpost in Tuscany. His task was relatively easy. Appiano was well aware of his reputation in Tuscany and of Florentine ambitions and it seemed to him rather more desirable to have a powerful but distant protector than a nearby ally whose constant need was a port. After a long conference he allowed himself to be placated. Pallavicino was released and, though it must have been a humiliating action, at Giangaleazzo's direct order he invested Gerardo Appiano with a military decoration. Then he and Savelli took the road to Pavia to report to their master. Diversi alone was left in prison until he managed to raise, without assistance from Giangaleazzo, the 50,000 florins fine. Sercambi threw scornful pity upon him. 'You, stupid one, why did you not take up your residence in Mantua or Siena to do the duke's work since you knew what the Pisans were like... You should have remembered that Pisans are not friends of the Lucchese and especially of you.' But it is all the judgement of God 'because man is born first to God and then to the commune and he who hurts the commune angers God'.[190] No Lucchese could ever forgive Diversi for freely abandoning his city for Milan.

The duke's prompt action enabled him to retain a foothold in Pisa; eight months afterwards he justified his self-humiliation with the smooth acquisition of the city in the correct manner. Jacopo Appiano died in the October of 1398. His treachery to Gambacorta had brought him little satisfaction for his five years of high office, propped up by the power of Milan, had been spent in a constant apprehension that a treachery as great as his own would send him tumbling. The son for whom he had fouled his name was dead and the son who inherited was a blustering coward. Even on the day of his father's funeral Gerardo Appiano declined to exchange his armour for mourning, certain indication to Sercambi that he

---

[190] Sercambi, DLXIII.

would be unable to retain even nominal power. Gerardo barely tried. He actually made overtures to the Florentines, offering to come to terms with them should they support him at home. But Florence, displaying an unusual altruism, declined; if Pisa could not be established as a true republic then the least that was required was the reinstatement of the Gambacorta. Florentine altruism was displayed at an inappropriate moment for Florentine ambitions. Giangaleazzo kept the closest watch on developments in Pisa and swiftly moved to take advantage of Gerardo's fears. This time there was no bungling, for the negotiations were in the hands of Pietro Filargo, supported by Antonio Porro, and Gerardo, a frightened, incompetent young man, grasped at the price offered for the relinquishing of his sovereignty. The duke would pay off all his debts, give him 200,000 florins for himself and invest him with lands wherein he could uphold what dignity he had left. The negotiations were carried out in secret; the Anziani suspected some such move and protested, but Gerardo was able to calm their fears while a large Milanese force moved down the coast and camped at Sarzana, waiting for the call. When it came the force 'rode the streets' of Pisa with little or no opposition, Gerardo signed the deed of cession and the Tuscan city for which three generations of Visconti had fought and intrigued was inducted into the Milanese state. The 800 lances which Porro brought down from Sarzana were more than enough to subdue an already confused and demoralized population, but Giangaleazzo, well aware of the value of tempering threat with bribe, immediately sent a large convoy of wheat into the city to relieve the near-famine conditions. There was little need for any threat of further force after that; the Pisans were Ghibelline, looking upon an enmity with Florence as part of the natural order of things, and after the shabby lordship of the Appiano family, the duke of Milan appeared a worthy master.

Immediately after Appiano had formally renounced his sovereignty, Antonio Porro despatched an embassy to Lucca to acquaint the citizens of the change of government in Pisa. Lucca was small and its citizens impoverished, but its closeness to Pisa made their goodwill of some importance even to the duke of Milan. Hearing of the embassy the Florentine Signoria hurriedly sent spokesmen to remind the Lucchese of their joint efforts against the Visconti, urging them to send representatives to Venice to complain of the Milanese coup which endangered all Tuscany. The Lucchese were unimpressed. 'You regard ever your own good and have little care for that of your companions. Do you think that others have failed to guess the reason why you have sent such an embassy?' Sercambi demanded and apostrophized his fellow citizens. What good have they had from the recent war, he asked and goes on to quote the fable of the lion who claimed the entire prey after having been assisted to bring it down. 'Thus Florence shall treat you. Better to live in peace than go to war at Florentine petition.'[191] Sercambi was not particularly popular with the Lucchese and he personally was merely awaiting the time when his protector Paolo Guinigi would turn Lucca into a despotism. His open hostility towards Florence was extreme, but it reflected with some accuracy the opinions of most members of the League of Bologna.

Signs of stress had begun to show in the League even before Pisa fell. In vain Florentine envoys at Venice insisted that the stalemate in Lombardy was but an interlude, that ultimately the defence of Venice itself rested on the continued existence of the League of Bologna. The Serenissima replied in effect: 'You

[191] Ibid., DCI.

have done much and the Count has repented of his sins. If you do not accept this then we will aid him, for we will not consent that he be destroyed.'[192] Dati was admittedly biased but the Serenissima judged even by their own standards, displayed a remarkable cynicism. Visconti had been made aware of their displeasure and had prudently checked his eastward advance; Visconti could therefore ravage where he would provided always that Venetian territory was left undisturbed. Trade had been dislocated quite long enough in Lombardy; the Venetians therefore now openly detached themselves from the League. On the insistence of the Serenissima a truce between Giangaleazzo and the League was arranged in May 1398; superficially matters were left much as they were before, the only positive enactment being that the destroyed bridge at Borgoforte should not be rebuilt. But in practice the truce spelt the death of the League; propped up by Venice it collapsed when Venice withdrew. Gonzaga was the first openly to desert the cause. He had never been a wholehearted supporter of a predominantly Tuscan alliance. The only direct result of his breakaway from Giangaleazzo had been the transference of the war to Mantuan territory, making of it a cockpit while the lands of his allies went unscathed. Now that Venice had made it clear that she would underwrite no more enterprises in Lombardy Gonzaga at last made his peace with Giangaleazzo. Ferrara inevitably followed Mantua. There was an element of truth in Dati's statement that Giangaleazzo would rather have been in outright possession of the two states than to be joined to them in an alliance which might again be broken. But 'it was enough for the moment that they should be leagued with him so that the Florentines should not have an entry into Lombardy,

---

[192] Dati, p. 50.

saying within his heart, "If you help me to defeat the Florentines I shall then be able to break you without trouble."[193]

Giangaleazzo was just forty-seven years of age when the last coherent opposition to him in Italy began to crumble. He had been reigning in Milan for thirteen years, and in the normal course of events could reasonably hope for at least another thirteen years of active life. His only will, dictated in 1388, had been made for reasons of politics and not of health, the sudden expansion of the Milanese state in that year invalidating all previous arrangements. Apparently he enjoyed good health, but the secluded nature of his life made it possible to conceal any personal facts which it was deemed politically undesirable to publish abroad. Nevertheless, outsiders were able to gain an impression that all was not well with the court of Milan. There had been the military errors of Mantua, the deposition of Capelli and the political blundering of Pisa, all indications that something in the heart of the smooth-running machine was not functioning as it ought. Then, some time during the course of 1398, he suffered either a grave illness or even an attempted assassination which gave rise to rumours that he was dead. The Annalist of Milan confused the occasion with the poison plot made against Giangaleazzo by Ricci in 1389;[194] no details whatsoever were released from Milan, but so certain were the rumours that, for the first time since a Visconti held power, factions again rose in the state. The Guelphs of Crema rose in arms, not against the central power, but against their ancient rivals in Bergamo, ominous indication of the conditions which would prevail upon the duke's actual death. Among the ever-turbulent hill people in the north a leader arose, a certain Giovanni Rozone who gathered to himself a group of semi-

[193] Ibid., p. 61.
[194] Annales Mediolanenses CLXI, col. 832.

248

bandits and proclaimed war against Milan. The disturbance in Crema was swiftly suppressed and Rozone's activities were not worth the expense of a protracted expedition among the hills, but throughout the state there was a feeling of unrest. In December an edict reminiscent of the dead Bernabò was published, prohibiting the approach of any person whatsoever to the current residence of the duke under penalty of losing a hand. For a year or eighteen months it seemed as though the firm hand of the duke was slipping from the controls of power, but the unknown cause of the disturbance passed and again he was master in his own house. Nevertheless, from the winter of 1398 onwards there was a hint of urgency in his actions and something less of caution as though he knew that time was running short.

The acquisition of Pisa was the beginning of an astonishing landslide. The city accepted him as sovereign in February 1399; within eleven months Siena and Perugia had followed suit, then the little lords of the Apennines and finally Paolo Guinigi, the newest despot in Italy, placed Lucca under Milanese protection. The landslide isolated Florence, ringing her round not with mere allies of Visconti but actual cities of the Milanese state. Yet though the change of the political map of Italy was dramatic enough, the fall of the cities swift, it was the end product of that same process which had eroded Pisa from its independence. And allied to the Visconti system of subversion was the beginning of the Italian acceptance of the monarch. Padua had heralded the acceptance, although Giangaleazzo's attempt to capture the city had been a decade too previous; Pisa's submission confirmed the wavering decision of the first of the republics who elected for peace under an hereditary monarch. But even the two processes in alliance could not have wrought the change with such speed had they not been assisted by that great wave of popular reaction against war which produced the penitential processions of the Bianchi.

THE PENITENTS

The century which had begun with the triumphant jubilee in Rome ended with a sudden emergence of the people themselves, in a movement which swept down the peninsula, halting war in its path, welding, if but briefly, the clashing cities into one great brotherhood. The Bianchi were not fanatics; no scourges were wielded as by the Flagellants of a century earlier nor was there the desire to purge sin by the slaughter of Saracens. For a brief period during the last months of the dying century the true voice of the people was heard, speaking for once direct without the medium of golden-tongued propagandists for republican or monarchial causes. Their governments had freely used their name in a thousand polemics but when, briefly, they spoke for themselves their slogan was neither 'Liberty' nor 'People' nor even 'Peace', but 'Mercy'

Misericordia, eterno Dio,
Pace, pace, signor pio,
Non guardare il nostro errore
Misericordia andian grindando
Misericordia non sia im bando
Misericordia Idio chiamando,
Misericordia al peccatore.[195]

---

[195] 'Mercy, eternal God/Peace, peace, gentle Lord/Look not upon our errors/Mercy we call upon/Mercy be not denied,' Mercy we implore/Mercy unto the sinner.'

There had been a series of natural catastrophes in that year. As late as April frost and heavy falls of snow destroyed the young crops and supplies of corn and wine were cut by half. Famine followed and, in the wake of famine, plague. The governments of the land were formally at peace save in the north, in Piedmont, where the *condottiere* Facino Cane was engaged in a war between Monferrat and Savoy. The fighting there was neither more nor less bitter than Italians had suffered throughout that century, but at some point the inarticulate agonies of the anonymous people took voice. In Cheiri certain citizens surged out into the main square crying spontaneously 'Misericordia'; others joined them, the milling crowd resolved itself into a unit and finally a procession winding through the hills, making pilgrimage to local shrines. There, as with so many manifestations, it might have stopped; instead, a group of them began to move southward, evolved a ritual and adopted a uniform. Sercambi, the most devoted chronicler of the movement,[196] described the uniform as being composed of a white habit and cowl, the whole covering the wearer from head to foot and with a great red cross emblazoned on the front. Corio's description of it as being a plain, rough sheet drawn over the head with holes cut for the eyes is more probable, considering the numbers involved; probable too is his dry remark that the wearers must have had difficulty in seeing where they were going.[197] No great leader arose, no committee planned their routes, but a routine became swiftly apparent. The movement did not snowball — had it done so the effect upon Italy would have been incalculable — rather was it in the nature of a transmission, the components of the

---

[196] Sercambi, DCXIII-DCLIV. He was probably the author of the penitential hymn.
[197] Giulini, Pt. III, p. 596.

wave ever changing. Bianchi from one city would pass to another, join the citizens there in a ten-day round of devotions and then return home, while their late hosts would in turn visit the next city en route, and so on down the peninsula. Both sceptical and enthusiastic recorders of the movement noted the astonishing fact that all strife ceased in its path. Citizens indeed made a point of visiting the cities of hereditary enemies, Lucchese to Pisa, Pisans to Florence, Florentines to Siena, men, women and children in their thousands flooding into foreign cities in an ecstasy of fraternal love. Sercambi devoted but four lines to the resurrection of a dead man and four and a half pages to the reconciliation of enemies; 'Minerbetti' was scornful about the many alleged miracles but freely admitted that the Bianchi brought peace wherever they came. The movement of great numbers of people brought problems to the administrative authorities; most accepted the dislocation of everyday life, but Giangaleazzo made a firm effort to control it. In the cities of the Milanese State alone the Bianchi were not allowed to enter; the processions were obliged to halt outside the gates and those citizens desiring to take part went out and joined them. On August 19th the duke gave a general permission to all those wishing to go on pilgrimage 'to visit churches, dressed in white — or in any other colour they are disposed to wear', but it was on the understanding that all citizens remained within their natural groups and did not mingle with the general processions and that the processions should end by September 5th in order that the harvests might be brought in. His reason for segregating the citizens of his own cities from each other and from the general procession was based less on fear of sedition than on a sensible precaution against the possible spreading of plague. The duke's cool approach to the Bianchi was in marked contrast with most other Lombard authorities. In Genoa the aged and crippled archbishop personally led the great procession of 30,000; the groups which reached Ferrara and Padua found themselves in each case joyfully welcomed by the Signore who with his family again personally led the processions through the cities. Venice shared Giangaleazzo's unenthusiastic view of the penitents and the blessed Dominici, defying the prohibition and welcoming the crowds, was exiled for his trouble. But such reactions were rare and the white flood moved on down the peninsula, drawing all classes to it, nobles and people, peasants, monks, citizens, until at last it came to its natural home. The first group, 10,000 strong, entered Rome on September 7th, made pilgrimage and departed; others followed throughout autumn, group after group in their thousands filling the city with a ferment which had not been known since the jubilee of 1300. Benedict IX was at first hostile but later wisely adapted himself to the flood, promulgated indulgence, channelling the emotions, making of it a respectable thing. And, falling into the hands of professionals at the end of the road, the movement came to an end, the people returning to their homes, leaving only a few enthusiasts to wear the white habit into the new century.

It was against this country-wide background of war-weariness that Giangaleazzo established the southern outposts of the Milanese State. Florence sent embassies to the Venetian stakeholders to complain of Visconti's violations of the truce, to reiterate again the dangers that he presented, but the Serenissima declined to trouble itself, to take part in open war for the sake of distant Tuscan cities. And well aware of the lengths to which he could go, before incurring the hostility of Venice, Giangaleazzo prepared to harvest that which had been sown. The ten-year alliance which he had signed with Siena in

1389 was on the point of expiry. Desiring nothing more than its renewal in fact, the duke nevertheless made difficulties, stating that he could not continue to protect them without a more formal relationship. The Sienese had the choice of either accepting the outward form of Milanese rule or being abandoned to the mercies of Florence. They accepted Milanese rule; it was in practice merely the demonstration of an existing fact for Siena was subsidized by Milan and key positions in the city had long been held by Visconti officials. On September 6th Siena became a city of the Milanese state, extinguishing its republican history, acknowledging the duke of Milan as sovereign. Sienese example made a deep impression upon Perugia. The situation there more closely resembled that of Pisa; again an ambitious man, Biordo Michelotti, had climbed to despotic power with the aid of Milan. He had fallen victim to an outraged republican spirit yet his assassination had merely sparked off partisan hatreds and Perugia found, as the Lombard cities had already found, that there could be no tranquillity without a single ruler. Florentine ambassadors again made their vain appeals to liberty; the Priors of Perugia voluntarily sought out Giangaleazzo and, at the hour before sunset on January 21st 1401, the Viper standard was broken out over the walls of Perugia to float above the most southern city of the Milanese empire. 'And now the duke could call himself Duke of Milan, Count of Virtue, Lord of Pavia and Pisa and of the city of Siena; and so the duke draws the net around Florence for which reason it is well that every person should look to himself.'[198]

---

[198] Sercambi, DCLIX.

IX: THE FINAL STRUGGLE

On August 20th 1400 the Electors of Germany, having deliberated for over eight months, formally deposed Wenceslaus IV and elected Rupert, Count Palatine and cousin of Isabella of Bavaria, Emperor in his stead. Their motives were domestic but their act conjured up yet again the ghost of the Empire to trouble the distant Italians. Wenceslaus had made two half-hearted attempts to restore order in the amorphous nation of which he was titular head, but the task had been altogether beyond him and he sank back into his drunken debauches. Twice his offended subjects imprisoned him but, incapable of choosing a successor, they released him and he continued his habits with a bland indifference to opinion. At the Conference of Rheims in 1398 when he and Charles VI met to discuss the simultaneous deposition of both popes, he was so drunk that the opening ceremonies had to be abandoned. The growing scandal could not be continually ignored. The Electors met, gave audience to his ambassadors and, not receiving satisfactory explanations from them, ordered him to appear in person before them on August 11th. He ignored the order and nine days later was deposed. His successor had many excellent personal qualities, but overshadowing them all in the eyes of the Electors was his close relationship to the queen of France. The Germans intended again to establish their mystic suzerainty over Italy, to tap again that rich source of revenue for the benefit of their impoverished land. Wenceslaus' alienation of a large area of that source by his creation of the dukedom of Milan bulked larger in the reasons for his deposition than his criminal folly at home. Rupert was charged with this new crusade and, specifically, with the annulling of the dukedom and the regaining of its territories for the Empire. But the mere withdrawal of Visconti's diploma would not be sufficient; force would be needed to expel the usurper and Rupert's family connections were an excellent medium to obtain the military support of France. A few weeks after the imperial election Stephen of Bavaria accepted a commission to go to Paris and obtain his daughter's sanction for an expedition against Milan. His mission was easy for Isabella needed no urging to support a Wittelsbach against the upstart duke of Milan. She charged her father to inform the emperor that he could count upon her wholehearted support and promised to win over the dukes of Berry and Burgundy. Orléans and Charles himself might prove a difficulty, for the deposed Wenceslaus was their cousin and Orléans still identified himself with Visconti, but she had her own measures for overcoming the difficulties. Over the following year Isabella devoted herself to this most excellent means of bringing about her long delayed revenge. Rupert relied almost entirely upon her to manipulate French opinion. In the spring of 1401 his personal secretary, Master Albert, curé of Saint-Sebald in Nuremberg, arrived in Paris and privately sought out the queen. The Emperor desired to know exactly what help he could hope for from France. An Imperial diet was to be summoned at Metz in June and he wanted his envoys to be accompanied by French theologians to discuss the possibility of ending the Schism — always a prerequisite of French aid. If Isabella agreed he would choose a favourable moment at this conference to raise the matter of the Italian expedition. Isabella plunged deep into the intrigue which was the breath of life to her, going to considerable lengths to cover the comings and goings of German ambassadors until the alliance was firmly settled. She even let it be known that The queen employs herself voluntarily and of good faith to bring about a marriage between a daughter of France and the eldest son of the duke of Milan'.[199] But progress was slow; all depended upon the success of Rupert's Italian expedition and his ability to persuade the Roman pope to crown him in Rome.

The deposition of Wenceslaus had created almost as many problems as it was meant to solve. Few were enamoured of him, but neither was there a wholehearted desire to see the Imperial Crown transferred from the house of Luxembourg to that of Wittelsbach. Rupert was crowned in Cologne on January 6th 1401; he should thereafter have been elected and crowned in Frankfort and Aquisgrana respectively, but both cities were in the hands of Wenceslaus' supporters who had declined to recognize the sentence of deposition, first clear indication that schism now existed in the Empire as well as the Church. Rupert, wiser or more energetic than his predecessor, resolved to descend in person into Italy and in the same month of his coronation sent envoys ahead. They came first to Florence, even as the envoys of Wenceslaus had come first to Florence seeking subsidy and had been repulsed. But the Signoria had learnt a bitter lesson. They were no longer the head of a powerful league as they had been six years earlier; the very city which had given its name to the League of Bologna was in the hands of a tyrant since March 1400 when Giovanni Bentivoglio, with due legality, took over the city of Bologna. Francesco Carrara alone remained faithful and he possessed little more than his stout spirit. There was formal peace in the land, but for most Florentines it was the brief lull before the storm for it was unthinkable that Visconti would not complete the engulfing of Tuscany. They grasped at the proposals of

---

[199] Thibaut.

Rupert's envoys, indifferent to the sarcasm of such as Sercambi who professed astonishment at Guelphic Florence's new-found enthusiasm for the head of the Ghibelline party. It was immediately decided to send an experienced ambassador to Rupert. The man chosen was Buonocorso Pitti, already well known to the Court of France and a confidant of Isabella and her brother Lewis; a man of considerable learning, wide ambassadorial and mercantile experience and totally devoid of scruples.

Pitti arrived in Amberg on March 18th and immediately entered into negotiations with Rupert's procurator. His instructions were to persuade the emperor to enter Italy that same year and he was authorized to offer 100,000 florins as first instalment of the subsidy. The procurator rejected the offer, claiming that at least 500,000 florins were necessary, a figure confirmed later by Rupert in person. He was hard put to hold his own against Wenceslaus' supporters; the Italians, if they wanted the support of the Emperor, must pay the whole cost. The request went far beyond Pitti's powers and he referred the matter back to Florence. The Signoria replied promptly, increasing their offer to 200,000 florins with promise of further aid during the actual campaign. Rupert remained unsatisfied; daily the difficulties of the enterprise were becoming more apparent to him. He said in effect that he would have to think it over and bring the matter up at the next Diet which would be meeting in Nuremberg. There it seemed that the matter would end; the Emperor would not move without money and Florence declined to invest half a million florins in an unknown German. Yet the coming of the Emperor was vital to their policy; something was required to move him into action. The Signoria was not long in discovering the required motive force. Pitti prepared the ground with some subtlety. 'While awaiting the reply from Florence and having a meal with him in one of his gardens and having seen that he made no guard against poison I said to him, "It does not seem that you are well advised as to the evil of the duke of Milan, for if you were you would take better guard of your person than you do. You may be certain that, when he knows that you have decided to enter Italy, he will attempt to kill you by poison or dagger".' The Emperor was genuinely shocked by the suggestion but Pitti had opened up unpleasant possibilities 'and amongst other things, because of the suspicion I had shown him, when he saw anybody near him that he did not know he immediately wished to know what that person was there for'.[200] Three weeks after Pitti's warning, by a remarkable coincidence, a stranger was apprehended near the Emperor as he was going to Mass. Rupert demanded his business and the man replied that he was on his way to Venice and had come merely to gaze upon the Emperor. He was taken into custody and after Mass Rupert questioned him personally. The man immediately confessed, spontaneously, that he was an intermediary between Giangaleazzo's personal physician Piero di Tosignano and Rupert's own doctor Herman Polein. Polein was summoned, tortured and ultimately confessed that he had been bribed by Visconti to poison the entire royal family. Rupert was enraged; spurred on by the affront which turned the destruction of Giangaleazzo from being politically desirable into an act of personal vengeance, he overrode all difficulties, accepted the Florentine offer and promised to bring by all possible means an army into Italy by the summer of that year.

On April 26th the Emperor wrote to Florence, Venice and other Italian powers, telling them of the plot against his life. The Venetians were silent but the Florentines replied, warmly

---

[200] ASL 21, 1894.

congratulating him on his escape, urging him into Italy to take revenge. The news came at last to Giangaleazzo who vigorously protested against the accusation. He wrote first to the commune of Nuremberg where Herman Polein and the informer were detained, asking that all judgements should be suspended until he could oppose the informer's statement with that of his own physician Tosignano. It was true that, three years earlier, Polein had been a student under Tosignano at the University of Pavia and thereafter corresponded frequently with him. But the accusation that Tosignano was coaching the German in poison was demonstrably absurd for Tosignano was about to pass into the service of the king of Portugal and had already sent his family and goods on ahead. The letter arrived either too late or was ignored; Polein was formally charged with the attempted poisoning of the Emperor at the instigation of Visconti and was executed. In Italy, Giangaleazzo enjoyed no better reaction to his protests, particularly with the important Serenissima. On July 26th they decided, by a very large majority, to accept his statement. But later there were second thoughts not because of additional doubts but because, as the Doge Michael Steno observed, their acceptance would make a bad impression upon the Emperor. Their ultimate reply said simply that they were sure that the duke would find some way of saving his honour. The Venetians were in a quandary, wishing to offend neither Visconti nor the Emperor. They had no part in Rupert's coming, nor did they particularly desire it, yet they were aware of its potential use in placing a curb upon Giangaleazzo's ambitions. Their double interest was to inhibit them during the whole period of the Imperial expedition and, reluctant to move to either side, they remained passive.

The reputation which Giangaleazzo had earned, partly justly, partly through Florentine propaganda, ensured that at this vital juncture he was condemned without a hearing. The entire plot against the Emperor was a Florentine fabrication whose audacity and scope, together with the extreme secrecy with which it was carried out, convinced almost every person who was not a party to it. So skilfully did they cover their traces that even a later, detailed, confession by one of their number did nothing to restore Giangaleazzo's reputation. The Florentine archives, together with Pitti's chronicle and the confession extracted from Niccolo Uzzano, present a story of a skilled and complex duplicity which, for once, outreached even the duke of Milan's.[201] Nothing could be clearer of Florentine intentions than the tenor of the instructions given to their four ambassadors — Tommaso Sachetti, Fillipo Corsini, Rinaldo Gianfigliazzi and Maso degli Albizzi — who were sent to meet Rupert on his entry into Italy. They were to congratulate the Emperor on the escape of himself, 'his most sacred and august lady and his glorious children from the evil plot designed by that most unjust tyrant, Ioan Galeaç (not Count of Virtue as he is entitled, but fount of all treachery)'. Next the ambassadors were to 'aggravate this most cruel attempt as much as you are able' by drawing the Emperor's attention to a list of similar crimes of Visconti's; he had poisoned a host of his own servants including Bevilacqua and Pallavicino, as well as Antonio della Scala, through the medium of this same Tosignano. It is just possible that the writer of the brief was so woefully misinformed as to believe that Visconti despatched some of his most able and loyal lieutenants out of blind evil; the four ambassadors could make no such excuse for each was

---

[201] The full range of Florentine duplicity was made public only in the nineteenth century as a result of a painstaking piece of detective work by Giacinto Romano (Giangaleazzo Visconti Avvelentore in ASL 21, 1894).

well acquainted with Milanese affairs. Final proof of the scale and nature of the Florentine conspiracy was supplied only two weeks after Giangaleazzo's death in September 1402. Niccolo Uzzano, a Florentine captured in Bologna by Milanese troops, made a formal declaration before Caterina, widow of the duke, Francesco Barbavara and other prominent members of the Court. Uzzano declared that in January 1401 he was a member of the Ten of War. Two of his colleagues conceived the idea of writing to Pitti to find a way of making the Emperor believe that Visconti wished to poison him. Uzzano stated, naturally enough, that he himself was opposed to the plot and knew nothing of the details at the time. A year later, however, he obtained the most detailed information from Maso degli Albizzi on the latter's return from his embassy to Rupert. Maso was a relative of Pitti and so was fully informed of all that had transpired in Germany. According to Pitti the plot was set in motion by the Florentine envoys there with the direct aid of Isabella's brother Lewis of Bavaria. They had engaged and briefed the alleged messenger between Tosignano and Herman Polein and later arranged his release from prison after his work was done. Pitti had urged Maso not to speak of the affair to a living soul 'in order not to compromise duke Lewis' and Pitti's own position in Germany, but Maso had been misguided enough to pass the information on to Uzzano, 'a man of sweet temper but a blockhead'. Doubtless Uzzano would have kept the secret had he not found himself in Milanese hands, but being no man to court martyrdom he divulged the entire story, probably hoping to gain preferential treatment. The truth of his deposition was borne out by his later treatment at the hands of his compatriots. Far from disowning him, the Signoria paid his ransom from the public funds and Uzzano continued in high office on his return to Florence, even becoming leader of the oligarchy in 1420. His statement came long after it could do Florence any harm. Rupert, quite unaware of the fact that he was a pawn in Florentine policy, prepared to enter Italy on the slenderest of budgets to repair the Imperial honour. As a preliminary he despatched a coldly insulting letter to Giangaleazzo, addressing him simply as 'Milanese knight' and ordering him to render back to the Empire the territories which he unjustly held. Giangaleazzo's reply was in similar vein, emphasizing Rupert's ambiguous position. 'To thee, Robert of Bavaria, we, Giangaleazzo Visconti, by the grace of God and of the most serene lord Wenceslaus king of the Romans and of Bohemia, duke of Milan, etc., and Count of Pavia and of Virtue… we reply that each city, castle, territory and place that we possess in Italy we retain and possess by authority of the aforesaid serene lord Wenceslaus, king of the Romans and canonically invested with the government of the sacred empire. And all these places we shall most heartily hold against you, invader of the Empire and manifest enemy of the aforesaid Wenceslaus and of ourself. We defy you if ever you should presume to invade our lands.'[202]

Giangaleazzo's preparations were on a scale commensurate with the challenge. Theoretically, the entire might of the Empire was to be hurled against Milan and it was reported that Rupert had a force of not less than 30,000 horse of those German veterans who, as mercenaries, had terrorized Italy for half a century. Opposing them the duke had perhaps 15,000 horse, but the list of their commanders was a roll-call of the most illustrious names in Italian warfare; Alberico Barbiano, Ottobuon Terzo, Galeazzo of Mantua, Taddeo dal Verme, Galeazzo and Antonio Porro, the marquis of Monferrat, Carlo Malatesta — each one of these men in their time had

---

[202] Corio, IV, 1.

commanded entire armies, sometimes against Visconti sometimes on their own account. Jacopo dal Verme held the command-in-chief, but Giangaleazzo, departing for the first time from his policy of military delegation, personally ordered the tactics. All troops were to remain behind walls until or unless a pitched battle was unavoidable; the war, if any, was to be a defensive, retaining operation. 'Minerbetti' alone records that uncharacteristic interference of the duke's,[203] but out of that decision arose Italy's most resounding military triumph of the century, freeing Italians from their lingering sense of inferiority.

Rupert appeared at Trento on October 21st. Even before he had left Germany half his force deserted and it was with barely 15,000 horse that he joined the Italian allies waiting for him. Nevertheless, it was a force concentrated to strike where its commander wished, whereas Milanese forces were obliged to cover many vulnerable points throughout the state. The command of the Imperial army had been confided to Francesco Carrara, a signal honour considering the minute force he was able to contribute and one tardily recognizing his steadfast opposition to the duke of Milan. The main attack was to be launched on Brescia where the rebel Giovanni Rozone with his 'army' of some 2000 semi-bandits had been conducting guerrilla warfare with Florentine subsidy. Rozone sent a company of guides to lead the army through the hill country and it arrived, unmolested, on the Bresciano on October 24th to find a force of only 6000 Milanese ready to oppose them under the command of Facino Cane. The Imperial army had chosen to attack probably the only city in the Milanese state where Giangaleazzo's defensive order could not apply. This city on the mountainous fringe of the state was

---

[203] 'Minerbetti', IX, A. 1401.

a Guelph island in a Ghibelline sea; ever in a state of unrest, Rozone's activities had created a new ferment, loosening the already uncertain loyalty of the citizens. It would have been a courting of disaster to attempt the withstanding of a siege and Cane decided to attack.

The battle of Brescia was a total and humiliating defeat for the Germans, the first time in that century that a foreign army was smashed in pitched battle by a purely Italian force — a force, moreover, just half the size of the invader. Both 'Minerbetti' and Gatari accounted for the defeat of the Germans because 'they did not understand the Italian method of warfare and fell thereupon into shame and damage'. But for at least fifty years German mercenaries had been fighting in Italy. Bruni, analysing the technical details of the battle, brought out the true reason for the defeat; the Germans used the old technique of the mercenaries who fought for pay while the Italians, fighting for their *patria*, desired a decisive end to each battle. Blood had been brought back into Italian warfare. The only contingent of the Imperial army which was not totally shamed was the Italian force commanded by Francesco Carrara; for the rest there was nothing but confusion, lack of direction and incentive until that moment when 'the baron of Storiche (Leopold of Austria) commenced to cry out "Vidron! Vidron!" which is to say "Fly! Fly!"[204] and commenced to flee'. Carrara saved the immediate situation, acting as rearguard while the demoralized army retreated, finished as a fighting force. Two of the German leaders, the bishop of Cologne and Leopold of Austria, immediately returned home taking with them the greater part of the army and leaving the Emperor in an acute state of indecision. It was shameful to return but it seemed useless to stay with a few troops and no money.

---

[204] Gatari, p. 473.

Francesco Carrara prevailed upon him to stay, offering him the hospitality of Padua while the possibility of obtaining more money from Florence was discussed.

Giangaleazzo was most quick to seize the moral advantage which the military victory at Brescia had given him. A few days after the battle his orators went to Venice to protest against the breaking of the peace by the Florentines. It was an expected charge and the Signoria had made no particular attempt to anticipate it, the Florentine ambassadors who were summoned to heat the charges against their city being in Venice for other purposes. But the Milanese speaker developed his brief into a damning and indeed noble indictment of the entire Florentine policy. The speech opened with the usual accusations of broken faith and an accurate enough summary of Florentine intrigues in Germany. 'They promised the Emperor a great sum of money with the express condition that it should be paid to him only when he entered upon the territory of he with whom they had only recently made a peace.' But from there the speaker went on to his main charge — the calling of foreigners into Italy. 'This same city, contrary to the customs of antiquity, have given opportunity to the French and Germans (strange and barbaric nations, enemy of the Italian name) to pass into Italy, calling upon Italian heads those which nature herself has excluded from Italy by the barrier of the Alps. And such is the blindness of their council that they do not understand that if the French and Germans are brought into Italy, it is to the common ruin of all Italians. The ancient Romans opposed and destroyed the Cimbri and Teutons when they entered Italy and for this they deserve especial praise. But these Florentines, these new Romans as they call themselves, by means of money have persuaded these transalpine nations to enter Italy... forgetting their *patria* and their people. They complain of Visconti's interference in Tuscany, but in truth this was done only at the direct request of the oppressed Sienese and Perugians and could not be compared with their own actions in making common cause with Germans. But to make brief conclusion, O Venetians, we are sent to complain of the violated peace and demand penalty upon the violators.'[205] The reply of the unprepared Florentines was painfully inept. The duke's boundless ambition was the cause of all troubles in Italy and, in any case, the army which had come to Florence's aid had not been composed of 600,000 wild Cimbri and Teutons but a civilized force under the command of the Emperor. The Venetians avoided imposing penalties upon either party, contenting themselves with a general and useless exhortation to good will.

The Imperial expedition was drawing to its inglorious end. As soon as Rupert had arrived in Padua he enquired if any Florentines were in the city, and upon being informed that there were not, displayed anger. But then it was learnt that an embassy was on its way from Florence and, believing that they were bringing gold, 'he was a little quieted. And from this one saw clearly that his coming to Padua was more for show than to prepare to go against the duke of Milan — and also to have money of the Florentines of which he stood in great need and not only himself alone but all his people who were with him.'[206] The undignified wrangle over money which accompanied every Imperial journey into Italy commenced as soon as the embassy arrived in Padua. The Florentines stated flatly that they would pay out no more money until the Imperial army was on Visconti territory; the Germans demanded payment on the grounds that the action at Brescia had constituted an invasion.

---

[205] Bruni, 1st. flor. XII, p. 601.
[206] 'Minerbetti', IX, A. 1401.

267

Neither would give way and, in high dudgeon, the Emperor took himself off to Venice 'to complain of the Florentines and ask financial aid of them (the Venetians) and council as to what he should do'.[207] He was received with the utmost respect. The Bucentaur, carrying the Doge, met him at San Giorgio; a palace was assigned to him and another for the empress; he was treated with reverence amounting to obsequiousness. But the Venetians absolutely refused to interfere either for or against Florence and declined to make a personal loan to the Emperor. In another of the sudden rages which his dealings with Italians seemed to bring upon him, Rupert broke off the discussions and departed without taking leave. The open manifestation of anger troubled the Serenissima, whose only desire was to avoid trouble, and a swift vessel was despatched to persuade him to return. He did so, remaining in Venice for six weeks as an honoured guest, at the end of which he returned again to Padua and made one more attempt to obtain money from Florence.

Pitti's plot had worked too well. Rupert had been spurred prematurely into action, committing himself to the Italian expedition without ensuring that funds would be forthcoming, expecting indeed that the wealthy Italians would contribute generously to their saviour. But those Italians opposed to Giangaleazzo, measuring the chances of the Emperor's success, declined the honour. Florence by herself could do no more, 'neither the Pope nor any other commune or lord of Italy wished to help — saving only the lord of Padua who offered what he could which was 200 lances and 300 militia. And this little force was insufficient to do that which was desired because Visconti had engaged 4500 lances of good Italian people.'[208] On April 15th 1402 Rupert admitted defeat

---

[207] Ibid.

and, deeply shamed, left Italy. Florence was alone 'saving only the lord of Padua'.

THE FALL OF BOLOGNA

In the January of 1399 Giovanni Bentivoglio and Nanne Gozzadino led a rebellion in Bologna against the dominant party of the Maltraversi with the aid of Giovanni Barbiano, count of Cuneo. The attempt was unsuccessful and Bentivoglio and Gozzadino went into exile where they made their first overtures to Giangaleazzo. In the interim, the Bolognese government captured and executed Barbiano. It was the most dangerous thing they could have done for it earned the immediate hatred of Barbiano's brother Alberico, the great *condottiere* then serving with Giangaleazzo. Alberico's desire for vengeance perfectly coincided with his employer's desire to place pressure upon Bologna without the declaration of war. Barbiano was no casual mercenary dependent upon Milan for the supply of troops and money, but a prime example of the new Italian *condottiere* who was to be reckoned with as a political force in his own right. A quarter of a century had passed since the youthful Barbiano, in response to the appeal of St Catherine of Siena, had formed the first Italian company of mercenaries and fought the terrifying Bretons of the Avignonese pope. Giangaleazzo privately gave him permission to march against Bologna while publicly disclaiming responsibility. Barbiano's task was simplified by the fact that plague struck in Bologna during the autumn, carrying off most of the leaders of the Maltraversi. A successful revolution overthrew the remnants of the party and recalled the exiles, but scarcely a month after their return Bentivoglio and Gozzadino, with Barbiano's aid, turned upon their benefactors and re-

---

[208] Ibid., I, A. 1402.

established their own party. Three revolutions in a single year, together with the plague, had utterly demoralized the Bolognese and they, as others had done before, succumbed to the attraction of peace imposed by the autocrat. In March 1401 Bentivoglio proclaimed himself signore of Bologna with little opposition and Gozzadino, seeing the republican principles of the revolution betrayed, abandoned his old comrade.

Bentivoglio had gained power largely through the support of Giangaleazzo's general and it was therefore not unreasonable for the duke to suppose that he could continue to control the new lord of Bologna. But Bentivoglio, though professing neutrality between Florence and Milan, was well enough aware of the dangers of being a protégé of the duke's. He was also Guelph enough to prefer the friendship of Guelphic Florence, and during the summer of 1401 relations between the two cities gradually returned to normal. The coming of the Emperor prevented Giangaleazzo from taking any active measures, but when finally the Germans trailed back through the Alps, leaving Italians to settle the affairs of Italians, the duke could turn at last to the enterprise of Bologna. The great army which had been conjured into being for the protection of the Milanese state against the Imperials was still mobilized; Gozzadino and the other Bolognese exiles were pleading with him to help them restore a republican government; the powers of Italy had shown themselves unwilling to oppose him — there could be no better time to attempt the achievement of the constant Visconti goal.

Bentivoglio's brief taste of power had transformed him from an ambitious republican into an unashamed autocrat. Already there were indications that the Bolognese were regretting their flirtation with despotism, yet Florence had no alternative but to send help when Bentivoglio appealed to them. The existence of a lord of Bologna might be a standing reproach to the whole Florentine philosophy, but the enemies of that lord were being supported by the duke of Milan. The Signoria therefore strained their very last reserves for the defence of Bologna. Nothing could better indicate the bankruptcy both of Florentine finances and philosophy than that the general whom they despatched to aid a despot was a foreigner, the Breton *condottiere* Bernadone da Serres. Bernadone was placed under the orders of Bentivoglio; it was unavoidable but it was the direct cause of the disaster which followed. The Milanese army was at least four times the size of the force commanded by Bernadone and he, in consultation with the Florentine Signoria, had wisely decided to limit himself to the defence of Bologna. But Bentivoglio, 'accustomed to being fortunate in all his enterprises and of his nature more ardent and courageous than wise or experienced, and moreover being young and vigorous of person, deemed it shameful to remain behind walls'.[209] He had an excellent additional reason for wishing to put the matter to the immediate test, knowing well that his fellow citizens were little disposed to suffer in his cause.

On June 26th, therefore, the entire army marched out and met the Milanese force at Casalechio. The Breton was inevitably blamed for the defeat which followed. 'Many who knew the place well thought Bernadone was very stupid to place his camp there, for it was ill-defended and was surrounded by a great number of vile enemies.'[210] But the issue was foredoomed. Bernadone disposed of barely 5000 horse while the Milanese had '15,000 horse and 20,000 foot and 12 captains and leaders of a kind that since the time of Charlemagne to this day there has not been a more wonderful

---

[209] Dati, p. 64.
[210] 'Minerbetti', VII, A. 1402.

army so that the victory was reasonable'.[211] The defenders retreated in total disorder to Bologna 'where the greatest terror possessed all the citizens, the people rushing hither and thither, astounded, as when slight minds are suffocated by too much wine. All took arms without knowledge of what they should do; there was neither order nor counsel in common.'[212] Bentivoglio did not long survive the defeat. According to Dati the Milanese killed him as soon as they entered Bologna, breaking their word, but Bentivoglio was in fact despatched by the people he had betrayed. Giangaleazzo received the news in the form of a terse postscript added to the report of the taking of Bologna. 'The late Giovanni de Bentivoglio was beheaded by the people of Bologna.'[213] In a manner so swift and simple as to seem to belie the long years of endeavour, Bologna, the gateway to central Italy, was again part of the Milanese State. As the duke had promised, the citizens were allowed to re-create their republican constitution, but Bologna was now incapable of governing itself, the deep and complex rivalries imposing too great a strain upon the constitution. Three weeks after Casalechio the new government voluntarily ceded its sovereignty to the duke of Milan, bringing to an end half a century of uneasy freedom.

There lay now no barrier between Giangaleazzo and the city which all deemed to be his helpless prey. Florence had used her last in the vain defence of Bologna and the powers who should have united with her for the defence of all Italy had left it too late. Why was this, Dati demands; why did not the Pope and the king of Naples and the Venetians and the Genoese and the rest combine in arms against the obvious common enemy?

---

[211] Dati, p. 65.
[212] Ibid.
[213] Giulini, Pt. III, p, 601.

The question was rhetorical for the answer was plain; selfishness and lack of foresight. Not until Visconti laid hands on Bologna, part of the lands of Holy Church, was the Pope troubled and even then ca great part of his cardinals were pensioners of the duke' and prevented any action against him. The king of Naples was a long way away and had his own troubles at home and counted on the fact that the Florentines were between him and the Viper. And as for the Genoese and Venetians 'they appeared to be bewitched by him' and also perhaps because these cities were governed not by the many but by the few so that it was simple for Visconti to seduce them. After the fall of Bologna 'the Florentines sent some valiant citizens to Rome to bellow so in the Pope's ear that he would awake and understand the shame that Holy Church sustained in that the tyrant occupied her territory' and there was talk of a holy league against Visconti.[214] But it remained talk and meanwhile Florence was slowly being throttled. Her sole access to the sea was Rimini and even that was by concession of an ally of Visconti, Carlo Malatesta, who defied him for the sake of revenue. Paolo Guinigi was tempted to extend similar privileges for a similar reason but Lucca was unpleasantly close to Milan and the appearance of a squadron of Milanese cavalry constrained him to change his mind. All the Apennine passes were in the hands of Visconti, and his subjects in Pisa, Siena, Perugia, eager for vengeance upon the arrogant Florentines, could be depended upon to hold the southern routes. Famine was abroad in Florence; there had been time to gather in the harvest but, unsupplemented by imports, it was insufficient for the needs of the State. Trade was at a standstill, the treasury was drained and, for the first time during their long struggle with Milan, the city had no

---

[214] Dati, p. 68.

military commander of ability. Hawkwood, the last of the great foreign *condottieri*, had died in 1394 and Florence, aware too late of the revival of Italian arms, had allowed her enemy to gather to himself all the Italians of note. Rumours abounded; the great army of Bologna was about to move in force into Tuscany and administer the conge; alternatively, Visconti was planning a simultaneous attack upon Padua and Florence, the twin core of resistance to him; he was about to make an alliance with Venice. Milanese envoys did indeed appear in Venice making such offers, but the Serenissima, making a belated attempt to bring about a balance, would accept only on condition that Florence and Padua were included and the Florentines were invited to send representatives to discuss the matter. The Signoria suspected fraud but, grasping at any straw, accepted, saying privately that if peace were made 'they would not pay much attention to Venetian demands afterwards.'[215] Venice had played safe for just too long. Nothing concrete came of the proposals — but neither did any great army march down through the passes of the Apennines to appear in the Tuscan plain. July passed into August and still the duke's army remained around Bologna, waiting for no one knew what. Then, towards the end of August, it was observed that Milanese troops were being withdrawn from Tuscany.

DEATH OF GIANGALEAZZO

There had been plague all that year in Lombardy. By the end of April it had entered the suburbs of Milan and the death-carts were again busy; by June certain indications were appearing in Pavia so that those who could sought healthier climates. But the pressure of work made it impossible for the court to disperse; Milanese arms had achieved the summit of Visconti

---

[215] Ibid, Bruni, 1st. flor. XII, p. 609.

ambition but Milanese politics were needed to consolidate the gains. The great danger of the possibility of Venetian interference, the restlessness of the *condottieri*, the wide-ranging plans to blockade Florence, the arranging for the induction of Bologna into the State — all these kept Giangaleazzo pent in Pavia. By July 26th the pressure had decreased and he was at last able to leave the dangerous atmosphere of Pavia, retiring to his country palace at Melegnano on the Lambro, some fourteen miles from Milan. It was not possible to cut himself off entirely from state affairs but he was able to combine recreation with business and for a week the court took on its usual relaxed appearance of the summer months. Then, on August 13th, the duke suddenly fell ill. Ironically, it was not the plague which he had sought to escape which struck him down, but a fever, presumably an occurrence of that malady which had caused rumours of his death four years before.[216] There was at first little apparent danger, but on August 23rd his condition worsened and the plans which had been made for the move of the court to Abbiategrasso were abandoned. In spite of later rumours which declared that traitors within the court had engineered the move to Melegnano so that, isolated, he would be beyond medical help, the duke did not lack the most skilled doctors which Italy could produce. His personal physician, Gusperto da Maltraversi, was in attendance upon him from the beginning, being a regular member of the court,

---

[216] Giulini's supposition that he 'carried the seeds of death within him' on leaving Pavia is incompatible with the circumstantial account of the last days given by Pietro Cinuzzi (in I manoscritti italiani del bib. nazonali di Firenze, T. III, p. 126, 1883). Cinuzzi's eyewitness account also disposes of the colourful theory that the duke was despatched, through Florentine intrigue, by means of a poisonous powder scattered over the pages of his favourite copy of Dante.

and Gatari believed that he was kept alive at all only 'with the aid of magical liquors and medicines made by that most famous man, Marsilio di Santa Sophia, the greatest doctor in the world'.[217] But Giangaleazzo had few illusions as to his condition. On August 25th he made his will, asked for his confessor and, statesman to the last, ordered that ambassadors should be sent to Venice to prepare some sort of peace 'in order that his young children should not be left in the midst of most grave peril'.[218] The fact that certain political measures were put into operation immediately on his death argues that, only too well aware of the danger in which that death would place the State, his last hours were spent in meticulous planning. He died, shortly after sunset on September 3rd, in a room overlooking the garden of the palace. He was not quite fifty-one years old.

There could be no clearer indication of the extent of Giangaleazzo's personal control of the State of Milan than the astonishing swiftness of its dissolution following upon his death. In spite of the fact that he had surrounded himself with most able lieutenants, in spite of his consistent policy of delegation, the State was formed by his own will, held together by the force of his personality. As an organism it was premature; there were no precedents to guide those on whom the burden of power fell with stupefying suddenness and the lengths to which they went to keep his death secret was a measure of their fear, of their knowledge of inability to cope. The natural sequence of events should have been the immediate publication of the name of the new duke, Giovanni Maria, followed by the reverent transportation of the remains of the old either to the capital or to his own beloved Pavia. But

---

[217] Gatari, p. 491.
[218] Bruni, 1st. flor, XII, p. 610.

the desperate need to ensure even a few days' freedom of action dictated the hurried disposal of the body in the nearest suitable place. This happened to be the obscure abbey of St Peter in the nearby hamlet of Viboldone, a far cry from the duke's own orders that he should be buried in the Certosa, the monument he had designed for the glorification of the Visconti.

The undignified interment and the speed and secrecy with which it was carried out led to the later reports of treachery and murder, that 'he had enemies and perhaps worse were those standing by his side... far from the city that was affectionate to him... far from faithful guards, from true friends'.[219] Additional emphasis was given to the rumours by the fact that the duke died alone, among only servitors. On that same day a letter was despatched to Wenceslaus, from Milan, giving the news in the name of Giovanni Maria and his brother. Giangaleazzo died some time after 9 p.m.; it would have obviously been impossible for the two young boys with their mother to have attended his deathbed, make the journey to Milan and despatch the letter on the same day. The family must therefore have been in Milan and were informed in the evening by fast messenger. Their absence was probably at the direct order of the duke to ensure that his son was in physical possession of the capital at the moment of his death, a move reflecting his fears for the immediate future. Wenceslaus alone was promptly informed for he had a vested interest in the continuance of Visconti dominance, the duke of Milan being the only certain ally he had in Italy. But news of such magnitude could not be long kept secret. The first indication

---

[219] Moiraghi, D., Il trasporto della creduta salma di Giangaleasgo Visconti (MSP Anno I, fasc. V-VI) where the theory of assassination is set out in full.

outside the State was the withdrawal of the troops from Tuscany; Paolo Guinigi, lord of Lucca, then claimed certain knowledge and so informed Florence, but the Signoria had been deceived before by rumours of Visconti's death and did not wholly believe. Nevertheless, an urgent messenger was sent to Venice, instructing the Florentine ambassadors there to suspend all negotiations until the truth of the matter be known. Confirmation swiftly followed. Francesco Carrara had long suspected that Giangaleazzo was ill and on September 6th apparently obtained certain word, for he then wrote to Rupert, telling him that the tyrant was dead and this was therefore an excellent moment for the Emperor to come into Italy and profit from the disorder into which the State of Milan must inevitably be thrown. Rupert had lost all taste for Italian adventure but the signs were already plain; the wolves were beginning to gather.

The Milanese were the last to hear officially of the death of their duke, being informed on September 10th in a letter issued in the name of both Giovanni Maria and his brother. The cities of the State were also ordered each to send ten representatives to the duke's funeral ceremonies, for the Council of Regency, as though atoning for the shamefaced burial in Viboldone, intended that the formal obsequies should be on the same scale as the coronation. Some 20,000 people took official part in Milan on October 21st and the rites lasted for fourteen hours; but it was a hollow ceremony. The coffin which was carried at the head of the procession was empty; empty too was the great, flag-bedecked mausoleum in the cathedral round which the final rites were held. There seems indeed to have been some attempt at deceit, for Gatari at least believed that the duke's body was actually present, but in fact it remained yet in its humble tomb at Viboldone, mute witness to the sinking splendour of the Visconti. A more obvious and so more ominous commentary on the prevailing conditions was the fact that the duke's immediate family were not present during the ceremonies. Caterina and her two sons remained within the closely guarded castle of Porta Giovia leaving Gabriele Maria, Giangaleazzo's favourite son by Agnese Mantegazza, to represent them. Gabriele had been legitimized but was nevertheless reckoned outside the line of succession and was therefore presumably of little interest to would-be assassins. The arrangement could have little diminished Milanese anxieties for the future.

Giangaleazzo's will of August 25th transmitted the dukedom to Giovanni Maria together with the county of Angera and direct dominance over twelve cities of the State; Fillipo Maria succeeded to the county of Pavia, Verona and the western cities; and to Gabriele Maria was given Pisa. Superficially, the provisions were a continuation of the old short-sighted policy of inheritance by division and Giangaleazzo was later so accused, but he in fact intended that the two younger sons should hold their lands feudally of Giovanni Maria. In the event the system worked smoothly, for Gabriele was swiftly eliminated by the Florentine conquest of Pisa in 1404 and Fillipo was content to lead a retiring life when he and Giovanni arrived at maturity. It was not this aspect of the will which was to bring final ruin upon the state, but that fatal clause in Valentina's marriage contract which ensured the transmission of the state to her descendants in the event of the male line failing. The duke having assented to it in the contract he had no alternative but to include it in the will which Giovanni Oleario, a notary of Pavia, drew up in Melegnano.[220] But in the

---

[220] Fifty years later Oleario's son Andrea was ordered by Francesco Sforza to find and destroy the will. Andrea defended his public trust,

autumn of 1402 the possibilities of French claims on Milan were merely academic. Surrounded by enemies though it was, the collapse of the State of Milan came from within. Giovanni Maria was barely fourteen years old and the Council of Regency over which his mother presided was from the beginning divided against itself. Giangaleazzo's policy of employing only the ablest men had helped him to create the largest state in Italy but, once his firm hand was removed, their very ability and ambitions rent the State apart. Caterina's first and fatal mistake was to accord too much honour, grant too much power to her fellow councillor and now open lover, Francesco Barbavara. Barbavara's progress from the social depths to the penultimate peak of Milanese society was entirely due to his own merits; Giangaleazzo never appointed '*ex affections*'. Nevertheless that progress had been at the cost of the bitter jealousies of the duke's other councillors, many of whom were of noble blood and resented the honour accorded to a plebeian. The rift within the court itself widened and as the central control lessened so the great families of the cities of the state reasserted their identities. And finally the *condottieri*, those military machines which the Count of Virtue had employed with consummate skill, proved their hidden danger. They desired, and took, not money but lands wherewith to found dynasties. Jacopo dal Verme alone remained loyal to the memory of the man whom he had served for over twenty years; the rest sought their fortunes some outside, some within, the State. One of the latter was Attendolo Sforza.

---

hid the will and claimed that it had been lost. Lodovico il Moro in his turn instituted the most thorough search for a document which was then assuming frightening implications, but he was no more successful. The will survived to give final legal support for Louis XII's claim on Milan.

The reaction of the chroniclers to the death of Giangaleazzo was divided in a curious manner. The Tuscans, though they might rejoice, were one and all sensible of the stature of the man who had been so suddenly removed and speculated as to what might have happened had he been given even a few more months of life. But the chroniclers of the cities of the Milanese State who had been so closely involved in his rise, and who were about to be tormented by the events resulting from his death, were quite incurious, merely recounting the bald facts of his death. The Lombard blindness was not only limited to them; the monk who pronounced the formal oration at the funeral totally ignored all that the man had actually done, preferring to elaborate a tedious conceit developed from the Count's so-called descent from the Counts of Angera.[221] The fact that northern Italy had been turned virtually into a Milanese dominated federation, the fact that only the hand of God had halted the inexorable process, the fact that the State itself had been radically re-formed — all these were ignored in favour of a ludicrous myth in which, it would seem, Visconti's greatest claim to fame was his descent from the goddess Venus by her son Aeneas. It was therefore his Tuscan enemies who pronounced the final judgement upon Giangaleazzo, particularly in shedding light upon his failure to march upon Florence immediately after the fall of Bologna. His indecision was an enigma for many of his contemporaries. At least two Florentine writers, the one a trained historian, the other an experienced politician, were convinced that only a miracle could have saved the city. 'If the enemy had followed up the victory with speed, the city would have fallen into irremedial peril. But they, either through negligence or discord, let the

---

[221] RIS XVI, cols. 1038-1050.

time pass uselessly.'[222] Such was Bruni's opinion and Buonaccorso Pitti was as positive. 'It is certain that he would have become lord of all Italy in a little time and that he would have conquered us; and this would have been in the natural order of things because he was already lord of Pisa, of Siena, of Perugia'[223] and of all central Italy. Bruni's hints at discord were based on reports of a quarrel between Carlo Malatesta and Alberico Barbiano over the latter's intention of establishing himself as lord in an area of interest to Malatesta. It was a copybook example of the dangers inherent in the employment of Italian *condottieri* with political pretensions. But it was extremely unlikely that Giangaleazzo, experienced as he was, would have been unable to establish harmony between his generals for the short time needed for the subjection of Florence. Bruni was uniquely equipped for the reconstruction of the entire struggle between Giangaleazzo and Florence; writing twenty years after Giangaleazzo's death he was able to view the whole with objectivity, supplementing opinions with documents drawn from the Florentine Chancery. He was probably even able to correct Florentine bias with the personal comments of the Milanese officials involved; he and Loschi were working together in the Papal Curia between 1409 and 1411. Nevertheless, Bruni's very credentials and objectivity result in a distortion. During that crucial summer he was in Rome and though reports doubtless came to him, pessimistic and indeed alarming reports, he could not have known of the true temper of Florence. It was Dati, the amateur, who gave the true reasons, twisting the facts to suit his thesis, eliminating some and exaggerating others with hindsight, but presenting the essential truths. The Florentines 'had made their reasoning

---

[222] Bruni, 1st. flor. XII, p. 608.
[223] Pitti, Cronica.

with pen in hand and talked as if this was a certainty — it can only last so long'. They knew that even Giangaleazzo's huge revenues were not inexhaustible, that even now they must be approaching their end, his overtaxed subjects 'wishing for his destruction almost as ardently as the Florentines themselves'. The Florentines expected his collapse and deliberately kept no more troops than they could afford to pay in the long run, expecting the duke to break down financially. 'And the Florentines made this decision with the intention of carrying on the war for a long time for they were resolved not again to make peace with the duke. Twice they had been deceived and betrayed and they did not wish it to happen for a third time; but they hoped that if they held out in the war they would see him consume himself... And the Florentines saw and understood that he must break down under the burden.' But surely the duke's financial councillors must have seen the same thing? Indeed they did, Dati replies, and they warned their master, but in the end emotion ruled reason and neither Florence nor the duke would give way. The duke's whole being was directed towards becoming lord and master of Italy and Florence was the hedge that stopped him. 'In consequence he believed that the Florentines were robbing him of his due and so he knew no restraint towards him... To be conquered and become subjects, this never seemed to the Florentines to be a possibility. Always they comforted themselves with the hope, which in their eyes was a certainty, that a commonwealth cannot die while the duke was one single man whose end would mean the end of his empire.'[224]

Such was Dari's assessment, based on personal knowledge, of the situation in Florence that summer. Giangaleazzo might not have known the details but he was aware of the temper.

[224] Dati, p. 69.

There was no real disaffection in the city and a formidable blockade was in process of erection. A frontal assault upon the city would have been against all Visconti policy. He intended to do what he had always done; wait until the city was starved into abject surrender or until the inevitable traitor arose. During July and August he was consolidating his position, recouping his strength, probably commencing the Visconti process of infiltration.

On August 25th he became gravely ill: by September 3rd he was dead. The Florentines gained their immediate freedom but the price they and all Italians paid was the continuing fragmentation of the peninsula so that, over the next five centuries the *oltremontane* — 'nations strange and barbaric, enemies to the Italian name'[225] — could ravage, pursuing their ambitions at the cost of Italian peace.

---

[225] Bruni, 1st. flor. XII, p. 601.

BIBLIOGRAPHY

Abbreviations

ASI: Archivio Storico Italiano

ASL: Archivio Storico Lombardo

ASN: Archivio Storico per la provincie Napolitane

FIS: Fronti per la storia d'Italia

RIS: Rerum Italicarum Scriptores: NS = New series

SMT: Fondazione Treccani degli Alfieri per la Storia di Milano

Annales Mediolanenses. RIS XVI.

Azario, Pietro. *Chronicon de gestis Principum Vicecomitum.* RIS XVI.

Baron, Hans. *The Crisis of the Early Italian Renaissance.* 1955.

Beltrami, Luca. *Storia documentata della Certosa di Pavia.* 1896.

Bonvesino dall Riva. *Le Meraviglie di Milano... traduzione del Ettore Verga.* 1921.

Bruni, Leonardo. *Istoria fiorentina: tradotto in volgare da Donato Acciajuoli.*

Bryce, James. *The Holy Roman Empire.* 1887.

Calvi, Girolamo. *Notice sulla vita e sulle opere deiprincipali architetti, scultore e pittore che fiorirono in Milano durante il governo dei Visconti e degli Sforza.* 1859.

Cibrario, Giovanni. *Della economica politica del Medio Evo.* 1839.

Cipolla. *Storia delle Signorie.* 1900.

Cochin, H. *Jean Galeaz Visconti et le Comte de Vertus* in ASL XXXII, I, 1905.

Cognasso, Francesco. *L'unificazfone della Lombardia sotto Milano* in SMT V, 1955.

Collas, Emile. *Valentine de Milan, Duchesse d'Orléans.* 1911.

Comani, F. E. *I denari per la dote di Valentina Visconti* in ASL XXVIII, 1, 1901.

— *Sui domini di Regina della Scala e dei suoi figli* in ASL XXIX, 2, 1902.

Corio, Bernardino. *Storia di Milano*. 1856.

Dati, Goro. *Istoria di Firenze*. 1735.

Donato di Neri. *Cronaca senese* in RIS NS XV, 1936.

Emerton, Ephraim. *Humanism and tyranny. Studies in the Italian Trecento*. 1925.

Frati, Lodovico. *La guerra di Giangaleazzo Visconti contro Mantova nel 1397* in ASL XIV, 1887.

Froissart, Jean. *Chronicles...*, translated by Thomas Johnes, 1849.

Gardner, Edmund G. *Saint Catherine of Siena*, 1907.

Gatari, *Galeazzo e Bartolomeo. Cronaca Carrarese confrontata con le redasfone di Andrea Gatari* in RIS NS XVII.

Giovio, Paolo. *Vita dei dodeci visconti... tradotto da Lodovico Domenichi*. 1645.

Giulini, Giorgio. *Memorie spettanti alia Storia... di Milano Continuasfonei*, 1771.

Gregorovius, Ferdinand. *History of the City of Rome in the Middle Ages*, translated by Annie Hamilton (Vol. VI, Pts. 1, 2). 1898.

Heim, Maurice. *Charles VI Le Fol*. 1955.

Jarry, Eugène. *La Vie politique de Louis de France, Duc d'Orléans*. 1889.

Luzio, Alessandro. *I Corradi di Gonzaga, Signori di Mantova* in ASL XL, 1, 2, 1913.

Magenta, Carlo. *I Visconti e gli Sforza nel Castello di Pavia...*1883.

Medin, Antonio. *I Visconti nella poesia contemporanea* in ASL XVIII, 1891.

Mesquita, D. M. Bueno di. *Giangaleazzo Visconti, duke of Milan*, 1941.

Minerbetti. *Cronica volgare di Anonimo Fiorentino… gia attribuita a Piero di Giovanni Minerbetti* in RIS NS XXVII, 2.

Monstrelet. *Chronique.* 1840.

Morelli, Giovanni. *Cronica.*

Muir, Dorothy. *A History of Milan under the Visconti.* 1924.

Muratore, Dino. *Bianca di Savoia e le sue nosgye con Galeazzo II Visconti* in ASL XXXIV, 1, 1907.

— *La nasccita e il battesimo del primogenito di Giangaleazzo Visconti* in ASL XXXII, 2.

Mussi, Giovanni de'. *Chronicon Placentinum.* RIS XVI.

Novati, Francesco. *Per la cattura di Bernabò Visconti* in ASL XXXIII, 1, 1906.

Osio, Luigi. *Documenti diplomatici tratti dagli Archivi Milanesi.* 1864.

Pastorelli, Ester. *Nuove richerche sulla storia di Padova… al tempo di Giangaleazzo Visconti.* 1908.

Petrarch, *Lettere (Fraccasetti).* 1869.

Religieux de Saint-Denys. *Chronique… in Collection de documents inédits sur l'histoire de France.* 1840.

Ricotti, Ercole. *Storia delle Compagnie di Ventura in Italia.* 1893.

Romano, Giacinto. *Giangaleastgp Visconti e gli eredi di Bemabo* in ASL XVIII, 1891.

— *Giangaleazzo Visconti Avvelenatore: un episodi della spedizione Italiana di Ruperto di Baviera* in ASL XXI, 1, 1894.

— *Tornandoci sopra: a proposito di alcuni recenti studi sul matrimonio di Valentina Visconti col Duca di Touraine* in ASL XXIX, 1, 1902.

— *Di una nuova ipotesi sulla morte e sulla seppultura di Giangaleazzo Visconti* in ASI 5, XX, 1897.

— *Il primo matrimonio di Lucia Visconti e la rovina di Bernabò* in ASL XX, 1893.

— *Niccolo Spinelli da Giovinazzo: diplomatico del Secolo XIV* in ASN XXVI, 1901.

— *Valentina Visconti e il suo matrimonio con Luigi di Turaine* in ASL XXV, 2, 1898.

Romussi, Carlo. *Milano ne' suoi monumenti*. Vol. II, 1913.

Sachetti, Francesco. *Novelle*.

Sade, Marquis de. *Histoire secrete d'Isabelle de Bavière*. 1953.

Salutati, Coluccio. *Lpistolario* in FSI Vols. XV-XVIII, 1891-1901.

Sercambi, Giovanni. *Le Cronache* in FSI Vols. XIX-XXI, 1892.

Seregni, Giovanni. *Un disegno federate di Bernabò Visconti 1380-1381* in ASL XXXVIII, 2, 1911.

Simeoni, Luigi. *Le Signorie*. 1950.

— *Due documenti sul sacco Verona del 1390* in ASL XXXIII, 2, 1906.

Sismondi, J. C. L. de. *Histoire des republiques italiennes*.

Symonds, J. A. *Renaissance in Italy. The Age of the Despots*. 1897.

Temple-Leader, John, and Giuseppe Marcotti. *Sir John Hawkwood (L'Acuto)*, translated by Leader Scott. 1889.

Thibaut, Marcel. *Isabeau de Bavière*. 1903.

Valeri, N. *L'italia nell'eta dei Principati dal 1343-1526* (Vol. IV of *Storia d'Italia:* Mandadori).

Verga, Ettore. *Storia della vita Milanese*. 1931.

— *Un condanna a morte contro Carlo Visconti figlio di Bernabò* in ASL XXXIX, 1, 1902.

— *Le sentence criminali dei Podestà Milanesi 1385-1419* in ASL XVIII, 2, 1901.

Vergiero, Pier Paolo. *Epistolario* in FSI LXXIV, 1934.

Villani, Matteo e Filippo. *Cronica*. 1825.

Visconti, Alessandro. *Storia di Milano. 1957.*

Volta, Zanino. *L'eta, l'emancipazione e la patria di Giangaleazzo Visconti* in ASL XVI, 1889.

Wilkins, E. H. *Petrarch's eight years in Milan*. 1959.

A NOTE TO THE READER

If you have enjoyed this book enough to leave a review on **Amazon** and **Goodreads**, then we would be truly grateful.

The Estate of E. R. Chamberlin

Sapere Books is an exciting new publisher of brilliant fiction and popular history.

To find out more about our latest releases and our monthly bargain books visit our website:
saperebooks.com

Printed in Great Britain
by Amazon

42864536R00165